Making Sense Of
Dying and Death

Making Sense Of
Dying and Death

Edited by

Andrew Fagan

Amsterdam – New York, NY 2004

The paper on which this book is printed meets the requirements of "ISO 9706:1994, Information and documentation – Paper of documents – Requirements for permanence".

ISBN: 90-420-1641-8
©Editions Rodopi B.V., Amsterdam – New York, NY 2004
Printed in The Netherlands

Contents

Welcome to a *Probing the Boundaries* Project

Making Sense of: Dying and Death is an inter-disciplinary and multi-disciplinary research project which seeks to engage in creative and innovative dialogues in focusing on the links between living and dying, and some of the contradictions and paradoxes which arise that we appear to accept without question.

Areas of interest will focus on different kinds of dying and death, the experience of carers and care workers, the changing role of medicine, palliative care, the work of the hospice movement, the work of the funeral industry, and the nature of grief and mourning. Interest will also focus on philosophical, ethical, and legal issues which surround the processes of dying and death, the role of religion, and the diverse range of historical, social, and cultural perspectives and practices.

The project will engage with and explore a number of core themes;

- contradictions and paradoxes
- dealing with and responding to different kinds of death and dying
- technology, dying and death
- institutions, dying and death
- issues confronting health care workers
- legal issues in dying and death
- philosophical and ethical issues in dying and death
- the management of dying and death
- the management of and changes within the funeral industry
- who deals with bereavement? Religious and non-religious counseling; bereavement, grief, and loss; forms of remembrance, sites of remembrance.
- religious issues; concepts of afterlife and their influence on the dying, rituals and practices in religious communities, theologies of death, near death experiences; the role of hope.
- the representation of dying and death in media - art, cinema, music, radio and television ; the portrayal of dying and death in all forms and types of literature
- death and dying in children's literature; children's concepts of mortality; the importance of narrative

Dr Robert Fisher
Inter-Disciplinary.Net
http://www.inter-disciplinary.net

Introduction

Andrew Fagan

This book aims to extend upon the growing body of literature concerned with death and dying. The book originated in a conference held in Brussels towards the end of 2002. The conference brought together scholars and practitioners from several continents, united by their interest and expertise in the phenomena of death and dying. The content of this volume reflects the broad, multi-disciplinary character of papers presented during the conference and consists of revised versions of some of those papers. This book aims to analyse various experiences and representations of death and dying from the perspective of academic disciplines as diverse as theology, philosophy, sociology, anthropology and literature. The rationale for this is simple. As objects of study, death and dying cannot usefully be reduced to a single academic perspective. One cannot hope to gain a deep and comprehensive understanding of death and dying by gazing at them through a single lens. Thus, a philosopher's perspective differs from that of the sociologist or anthropologist, whose own perspective is likely to differ again from that of a literary scholar or theologian. Bringing these perspectives together in a single volume fundamentally aims to both accurately record those enduring properties of the phenomena, such as mourning and fear whilst comprehensively analysing the diversity and heterogeneity of human beings' attempts to come to terms with this most forbidding of existential horizons, as witnessed, for example, by different conceptions of when death occurs and recent developments in funereal rituals within Western societies. The broad, multi-disciplinary character of this book aims to do justice to the phenomena of death and dying and distinguishes it from those other volumes on the subject that take a narrower, more academically restrictive approach. The book itself is divided into three sections.

The first section comprises chapters by Kasher, Weaver and Ford, all of whom are concerned with the experience of grief and mourning. The chapter by Kasher, a moral philosopher, focuses upon the question of how to deal with death, especially the death of loved ones. He argues against what he refers to as a 'naturalisation of forgetting' and outlines an alternative view of mourning and death that, he believes, can be addressed to the religiously and secularly minded alike. Kasher argues that the dead live on in those who love them and that this reveals something profound about how that life was lived. Thus he defends what he terms a view of 'life in the heart' through which the dead live on and retain their characteristics for us. He proceeds to identify different degrees of life in the heart and locates a cognitive precedent in the existence of children's imaginary companions as exemplifying the image of a person who lives on, not in the 'real world' but in the heart. Kasher argues that the persistence of our loved one's life in our hearts stands opposed to and places a limit upon the utility of those who argue that the best mode of mourning is one in which the presence of the deceased gradually fades away so that life 'can return to normal'. Kasher's chapter suggests precisely the opposite: that one's mourning testifies to the gravity of the loss and should not be dissolved or diffused through repressing the memory of those we continue to love, even after death.

Weaver's chapter is similarly concerned with mourning and also addresses the question of how to 'mourn well'. Western culture views inconsolable grief and sorrow with suspicion. The central adage those of us who continue to survive are expected to live by is 'life must go on'. Eventually, after some suitable period of grieving, we are expected to return to 'normal'. This attitude is reflected in many contemporary psychological models of sorrow and grieving which view a 'healthy approach' as one where the person eventually overcomes their sorrow at the loss of someone close. Like Kasher, Weaver challenges this orthodoxy by raising a more general question of how we ought to respond to our feelings? What is an appropriate form of attitude to adopt towards one's feelings of grief and sorrow? In contrast to the dominant approach she sees value in a sorrow that refuses 'to get over it'. Through one's grief and sorrow, she argues, one retains a relationship with the particularity of the actual person and forsakes gaining any consolation in the universality of death. Yes, we are all going to die, but that should not, she insists, diminish our grief at the loss of this particular person. She develops her approach through a comparative analysis of depictions of grief in St.Augustine's *Confessions* and Nicolas Wolsterstorf's *Lament for a Son*. St Augustine points to achieving a consolation for loss in God - the existence of God and the promise of an after-life serves to place our grief and sorrow in a context - an inconsolable sorrow, on this view, might be perceived as an affront to god. In contrast, Wolsterstorf points to the enduring value of an inconsolable sorrow, where the extent of one's sorrow serves as a testament to that which one has lost. The ultimate point is not to overcome sorrow at the world's imperfections but to live in and through it - death is part of the fabric of this world.

Ford's chapter completes the first section and takes a close look at a much neglected area of research into the contemporary experience of death and dying: grieving amongst the African American communities of the United States. Grieving for the dead may be a universal human phenomenon. However, as with so many other universal phenomena there exists profound social and cultural diversity in precisely how grief and sorrow are expressed. Ford primarily focuses upon African American women who, she argues, are generally exposed to far higher levels of premature death among, for example, their children as the victims of violent crime than other communities within the United States. Among some African American communities within the United States the average male life expectancy is lower than that of their counterparts in sub-Saharan Africa: within these urban communities the loss of at least one child or partner has become an expected life event of many women. Despite the widespread occurrence of these personal tragedies this remains a highly neglected area of study and Ford's chapter aims to clear some important ground in preparation for her own (and others) future research. Among a number of other themes she explores Ford focuses upon the myth of the strong Black woman and claims that the persistence of this myth serves to obscure the depth of grief experienced by many such women at the premature deaths of their sons and husbands.

Section two comprises chapters by Arthur, Johnson, McKenzie, and Crouch. The content of section two is more diverse and eclectic than that of the first section. It is common place to claim that the events of September 11th. 2001 (9/11) changed the world. Arthur's chapter analyses this claim in respect of North America's attitude towards death and its inevitability. Describing the United States as a society fundamentally based upon a collective denial of death, she questions whether the demonstrably horrifying images of 9/11 have 'brought death home' for Americans and whether death, through 9/11 has now been accepted by the peoples of the United States. If the collective psyche of the United States was genuinely based upon a denial of death and a corresponding myth of immortality then one might expect the events of 9/11 to have had a fundamental effect upon this general attitude towards death. In the face of previous similar catastrophes some have argued that being so directly confronted with death can lead to the development of a more mature attitude towards the inevitability of one's own death. It has been further assumed that the establishment of such an attitude encourages the development of a more empathetic attitude towards the suffering of others. Arthur finds little basis for such optimism. If anything, she argues, the response to 9/11 in the form of the war on terror points to a perpetuation of old ways: an attempt to banish death from American society with little real concern for the deaths caused in the process. In explaining her position she draws upon the work of Ernest Becker and his argument that human violence is ultimately rooted in a repressed fear of death: an inability to accept the inevitability of one's own death is manifested through a sense of self-importance and immortality that is pursued through the denigration of others. Not content to simply diagnose the problem, Arthur points to possible ways of responding to and eventually remedying the problem. She argues that we must first learn to accept the inevitability of our own death. In so doing, she hopes, we will all become better able to appreciate the value of life.

McKenzie's chapter might also been thought of as concerned with the denial and fear of death. She presents a sociological analysis of the social and emotional plight of cancer survivors in her native Australia and paints a disturbing picture. She posits a relationship between the fear of death among cancer survivors and the wider, collective fear of cancer: a fear which serves to marginalize and even alienate many cancer survivors from family and community. McKenzie identifies the source of the fear of cancer as emanating from a essential feature of shared practical consciousness: a belief that the future is taken for granted - that we can make medium term plans and projects free from any consideration of death. Cancer survivors cannot, she argues, fully share in this since it requires exclusion of the fear of death. She proceeds to criticise the general lack of social resources available to cancer survivors who have to deal not just with the physiological effects of the disease but the social consequences also. She identifies this feature of practical consciousness as coinciding with the specialisation of death and the removal of death from the life-world. As many have argued, complex, 'developed' societies are increasingly characterised by the removal of any direct experience of death. We have little direct experience of others' deaths, despite the prevalence of simulated depictions of death in various media. She analyses the effects of this twin predicament through studying women with breast cancer and presents a disturbing picture of the social and emotional plight of cancer survivors as suffering from deprivations that do not ensue from their physiological symptoms. As a potential remedy to the problem, she advocates a far more compassionate response towards cancer survivors and insists that this requires developing a sense of community between ourselves and cancer survivors. The obvious obstacle to this, however, is that it will require us facing up to the possibility of our own untimely death and suffering through cancer. A more compassionate attitude towards those considered to be closer to death than ourselves requires an acceptance of the inevitability of our own deaths.

Crouch's chapter continues the sociological temper of McKenzie's analysis but focuses attention upon recent developments in ritualistically marking the deaths of others. Anthropologists have long stressed the importance of funerary rituals for affirming the continuity of the community of people who survive - through the collective rites of death, communities reaffirm themselves. Funerals performed the social function of demonstrating the inevitability of death whilst seeking to secure the continuing life of the community. Crouch's chapter provides a sociological analysis of contemporary trends in funeral rituals, in particular so-called "DIY funerals" and funerals that intentionally cast aside the solemnity of the traditional funeral in favour of some more personalised event. Her interest is in those funerals which, on the surface, appear to have broken loose of the bonds and constraints of tradition so as to more authentically express the identity of the deceased. Far from welcoming such developments as the extension of individual choice to yet another area of 'life' and death, she criticises the development as a commodification of death and an attempt, founded upon a denial of death, to make death seem palatable. She argues that such personalised DIY funerals become a spectacle or a show and the success or failure of the event is judged in terms of entertainment. She argues that this fundamentally misses the point of funerals. Such funerals no longer express communal values and ideals and so are no longer capable of performing the collective functions required of them. As such, developments within funerary practices merely serve to express a far wider phenomenon of contemporary societies, the general loss of communal ties and relations. One might argue, from a structural perspective, that such developments more accurately reflect changing social conditions. Criticism of such practices might therefore be dismissed as founded upon a conservative desire to preserve the past. However, Crouch goes further in arguing that funerals exist to remind us all of an unavoidable, existential constant: the inevitability of death. She ultimately condemns DIY funerals as pathological precisely because they aim to obscure this fact, aim to take the edge off death.

Johnson's chapter completes section two and differs from the previous contributions to this section in the approach it takes to the analysis of death. Johnson's chapter presents a philosophical critique of a highly influential conception of death and its relation to life within the Continental tradition of philosophy. He focuses upon the claim presented separately be Heidegger and Bataille, two leading philosophers within the Continental tradition that one may only hope to live an authentic life upon fully accepting the inevitability of death. As other contributions to this volume indicate, death denial is a principal feature of contemporary, complex societies. David's chapter introduces us for the first time to those philosophers who present the denial of death as pathological, a condition which, if not overcome, serves only to severely constrain the living of life. The insistence that one must face death directly is absolutely central to the thought of both philosophers. However, Johnson argues that this is simply not possible. He draws upon the writings of Kafka in supporting his claim that one cannot experience death since death is the limit of all experience, the terminus of experience. Nor, he argues, can one conceptualise death, think of it prior to its occurrence, since death is not a concept. He suggests that we should orient ourselves towards time and not death. Ultimately what stands between us and our deaths is time and its passage. For us as individuals, death stands outside and beyond time, experience and thought. It therefore, simply cannot perform the service sought after by existentialist philosophers. Johnson's chapter is important, ironically perhaps, precisely because it advises us to steer away from a concern to conceptualise death in terms acceptable to us. The affirmation of life, he appears to suggest, has little to gain from a preoccupation with death.

The content of section three is as diverse as that of the previous section, comprising chapters by an anthropologist, two philosophers, a legal theorist, and a literary scholar. The first contribution to the section is provided by Kalitzkus and her examination of the medical determination of the occurrence of death. She examines the question of when death can actually be said to have taken place. Drawing upon cross-cultural research, she argues against the claim that death can be determined by recourse to some 'natural', purely biological criteria. Different cultures and societies exhibit different forms of determining death. While some cultures and societies have emphasised the death of organs such as the liver or kidneys as fundamental in determining death, other, more Western-oriented cultures and societies focus upon brain death as the principal measure of proclaiming the occurrence of death. She insists that actual death is best thought of as a process, rather than a single event or moment in time - a process which may last over considerable periods of time. Set against this context, she presents findings of the research she conducted into organ transplantation in Germany. The demand for viable organs, she insists, is exerting very real effects upon clinicians' willingness to pronounce someone as dead and the patients' surviving relatives experience of the death of their loved ones. In particular, she discusses those cases where brain death has occurred but the patient still shows signs of physical activity - the so called "living corpses", individuals who appear to relatives to be neither dead nor alive. While many relatives are pleased that the death served some purpose, where some other individual benefited from an organ, others have described very real problems coming to terms with their loss, precisely because they did not appear to be demonstrably dead. Kalitkus's chapter is important for the light it sheds on those cultural influences underlying our experiences of death and our ability to accept the actual occurrence of death. In emphasising death as a process, rather than an event, she raises fundamental questions for the ethics of organ transplantation, amongst other things.

Fagan's chapter presents a philosophical analysis of a situation that increasingly confronts medical clinicians: patients' expressing a wish to die rather than be subject to medical treatment that wholly violates some aspect of their religious or cultural commitments and beliefs. Thus, he focuses upon a contemporary issue in bioethics: the application of the principle of patient autonomy within medical treatment. He argues that a largely unrecognised problem has arisen with the application of the principle to patients' refusal to consent to life-saving treatment on the grounds of their religious or cultural beliefs. As it stands, many medically preventable deaths occur as a result of the application of the principle of patient autonomy to such cases. The problem arises, however, from the existence of cultural and religious communities that do not recognise the value of personal autonomy. Given the existence of such communities and the possibility that at least some of their members may not have the opportunities for acting autonomously, the principle of patient autonomy may be being applied invalidly, thereby sanctioning the medically preventable deaths of individuals acting in accordance not with their autonomous will necessarily, but more in accordance with the imperatives of their community. Fagan does not attempt to identify any detailed solutions to this problem. Rather, the chapter principally aims at identifying an existing, though largely unacknowledged, problem: for some people there are apparently worse things that can happen to them than dying from a medically curable condition.

Magnusson's chapter approaches the problem of death and medical treatment from the opposite direction to that pursued by Fagan. Magnusson's chapter focuses upon the practice of euthanasia and aims to challenge the conventional terms of the euthanasia debate through demonstrating the existence of what he refers to as the 'euthanasia underground' among medical clinicians in Australia and the United States. He argues that the question of whether or not euthanasia should be permitted ultimately fails to protect those involved in the euthanasia underground. His empirical study reveals the existence of health care professionals, undertakers, and others who practice voluntary euthanasia among the HIV populations in cities such as Sydney and San Francisco. While many deaths occur without incident, some do not and these, in particular, raise very serious ethical concerns. Having demonstrated the existence and effects of the underground, Magnusson proceeds to raise a number of questions of policy and of how the practice might best be responded to. He insists that an intelligent and considered response to the problem excludes either resorting to existing criminal measures or placing one's hopes in the possibility of widespread legalisation of euthanasia. Rather, he argues that we should aim to minimise harm to the likes of those who presently have no option to expose themselves to the 'underground' through education and, to some extent, legal regulation of the practice. Ultimately, he argues that we must begin by making the euthanasia underground visible, accepting its existence without seeking either to punish or redeem its participants through the deployment or revision of existing law. His chapter marks an important stage in that process.

In contrast to the previous chapters in this section, Clifford's contribution approaches death and dying from a very different perspective whilst simultaneously broadening the scope of the volume through her study of the confessional poetry of three 20th. Century American poets and suicides: Anne Sexton, Sylvia Plath, and John Berrymann. She analyses the writings of the three poets for the light they may shed on modern attitudes towards suicide. She thus situates their poetry in a distinct social context. Clifford argues that the general social attitude towards suicide is one of a taboo. In contrast, the poetry of her three poets testifies against the depersonalisation of death in mass society. Each in their respective way attempts to individuate death and dying through the representation of suicide as the most personal and self-defining of acts. Suicide is not represented as a 'good death' but a death that is one's own, that belongs to and expresses oneself. She proceeds to identify certain distinct benefits from engaging with their poetry, despite the melancholic reputation it has long enjoyed. Thus she argues, for example, that their poetry helps to alter our view of the suicidal person, helps to alter the stereotype of the suicidal person as hopelessly out of control. It thereby re-personalises the suicidal person and forces us to look more carefully at a presumed type of person that has long been excluded from the consciousness of what might be termed 'polite society'. In addition, she also emphasises the potentially therapeutic benefits of writing poetry as a means for confronting despair, so that when one writes of suicide, one may thereby help prevent, rather than ensure, its occurrence.

Peters's chapter concludes section three and, with it, the book as a whole. He presents a philosophical examination of the relationship between irony and death within the philosophical writings of the likes of Hegel and Kierkegaard. Specifically, Peters focuses upon the phenomenological philosophical tradition and the enduring problem of solipsism that philosophers working in this tradition have long been beset by. He questions whether a conscious awareness of the inevitability of death can provide the constitutive ground for inter-subjective experience. Does the very fact of death, ironically, help us escape from the philosophical prison of the pure ego which many phenomenologists confine us to? Like Johnson's chapter before it, Peters argues that one cannot have a direct experience of death. However, he insists that the proximity of death does exert a direct effect upon our experience of time and its passing and this provides the potential ground for the inter-subjective experience lacking from phenomenological philosophies. Phenomenologists, he insists, would benefit from directing their attention towards the issue of temporality and death. The irony residing in the contribution death may make to an understanding of the living.

Life in the Heart

Asa Kasher

"I am searching," says a certain stranger, in a story by Borges, "I am searching for the secret river which purifies man of death" [1]

"We cannot find it," say countless people to themselves, both strangers and friends. "We cannot find this hidden river which purifies man of death."

"We cannot find it, such a shame," say many to themselves. A few, though, tell us, "We cannot find it, no big deal." The former offer us one image of death, so that we may live in its shadow. The latter offer us a different image of death, so that we may live by its light. Both depictions are ancient; both have carried people along. Each has its own place in the museum of the great images of life and death, but neither one of them does us much good. We will examine them both now, briefly, to set the stage for our view, the third one.

At the heart of one image of death stands "destiny," an inescapable fate that is a consequence of man's very nature according to some, or of a "decree" of the Creator, according to others. Either which way, says this perception of death, it is the way of the world that "the deceased is forgotten from the heart" and there is nothing in the world that can stop this. In ancient times the essence of this view, there was already a Jewish sage, Rav, who considered this image to be in essence though not in full detail self-evident: "The deceased is not forgotten from the heart, only after twelve months" (*Babylonian Talmud*, Tractate Berachoth 58b). Other ancient sages not only acknowledged the truth of this view of death but declared it essential for man's existence, "otherwise man would not exist". "Three phenomena were part of the plan at Creation ... and it is fitting that they should be part of the plan ...". One of them is "that the dead will be forgotten" (*Babylonian Talmud*, Tractate Pesahim 54b).

Put differently, in modern verse, seven dead persons say in the Israeli poet Nathan Zach's "Shiv'a [Hebrew for seven, as well as first mourning period]": "Will remember us those who cannot forget. Our figure fades by the hour".[2] They "know" that sooner or later, each of them will be forgotten from the hearts.

The tendency to forget has not passed from this world, and many take this path without even realizing it. Such is anyone who describes his attendance at another's funeral as paying "last respects", as if after the funeral there will no longer be room for respect since there will no longer be room for the person to pay respect to. Such is anyone who "bids farewell" to the deceased, as if afterwards there will be no further affinity, since a person who was, and is no longer, will no longer play a part in the life story of a person who was and still is.

I once had the opportunity to purchase many special books, as many as I wanted. I visited a bookstore that specialized in antique and used books, and also warmly welcomes all visitors. I asked to see memorial volumes that were written in honour of deceased soldiers. They took me to a nearby place that was packed with used books, and they pointed to the ceiling and showed me everything that lay between it and the shelf below it, telling me: here are hundreds of memorial volumes. I asked to see them all and they took them down for me, dozens at a time. I opened them all, leafed through most of them and put many aside for myself. Each and every book was written with a broken heart, with a trembling hand, and with unmistakable love in honour of a dear person, loved most dearly, second to none. To my mind, each of these books is a human gem, incomparably pure, but at the same time, each of them lay there as a stone that no one would turn.

I was consumed with pity. A book about a person, if its story is forgotten, not only is the book forgotten, but possibly also the person who is its subject. That day, I bought nearly a hundred of those books, and I have looked, at some time or other, through each. Three copies of one book lay there, all given by the parents of the deceased to their friends, in memory of their son, Eli, each of them inscribed and signed.[3] I took all three, not wanting to leave them there, offended, so to speak, coming from where they had come and reaching the place they had reached, as if forgotten three times.

Then and there, I saw the process of forgetting for what it is. At first glance, it appeared to be an obvious path. Here are the forgotten books and here are the forgotten dead. In truth, however, it is a miserable path. There is no "decree" on any book that it should be cast aside, left as a stone unturned. The path of forgetting is a bad, painful, irritating and unnecessary one. There is no "decree" on any person that he should be forgotten by the heart. No man is forgotten, if there is someone who resolved not to allow him to be forgotten, if there were someone who did not succumb to the temptation to forget. This is not a temptation that is difficult to resist and it is not beyond our power to defeat the cancerous forgetfulness. When I brought a memorial volume into my house, I brought a person into my heart, so here is a person who now is not forgotten by the heart, for he has a place within my heart. I wanted that person not to be a person who was forgotten by the heart; I made him a man who was not forgotten by the heart, and now, indeed, he is a man who was not forgotten by the heart.

There is no sense in the path of forgetting. The great image of death, that views the dead "being forgotten by the heart" as an unavoidable "decree," is a false image. There is another option, and there is no decree; one can choose to forget or not to forget. The reality is not, as the poet describes it, on the behalf of those who have died, regarding those who are alive, "will remember us those who cannot forget," but rather the reverse, said on the behalf of those who are alive, regarding those who have died, "they who do not wish to remember will forget them."

An alternate image of death views it as the passage from the vestibule that is life in this world, to the banquet hall, which is life in the World to Come. An ancient Jewish sage, Rabbi Yaakov, said: "This world can be compared to a vestibule before the World to Come. Prepare yourself in the vestibule so that you may enter the banquet hall" (*Mishna*, Pirkey Avoth IV,21). The Jewish philosopher, Rabbi Yosef (Joseph) Ibn Kaspi, presented an exceptionally sharp formulation of this view in *Sefer Hamusar* [*Book of* Admonition] an ethical will to his son, written in the fall of 1332. "I am thy surety, my son," he says, "that if thou dost fulfill all my behests, thou wilt after thy death reach the highest degree of good appointed unto us for the world to come, and the expression 'after death' will be only a figure of speech, and when thy house-hold think thee dead, then wilt thou be truly alive".[4] The great show that is called life is only a general rehearsal for the true life. The story of man's sojourn in this world is only an introduction to the real story, which takes place after man has finished his journey here.

The image of "passage" is not the sole one in this image of death. In fact, it is just one piece of a great, religious, intricate and special mosaic. This mosaic contains not only the image of "this world" as a vestibule leading to the great banquet hall that is the "World to Come," but also an image of the "virtuous and just" life in "this world", alongside an image of the reward received in the World to Come for being virtuous and just as well as, in contrast, an image of the punishment received for not fulfilling this ideal. All these images surround the mosaic's central image of the "thick darkness where God" is (*Exodus* 20:21).

We do not relate to this conception of death. Whenever we have discussed the meaning of life we have dealt with the meaning of life on earth.[5] Likewise, whenever we will discuss here the meaning of death, we will deal with the meaning of death on earth. Whatever we have said about the meaning of life was not expressed on the background of any ready-made grand picture of existence. Whatever we have said about the meaning of life can be realized in the life of a person who, wittingly or unwittingly, has not accepted any religion and its commandments, just as it can be realized in the life of a religious person who has accepted upon himself some religion and its practices. Similarly, whatever we will have to say about the meaning of death will find expression both in the life of a religious person and in the life of a deliberately or inadvertently irreligious person. Therefore, the vague image of the "passage" is also not our view.

We want to propose a third approach. In his life, man writes the story of his life. In death, according to the first approach, the story of man's life reaches the final page, the final line. The back cover of the book is reached, and the book ends and is put away, "forgotten by the heart." The third approach views death differently. In his life, man writes the story of his life, and in his death, the story of his life continues, not by itself, but within the life story of one who loves him. The one who loves him writes his own life story during his lifetime, and in it, also, the continuation of his beloved's life story. When he, too, ultimately dies, his life story is perpetuated, not on its own, but in the life stories of those who love him, and within it the story of his beloved who had lived within his heart. Thus, a person's life story continues in the life stories of those who love him, and those who love the ones who loved him and those who love those who loved the ones who loved him. In this way, as long as there is love in this world, those who are loved live in the hearts of those who love them and in the hearts of those who love those who loved them and in the hearts of those who love those who loved the ones who loved them, endlessly.

This third approach differs also from the second approach. According to the second approach, man writes the introduction to his life story during his lifetime. In his death, the introduction reaches the final page, the final line. The back cover of the introductory volume is reached and this volume closes and the introduction is as if it never was. Then the real book, the book of life opens. According to the third approach, however, man writes the story of his life during his lifetime – not an introduction, but the story itself. Death stops man from developing the story, from continuing the story from the place where it was cut off. For this reason, man's death is a terrible end, a bitter tragedy, and total devastation. Yet despite this, his life's story continues – beyond the back cover of his book – within the life stories of those who love him. His life story continues and he lives, not on his own but within the hearts of those who love him, he lives in the hearts.

A dear, loved, unique person who lives in the heart of someone who loves him continues to be a dear, loved, and unique person in that person's heart. A wise, brave, outstanding human being who lives in the heart of someone who loves him, continues to be a wise, brave, outstanding human being in that person's book of life just as he was in his own book of life. A modest individual who lives in the heart of someone who loves him remains a modest individual, the embodiment of modesty, in that person's heart just as he was a modest individual and the embodiment of modesty in his own right. A virtuous man is a virtuous man is a virtuous man, in his life, in his death, and in the heart of someone who loves him.

This third conception of death, of "life in the heart," appears, at first glance, to be a completely new conception in a bold, perhaps even too daring style. Upon further inspection, however, this conception turns out to be a new mosaic, made of many tiles, some ancient, others the work of other generations, but all fitting together, as if they are ready-made. The tiles of this mosaic together form a picture of an individual, who is a complete world, who lives in the heart, while each of these tiles alone is only the picture of one specific silhouette of a complete being, a silhouette that lives in the heart. In different times, places, and cultures, different silhouettes, living in the heart, reveal themselves, as will be seen in the sequel. The image of "life in the heart" is not an image of one individual silhouette, or one of just certain special silhouettes, but a full image composed of all the silhouettes and profiles at one time, an image of a complete person who lives in the heart.

Talking about silhouettes of a dead person is using a metaphor that needs some clarification. Anthropologists tell as about the Batek of Malaysia that they see a person as composed of body, life and shadow, a transparent entity which inhabits the body, determines personal identity and leaves the body upon death.[6] Thus, a person's shadow is, in a sense, one's presence. Accordingly, a silhouette, in a related sense, is an aspect of one's presence, whether it resides in a body or not.

Man's name is one silhouette of his life. Every person has a name that his life has given him, which began as a tag on the tiny arm of a baby, "the name given by his father and mother",[7] but which over time becomes a silhouette of the person, and part of his identity. When man dies, this silhouette can live in others' hearts. Man's name endures, not as a name in a list of names, but as it was, the name of the person whose name this was, whose name this is.

Man's name is written after his death on his tombstone. If a cemetery can be compared to a forest, it is first and foremost a forest of names. Yet cemeteries have not always existed and even when they were first built, graves were not always marked. The decision to engrave the deceased's name on a tombstone, historians explain, reflected a certain outlook on death: "The erection of a tumulus crowned by an upright stone or by a planted wooden post marked the desire to inscribe the presence of the dead on the surface of the ground, too, and to mark it out to the living forever".[8] In Rome, during the first centuries AD, for example, "the inviolability sanctioned by the law was meant not only to ensure the inviolability of the bodies laid in tombs, but also, if not especially, was aimed at guaranteeing that the 'nomen' of the dead man, his memory, his personality in all its different manifestations, private and public, would endure through time".[9] Thus, a precious individual did not fade away, his memory was not extinguished; he was not forgotten. His name on his tombstone perpetuates the fact that such a person lived and that this was his name. A passer-by seeing the name on the tombstone, knowing that "every name has a person," recognizes that before him is the tombstone of the man who possessed this name. If he takes the impression of the name on the tombstone with him when he leaves the cemetery, he gives this silhouette of the person a place in his heart; he gives it life in his heart. Possibly, he may even give the entire person, and not merely his silhouette, life within his heart.

This silhouette of man lives on not only in the cemetery, in the form of a name on a stone. A man's name can live on when another person is named after him. In certain cultures, in the early part of the Middle Ages as well as in our days, in the island of Carpathus, between Rhodes and Crete, among other places, a man's name passes on through inheritance by a set formula: the firstborn son is named after his paternal grandfather while the eldest daughter is named after her maternal grandmother.[10] In naming a child the name of the deceased, we give his silhouette a place among the living, and life in the hearts of others, also in his death. A woman by the name of Zohar once related to me that she was named after her mother's brother, who was killed before she was born. Her name is her own name, but it is also *his* silhouette. Her name opens a small door in the path to him. Whoever remembers that she was named after him, gives Zohar's silhouette, and perhaps even Zohar himself, life in his heart.

Based on this conception of man's name as a living silhouette of the man himself, we understand the known phrase "may his name be obliterated" (similarly "may his name and memory be obliterated"). The curse is that that name should be obliterated from every place that it is written. In other words, that that man's silhouette should cease existing the moment he departs this world. If in fact this curse comes true, then it is reasonable to presume that that man will not be present in anyone's heart and, certainly, that he won't live in the heart.

The opposite of this curse is the blessing expressed by Ben Sira (Ecclesiasticus): "Their bodies are buried in peace, but their name liveth for evermore" (44:14). The blessing is that each person's silhouette should "live for evermore", and, perhaps, in this way he too will "live" in people's hearts "for evermore." The famous poet, Rudyard Kipling, who lost his own son in the First World War, recognized the significance of that blessing, and chose the verse from Ben Sira to be inscribed in all WWI British military cemeteries in the care of the Imperial War Graves Commission [later, the Commonwealth War Graves Commission].[11] The first part of the verse is apparently self-evident, though not in the case of Kipling's son, John, and in many other similar cases,[12] but the second half of the verse is a deep and moving blessing: "their name liveth for evermore".

Man's name is a complete silhouette, a silhouette of the entire man, body and soul, his views and feelings, his hopes and memories. Not every silhouette of a man is complete. There are narrow silhouettes, there are broad ones, and there are complete ones, all depending on what is reflected. Man's name is a full silhouette; his will is a broad one since it reflects – in life and in death – his values, his character, and his dreams.

Man's conclusive will, in the sense of the things that he desired in his lifetime and achieved, as well as the things that he desired in his lifetime and failed to achieve, can be given a place in our lives, if we so choose. In his death too, we can honour his will, honour a unique silhouette of his, honour him. In his death too, we can find a place in our hearts for that particular silhouette, and perhaps even for the man casting that silhouette.

Though people do not notice it, they often give life to another's silhouette when they carry out his last will. Such is the way of the proper world – if a man writes a will in his lifetime, his heirs carry it out after his death. He himself may have departed from the world, but his silhouette remains in this world, and his will endures in this world. By honouring a last will, one honours the person's wishes, and the person himself, in his death.

A man's last will can indicate his wishes concerning financial assets and property, or, alternatively, concerning values and virtues. Either way, those who survive him respect it, both by giving his silhouette life in their hearts and by giving his desires a place in the world of the living. "Man's will is his honour".

What a man wants in life is what brings him honour in death, even if he didn't leave a will, even if he never made his desires known, and even if he never considered how the world would look after his death. Man's will, even if he left not a word regarding the days following his death, is nevertheless his will, his silhouette, that can be honoured, though he is no longer. On November 6, 1817, Princess Charlotte, the British crown prince's only daughter, died, after giving birth to a lifeless son. The day after the funeral, the Earl of Lauderdale came to Claremont to offer his condolences to Prince Leopold, her husband. "I will live and die at Claremont," Prince Leopold vowed to his friend, "I will devote every moment of my future life to carry into effect all the ideas of that blessed angel whom I have lost forever" and he burst into a flood of tears.[13] Leopold resolved to dedicate his life to fulfilling every one of his wife's wishes, to giving her silhouette, after her death, life in the real world of practice, to giving his Charlotte life in his heart, all his days until his own death.

Man's will projects a wide silhouette. Man's personal soul-searching, his self-evaluation in a moment of truth, can also cast a wide silhouette. On occasion, man's will, in his life, to find clear expression in his death for his self-evaluation, can throw a special, double silhouette. Rabbi Eleazar ben Shmuel Halevi (son of Samuel the Levite) from Mainz wrote in his will in 1356, "I beg of you, my sons and daughters, my wife and all the congregation, that no funeral oration be spoken in my honour … At a distance of thirty cubits from the grave, they shall set my coffin on the ground, and drag me to the grave by a rope attached to the coffin. Every four cubits they shall stand and wait awhile, doing this in all seven times, so that I may find atonement for my sins. ..."[14] Rabbi Eleazar considered himself a Jew who had been defiled by sin, a Jew whose sins had not been forgiven, and who therefore deserved to be disgraced in death in order to atone for his past sins. Whoever accompanied Rabbi Eleazar to the cemetery, if he fulfilled his last request, dragging his coffin on the ground four cubits seven times, gave two of Rabbi Eleazar's silhouettes, for some time at least, a place in the real world: the silhouette produced by his personal soul-searching, within a second silhouette born of his will to see that penetrating appraisal come to clear expression after his death. If, indeed, they treated him thus in his death, Rabbi Eleazar had, at that time, life in the hearts of his loved ones – exceptional life.

Rabbi Eleazar understood what it is to live in another's heart. He further wrote in his will: "Put me in the ground at the right hand of my father, and if the space be a little narrow, I am sure that he loves me well enough to make room for me by his side".[15] Not only his father's love lived in his heart – his father lived in his heart.

In his lifetime, man has many faces; in his death, he has many silhouettes. The ways in which man can give his beloved's silhouette life in his heart – so that he will be among the living, so that he will be among those who live in the heart – are wondrously diverse and too numerous to reckon.

Some will carve out their own path, while others will take paths already paved by others and which are open also before them. Language readily provides such pre-paved paths. Any person who is fluent in a language can easily, almost without noticing, take these paths. Every language has an abundance of expressions that convey the idea of life in the hearts.

Every language is replete with euphemisms, stock phrases, which make it easier to express oneself in special circumstances. There are many such phrases that make it easier for a speaker to express himself regarding a person who has passed away.[16] Some say: to allow the speaker to get around the language of death. We say: to allow the speaker to articulate in the idiom of life in the heart. When three sentences ago we described a person as having passed away the image was of a person alive, still on his feet, journeying as he is into his next world. So too for other death euphemisms such as: "entered his eternal home," "gathered unto his fathers," "went to his world", "come to his people" and "summoned by the heavenly academy." These also paint an image of life. When a person who is careful with his words chooses one of these phrases, one may presume that it is because the deceased lives in his heart.

This is true in Hebrew, as well as in other languages, like English: "to lower the curtain", "to hang up one's hat", in the footsteps of Hebrew, also "to go the way of all men" and "to cross that river",[17] and in the footsteps of Greek, "to join the immortals", and so on and so forth.[18] These are all life images.

The abundance of such expressions, which is an abundance of images, is actually inexhaustible, as much as the abundance of images in the language is inexhaustible. In a cemetery of a village on the shores of Scotland, a tombstone for an 11 year old boy, Andrew Adam, was erected in 1758, saying: "…I harrbour here below, \ Where now I lie at anchor sure, \ With many of owre fleet, \ Expecting on[e] day to sail \ My admiral to meet ".[19] It is quite reasonable to assume that those who loved Andrew, by creating the image that emerges from what they engraved on the tombstone of their beloved Andrew, meant to express a broader image of Andrew, living in the hearts, anchored, speaking.

It is important to understand that euphemisms do not deny death, dull the pain, or console the inconsolable. The Hebrew expression "*nafal*" (fell) does not cloud the image of death, neither in the mouth of King David in his lament over Saul and Jonathan, "How are the mighty fallen," nor for any of the visitors to the military cemetery in which each buried soldier is described on his tombstone as having "fallen." Nevertheless, the image of a person who has fallen is an image of a person that one can stand beside, that one can assist and keep the light in his eyes from going out – and all in spite of his death.

To "fall," to "sleep the eternal slumber" – neither phrase eases the bitterness of death, not even a bit, yet each offers an image of life in the heart. "One who sleeps" must be alive; one who "sleeps the eternal slumber" lives in the heart, in his death.

"...To die! to sleep!", Hamlet says in his famous speech, "To be or not to be," "To die! to sleep! / No more! and by a sleep to say we end / The heart-ache and the thousand natural shocks / That flesh is heir to!...To die! To sleep! / To sleep; perchance to dream!..." (*Hamlet*, III,I,60-65).

Voltaire formulates Hamlet's speech in this way: "...And what is death? \ It is an end to our troubles, my personal sanctuary; \ After long suffering, peaceful rest. \ We sleep, and it is the end to everything..." (translated from Voltaire's French translation of Hamlet's soliloquy, Voltaire, 1909-14, Vol. XXXIV, Part 2).

The poet Alexander Pope writes in similar vein, "Heroes and kings! Your distance keep: / In peace let one poor poet sleep," words which later were used in an epitaph on his tombstone after his death in 1744.[20] Similarly, as the sign on the entrance to every cemetery in France after the Revolution read, according to a 1793 decree by Fouchet, "Death is the eternal slumber".[21]

"To sleep an eternal sleep," "to rest an eternal rest" – both are visions of a man who lives in death too. A person who does not view the dead as living in the heart will not distinguish between these phrases because, in his weak eyes, both merely depict death. However, a person who sees visions of life in the heart will distinguish between the two phrases. There are more signs of life in the image of a person resting than in that of someone sleeping. Regarding the righteous, Raban Shimon ben Gamliel said, "Their words are their memorial" (*Jerusalem Talmud*, Tractate Shekalim II 37a), for when people mention the words of a particular righteous person, "his lips move in the grave" (*Babylonian Talmud*, Tractate Yevamoth 97a). Or, in the first person wording of the commentator, "my lips move in grave, as if I am alive" (Rashi, *ibid.*). This might be an image of a man resting; surely not the image of a man sleeping.[22]

Just as language in general is full of expressions of life in the heart, so too, traditional usages in special circumstances can generate terms of life in the heart. Such is the tradition of eulogy, a special usage of language in honour of the deceased, in particular during his funeral. An ancient tradition has the eulogizer turning to the deceased and speaking in second person, as in "you have been very dear to me my brother Jonathan" or "that I should die instead of you." In our days as well, though generally no one believes, as was once taken for granted, that the deceased himself hears the cries and the mourning, we still address the deceased to praise, honour, and show love for him. The funeral orator, facing the beloved, deceased person, knows beyond any doubt that the beloved one is no longer alive, yet he still speaks to him directly because he lives in his heart. Within the image of his beloved living in his heart, he turns to him, naturally, speaks to him, movingly.[23]

The poet Giovanni Gioviano Pontano, a citizen of Naples, at the end of the fifteenth century, is considered the last of the great Latin poets. On his unique tombstone one can read dialogues between visitors and the deceased, or his singular spirit.[24] Within the image of the poet living in the hearts of those who loved him or admired him, just as they can speak to him, so he can address them as well as anyone who passes by. More than that: just as they can start a conversation with him, he – who lives in the heart – can open a conversation with them. Indeed, that is how the dialogues appear on the tombstone of this humanist poet.

A silhouette can sometimes be quite narrow. One of Dali's sculptures is called "A Gesture to Newton" (1969). It is an image of a man holding in his right hand a simple pendulum. His head and chest are holed through, totally empty. The name "Newton" is presented in this sculpture as the name of a piece of science, not as the name of a man, a man with the breath of life, a man with his own personality. If in your world the name "Lincoln" is not a street name, but a man's name, after whom the street was called, it could be that Lincoln's silhouette has a place in your heart, but it still may be narrow and faint.

A stranger's silhouette in another's heart need not remain faint. I once lived on Balzico Street, on the outskirts of the city Torino (Turin) in Italy. I imagined that the street was named after a person and every time I uttered the name of the street, I did so with the knowledge that it was the name of a person, so his pale silhouette found a place in my heart. When I soon noticed a note on one street sign that Alfonso Balzico was a sculptor, I told myself that one day I would find one of his sculptures and so his silhouette would expand in my heart. Eventually, I read that he was a nineteenth century sculptor in the court of King Vitorio Emanuelle II and that his sculptures are prominently displayed in Rome and other cities, information that further sharpened his silhouette in my heart. Eventually, I saw one of his sculptures, "Ferdinando, Duke of Genoa" in Torino, and his silhouette expanded even more within me.

The image of life in the heart can be a broad, expansive silhouette or even a complete silhouette. But there is an image of life in the heart that is even deeper and more complete, possessing more life than a silhouette can contain. This image of life in the heart does not contain a silhouette, but rather a whole person, as he is.

In this clear depiction of life in the heart, man lives in the hearts of those who love him in his death exactly as he lived in their world in his lifetime, to the extent that is possible. Once again, language can help us distinguish between this clear image of life in the heart and other representations of life in the heart. Someone who speaks of his loved one from within the clear image of life in the heart, speaks in the present, not in the past tense, as much as possible. I love Yehoraz, my firstborn son, my late son – in the present; I am proud of Yehoraz – in the present; I learn from Yehoraz – in the present; I long to Yehoraz – in the present; Yehoraz lives in my heart, in death, just as he lived in my world in his lifetime, to the extent that that is possible. To the extent that it is possible, for I once had constant joy seeing Yehoraz develop – in the past; seeing his hopes fulfilled – in the past; seeing his future spread out, like a red carpet, at his feet – in the past. "To the extent that it is possible" means without constant joy; means memory in the present of past joy; means present joy of memories from the past; but nothing more.

"How many children do you have?" One who has a clear image of life in the heart still counts a dead child as one of his children. If he once had three, he does not now respond "two," nor does he answer, "three but now two." All three live in his heart. One lives only in the heart, while the two live also in the heart. Essentially, in the hearts of those who love him, in his death too, a beloved person is alive.

Our conception of life in the heart is integrative. A family of separate silhouettes is expected to turn into a unified, fully-fledged image of a person, living in one's heart. At this point, it would be only natural to consider what can be dubbed *the cognitive problem of integration*. We seem to have the required cognitive and emotional facilities for maintaining in our hearts viable silhouettes. We have just shown it, by pointing out some examples. However, do we really have the facilities required for maintaining in our hearts viable images of persons, rather than some of their silhouettes, images that are as intricate and as independent as persons who are alive?

Consider your image of Job. One may safely assume that some people have a viable cognitive image of Job in their minds. When asked questions of the form "What would have Job said, facing a certain question or argument", they are able to provide us with answers that make sense as Job's answers. Not only are they compatible with Job's views and appropriately intricate, but in a sense they are also independent of the speakers who have an image of Job in their minds. Their Job's reactions could be quite different from their own reactions, facing the same challenges. Moreover, one may safely assume that some people have a viable cognitive as well as emotional image of Job in their hearts. They have an operative image of both Job's views and emotions and they can appropriately express both.

Interestingly, according to one Talmudic interpretation of the book of Job, the figure of Job is a religious fiction and the book of Job is a parable. Accordingly, at least some people have cognitive and emotional images of Job, whom they have never met, in person, either because he died long ago or because he has never lived on earth.

It is, then, reasonable to assume that if some people have the ability to maintain cognitive and emotional images of persons such as Job, whom they have never met, for one reason or other, then at least some people have the ability to maintain a cognitive and emotional image of a person they did meet, either in person or under suggestive circumstances such as those of a novel or a play.

Consider now a related kind of evidence. Some developmental psychologists have recently been interested in *Imaginary Companions and the Children Who Create Them*, to use the title of Taylor (1999). Imaginary companions of a person are those that (i) are clearly recognized by the person as being imaginary, and (ii) hold the person's sincere interest for a significant period of time. Some reports show that about 40% of 3- and 4-years-olds and 63% of children up to the age of 7 have imaginary companions, whether created or impersonated.[25] Since the interaction of a child with one's imaginary companion is clearly on a par with one's ordinary intricate interaction with an independent person,[26] it would be reasonable to assume that most of the children have the abilities of maintaining a cognitive and emotional viable image of a person, which they recognize as an imaginary person.

To be sure, imaginary companions of various kinds play a role in the life of adults as well. It has been claimed that most people experience having a personal relationship with some famous individuals they have never encountered outside books, movies and media, where the maintained interactions are not unilateral but rather involve, for example, imagined conversations and meetings.[27] More recent work shows that creative activities in adulthood, such as writing, involve the presence of independent *Invisible Guests*, to use the title of Watkins.[28]

We suggest that such abilities have to do with the abilities of adults to maintain a cognitive and emotional viable image of a person who does not exist in the real world, that is to say, a person who lives only in the hearts of some people.

Our abilities to maintain an intricate and independent viable image of such a person, our abilities to preserve and protect, express and manifest the personal point of view of such a person, our abilities to practice a form of life in the heart, are actually abilities to maintain, with dear persons who have passed away, *Continuing Bonds*, to use the title of a certain collection of studies by bereavement scholars Klass, Silverman and Nickman.[29] I have read or heard many keen suggestions "to let go", numerous apparently professional advices "to cope with death and depart from the dead", innumerably many rhetorical questions as to "whether I have already overcome it". I take it for granted that each and every one of those remarks has been well meant, however, to my mind, it has also been inapt, insensitive, misdirected, even cruel and oppressive. Thus, it was a relief to read a collection of papers by scholars who have eventually gained the insight, long known to so many persons in grief, that continuing bonds with the deceased are possible, natural, common, significant, and meaningful. They are neither denial nor "pathological", that the dominant twentieth-century model which holds that the function of grief and mourning is to cut bonds with the deceased is based more on some particular values than on substantial data or professional insights. Continuing bonds are manifestations of love, expressions of life in the hearts.

In the clear image of life in the heart, those who remain alive wish to bestow the gift of life upon their deceased loved one, not only in their own hearts, but in others' too, first, with him, then, somewhat after him, eventually much after him, eternally, in the hearts. One who lives with a clear image of life in the heart does not shrink from "eternity," for love offers the deceased eternal life within the hearts of those who love him.

Countless are all the expressions of love and innumerable are the expressions of life in the hearts of people who love a deceased person. "Do not stand at my grave and weep / I am not there. / I do not sleep. / I am a thousand winds that blow / I am the diamond glints on snow. / I am the sunlight on ripened grain / I am the gentle autumn rain. / When you awaken in the morning's hush / I am the swift uplifting rush / Of quiet birds / in circled flight. / I am the soft stars that shine at night. / Do not stand at my grave and cry, / I am not there; / I did not die".[30] An unknown poet wrote it. A British soldier, Steven Cummins, saved it in an envelope in his pocket, labelled "For my loved ones", when he died, being 24 years old, during active duty in Londonderry, where his armoured vehicle activated a hostile mine.

A man who is loved lives in the hearts of those who love him, in his death too. This is generally how a clear image of life in the heart is drawn. There is another possibility, similar but different, that arises from the tombstone of an RAF pilot, G. Hodges, who fell in battle in 1944. Thus reads the inscription at the bottom of the grave, in the Brookwood Military Cemetery: "To live in the hearts / of those we love / is not to die".[31] The clear image of life in the heart allows a man who is loved to live in the hearts of those who love him, in death, and allows a man who loves to live in the hearts of those he loved, in death. Sometimes, those he loves and those who love him are the same, and these two possibilities are identical, but occasionally they are not and both can derive from the clear image of life in the heart.

D. Yalom depicts in his story, *When Nietzsche Wept* (1992), Breuer, the doctor, and Nietzsche, the philosopher, visiting a cemetery. Breuer gestured to the fresh wreaths of flowers lying on many graves, saying that was the Land of the Dead, those were the dead, and those, he added, pointing to the old abandoned and neglected section of the cemetery, were the truly dead. No one took care of their graves because no one who had known them was still alive. They knew what it means to die".[32]

The contrast between well-tended tombstones and abandoned ones, even within the same cemetery, is a called-for distinction, but Breuer's explanation as presented in Yalom's book is incorrect. If it were true then the memorial that stands in the heart of London erected "by their friends and officers" in honour of those who fell in WWI would presumably also be neglected since all their "friends and officers" have long since passed from this world. Yet that memorial is well taken care of. Recently I saw it adorned with wreaths of fresh flowers. One does not need to have known a person in his lifetime in order to place a flower on his tombstone or on a memorial in his honour, to honour him in his death, to give him a place in his heart, or even life in his heart. Not only those who loved and were loved, relatives and friends, can give a person life in their hearts. On a memorial in memory of the British general, Charles George Gordon, who was killed in Sudan in 1885, the words of the Poet Laureate Lord Tennyson appear, in honour of Gordon, in his death: "Warrior of God, man's friend, and tyrant's foe, / Now somewhere dead far in the waste Sudan, / Thou livest in all hearts, for all men know / This earth has never borne a nobler man".[33] Not only those who loved Gordon, not only those Gordon loved, but "everyone," not because they loved him, but because they "knew" him, because they valued his nobility of spirit.

In their esteem for his nobility, while he still lived in their hearts, perhaps some of that nobility adhered itself to them. As the writer George Eliot wrote in the poem, "Oh, May I Join the Choir Invisible"," song during her funeral and inscribed on her tombstone: "Of those immortal dead who live again / in minds made better by their presence".[34] The clear image of life in the heart is not an image of a man who has in his death, in the hearts of those he loved, those who loved him, and others, refuge from absolute gloom, from complete oblivion. The clear image of life in the heart is an image of a person who in death lives in the hearts of loved ones and those who loved him and others just as he did in his life. To give a cherished person life in your heart means giving life in your world to his values, virtues and customs.

To give life in your world to values, virtues and customs means putting them into practice, including them in the principles that govern your life, giving them a real place in what gives meaning to your life. To give man in his death life in your heart is giving him in his death a place at a focus of the meaning of your life.

Man who lives in the heart, in his death, is a man whose life continues past the back cover of the book of his life in this world.

Man who lives in the heart, in his death, is a man who has life as a hero, as family, between the pages of another's life story.

Man who lives in the heart, in his death, is a man who lives through the meaning of life of a close person, in his life.

Man who lives in the heart, in his death, lives in the heart when he no longer lives on earth.

Man who lives in the heart, in his death, gives meaning to lives upon this earth.

Bibliography

Abrahams, I., *Hebrew Ethical Wills.* (Philadelphia: Jewish Publication Society of America, 1926.

Anonymous. *Do Not Stand at My Grave and Weep.* Special edition, illustrated by Paul Sanders. London: Souvenir Press, 1996.

Ben Zvi, I [President] and Yanait Ben Tzvi, R. *Eli.* Jerusalem: Kiriath Sefer, 1957.

Borges, J.L. Labyrinths, Selected Stories and Other Writings. New York, New Directions, 1964.

Boyer, P. *Religion Explained.* New York: Basic Books, 2001.

Castle, J. and Phillips, W.L. Grief Rituals: Aspects that Facilitate Adjustment to Bereavement. *Journal of Loss and Trauma* 8:1. (2003)

Caughey, J.L. *Imaginary Social Worlds: A Cultural Approach.* Lincoln: University of Nebraska Press, 1984.

Endicott, K. *Batek Negrito Religion.* Oxford: Clarendon Press, 1997.

Frost, K.M. and Frost, C.J. On Loss and Melancholy: An Autobiographical Essay. *Journal of Loss and Trauma* 7:3. (2002)

Gad, D. Attitudes Toward Death in the Mishnaic and Talmudic Periods. Ph.D. thesis, Tel Aviv University, Vols. I-II. 1997

Geary, P.J. *Living with the Dead in the Middle Ages.* Ithaca: Cornell University Press, 1994.

Holt, T. and V. My Boy Jack? The Search for Kipling's Only Son, Barnsley: Leo Cooper, 2001.

Kasher, A. The Jewish Eulogy. In T. Brosh (ed.), *A Speech for Every Season.* Tel Aviv: Open University and Yediot Aharonoth, 2001.

Kasher, A. A Little Book on the Meaning of Life. In A. Kasher (ed.), *Meaning of Life.* Tel Aviv: Hakibbutz Hammeuhad and Yehoraz Association, 2001.

Kasher, A. *Spirit of Man.* Tel Aviv: Am Oved and Yehoraz Association, 2001.

Kasher, A. *A Little Book on the Meaning of Life.* Tel Aviv: Hakibbutz Hammeuhad and Yehoraz Association, 2002. [An extended version of Kasher (2000).]

Klass, D., Silverman, P. and Nickman, S. (eds.) *Continuing Bonds: New Understandings of Grief.* Philadelphia and London: Taylor & Francis, 1996.

Lerner, L. Angels and Absences, Child Deaths in the Nineteenth Century, Nashville: Vanderbilt University Press, 1997.

Murray, J.A. Loss as a Universal Concept: A Review of the Literature to Identify Common Aspects of Loss in Diverse Situations. *Journal of Loss and Trauma* 6:3.(2001)

Neaman, J.S. and Silver, C.G. *A Dictionary of Euphemisms*, London: Unwin Paperbacks, 1984.

Petrucci, A. Writing the Dead: Death and Writing Strategies in the Western Tradition. Stanford: Stanford University Press, 1998.

Rees, N. Epitaphs, a Dictionary of Grave Epigrams and Memorial Eloquence. London: Bloomsbury, 1993.

Sharvit, S. Expressions of Blessing for the Deceased. *Hebrew Linguistics,* 48. 2001

Taylor, M. *Imaginary Companions and the Children Who Create Them.* New York and Oxford: Oxford University Press, 1999.

Voltaire, F.M.A. de (1909-14). *Letters on the English*. In C.W. Eliot (ed.), *The Harvard Classics*, Vol. XXXIV, Part 2. www.bartleby.com/34/2/18.html.
Watkins, M Invisible Guests: The Development of Imaginal Dialogues. Boston: Sigo Press, 1990.
Willsher, B. Scottish Epitaphs, Epitaphs and Images from Scottish Graveyards. Edinburgh: Canongate Books, 1996.
Yalom, I.D. When Nietzsche Wept, A Novel of Obsession. New York: Basic Books, 1992.
Zach, N. *Northeastern*. Tel Aviv: Hakibbutz Hammeuhad, 1979.
Zelda. *Zelda's Poems*. Tel Aviv: Hakibbutz Hammeuhad, 1985.

Notes

1 Borges, J.L., Labyrinths, Selected Stories and Other Writings. (New York: New Directions. 1964)
2 Zach, N., Northeastern. (Tel Aviv: Hakkibutz Hammeuhad, 1979), p.124
3 Ben Zvi, I., & Yannit Ben Tzvi, R., Eli. (Jerusalem: Kiriath Sefer, 1957)
4 Abrahams, I., Hebrew Ethical Wills. (Philadelphia: Jewish Publication Society of America, 1926), p.159
5 See Kasher, A., A Little Book on the Meaning of Life. In A.Kasher (ed.) Meaning of Life. (Tel Aviv: Hakkibutz Hammeuhad and Yehoraz Association, 2000)
6 See Endicott, K., Batek Negrito Religion. (Oxford: Clarendon Press, 1979) and Boyer, P., Religion Explained.(New York: Basic Books, 2001), pp.211 & 227
7 See Zelda, Zelda's Poems. (Tel Aviv: Hakkibutz Hammeuhad, 1985), p.117
8 Jean-Pierre Vernants cited in Petrucci, A., Writing the Dead: Death and Writing Strategies in the Western Tradition. (Stanford: Stanford University Press, 1998) p.6
9 Petrucci, op cit. p.19
10 Geary, P.J., Living with the Dead in the Middle Ages. (Ithaca: Cornell University Press, 1994), pp.88-89
11 Rees, N., Epitaphs, a Dictionary of Grave Euphemisms and Memorial Eloquence. (London: Bloomsbury, 1993), p.247
12 Holt, T., My Boy Jack? The Search for Kipling's Only Son. (Barnsley: Leo Cooper, 2001)

[13] From The Times, 19 November 1817, quoted in Lerner, L., Angels and Absences, Child Deaths in the Nineteenth Century. (Nashville: Vanderbilt University Press, 1997), p.8
14 Abrahams, op cit. pp.217-18
15 Ibid
16 See Neaman, J.S. & Silver, C.G. A Dictionary of Euphemisms. (London: Unwin Paperbacks, 1984)
17 Sharvit, S., Expressions of Blessing for the Deceased. Hebrew Linguistics. 48, 2001, pp.85-86
18 Neaman & Silver, op cit. pp.143-161
19 Willsher, B., Scottish Epitaphs, Epitaphs and Images from Scottish Graveyards. (Edinburgh: Canongate Books, 1996), p.8
20 Rees, op cit. pp.183-184
21 Petrucci, op cit. p.104
22 On the practice of time see Gad, D., Attitudes Towards Death in the Mishnaic and Talmudic Periods. Ph.D. Thesis. Tel Aviv University, Vols. 1-2, Vol 1. p.104
23 See Kasher, A., The Jewish Eulogy. In T.Brosh (ed.), A Speech for Every Season. (Tel Aviv: Open University and Yediot Aharonoth, 1993)
24 Petrucci, op cit. p.82
25 Taylor, M., Imaginary Companions and the Children Who Create Them. (New York & Oxford: Oxford University Press, 1993), 27-33
26 Taylor, op cit. p.153
27 See Caughy, J.L., Imaginary Social Worlds: a Cultural Approach. (Lincoln: University of Nebraska Press, 1984) and Taylor, op cit.
28 Watkins, M., Invisible Guests: The Development of Imaginal Dialogues. (Boston: Sigo Press, 1990)
29 Klass, D., Silverman, P. & Nickman, S., (eds.) Continuing Bonds: New Understandings of Grief. (Philadelphia & London: Taylor & Francis, 1996). See also Castle, J. & Phillips, W.L., Grief Rituals: Aspects that Facilitate Adjustment to Bereavment. Journal of Loss and Trauma, 8:1, 2003 and Murray, J.A., Loss as a Universal Concept: a Review of the Literature to Identify Common Aspects of Loss in Diverse Situations. Journal of Loss and Trauma, 6:3, 2001, pp.51-55
30 Anonymous. Do Not Stand at my Grave and Weep. Special edition, illustrated by Paul Sanders. (London: Souvenir Press, 1996)
31 Rees, op cit. pp.125-26
32 See Frost, K.M. & Frost, C.J. On Loss and Melancholy: An Autobiographical Essay. Journal of Loss and Trauma, 7:3, p.191
33 Rees, op cit. p.106
34 See Rees, op cit. pp.80-81 and Lerner, op cit. pp.60-61

Asa Kasher is Laura Schwarz-Kipp Chair of Professional Ethics and Philosophy of Practice at Tel Aviv University, Tel Aviv, Israel

Sorrow Unconsoling and Inconsolable Sorrow: Grief as a Moral and Religious Practice

Darlene Fozard Weaver

In an essay on anger, Christian social ethicist Beverly Wildung Harrison makes a claim about feelings and the moral life which perhaps expresses a widely shared perspective: "Feelings deserve our respect for what they are. There are no 'right' and 'wrong' feelings."[1] According to Harrison, "feeling is the basic bodily ingredient that mediates our connectedness to the world."[2] Feelings, then, are sources for moral evaluation, not objects of such evaluation. "The moral question is not 'what do I feel?' but rather 'what do I do with what I feel?'"[3] Of course, what we may do with our feelings encompasses more than how we express them in action, for we can and do make choices about how to understand and evaluate our feelings, nurture or wean them, and, importantly, whether or not to dispose ourselves to feeling them. Consider, for instance, the feelings associated with romantic love. In a long term romantic relationship, we might endeavour to reawaken feelings of appreciation for and delight in the beloved through practices of remembering the early days of courtship, directing our attention to qualities in the beloved that we prize, engaging in activities that may enable—at least one hopes they will—a sense of closeness and excitement. Conversely, if we seek to "get over" a person we love, we may discard photographs and possessions that bring him or her to mind, busy ourselves with work, avoid sentimental love songs or re-narrate the relationship so as to convince ourselves that its end is "for the best." Feelings may happen to us, and thus are in some measure beyond our control, but we may nevertheless court some feelings and scorn others.

Harrison does not deny that we can seek and avoid feelings. Her claim is that we ought not to do so.[4] It is helpful for our purposes to note that Harrison makes this claim as part of a project which identifies, analyzes, and assesses attitudes toward anger within Christian tradition. Her aim is to show what is mistaken about these attitudes in part by reinterpreting Christian beliefs and practices that underlie, elicit, and warrant them. Harrison recognizes that ethical inquiry includes the articulation and evaluation of beliefs and practices that explain and commend or denigrate feelings. And since she understands that feelings are basic elements "in our relational transaction with the world," she grasps that our capacities to know and value depend on our capacities to feel.[5] Thus, beliefs and practices that stunt our capacities to feel disable us and ought to be rejected. Feelings or affections may not be right or wrong. Nonetheless, I do not share Harrison's insistence that we "should never seek feelings," precisely because I agree with her that they are ingredients in our relational transactions.[6] Since our capacities to know and value depend on our capacities to feel, we can feel in better and worse ways, that is, in ways that fittingly dispose us to know and love the good, or do not.[7]

This essay considers the affection of sorrow, particularly sorrow over the death of a loved one, with the aim of describing what it might mean to sorrow well. Perhaps we already know what it means. Psychologists tell us that grief over the death of a loved one generally consists of various stages, such as denial, anger, bargaining, depression, and acceptance.[8] It is easy to find books, support groups, and other resources that appropriate this understanding of grief as an emotional process in which the mourner's protest against death, in its varied stages of denial, anger, bargaining, and depression, is understandable and "normal." But a psychologically "healthy" experience of grief is one in which such protest terminates in acceptance. Thus, a vast array of books and support groups ostensibly enable us to deal with grief so as to "move on." To sorrow well is eventually to cease to sorrow, so as to be capable of delighting in the goods that life continues to offer.

The belief that grief runs such a course, and that grieving well means ceasing to grieve, thus directs us to other beliefs that may console sorrow. A young widow may be told with the best of intentions that she will marry again, or a couple who mourn a miscarriage may be reminded that they will yet have children. About the dead we may say that "it was her time," or that "he is in a better place." Christian burial practices include appeals to God's mercy, and petitions to strengthen the bereaved's hope in the resurrection.

But what if sorrowing well has something to do with refusing consolation? Jody Bottum suggests as much in his essay "All That Lives Must Die."[9] Bottum argues against consolations that cheapen loss and obscure the particularity of the dead by referring them to a more impersonal, universal fate and fellowship. He points out the oddity of finding consolation for the death of a loved one in the knowledge that death is universal, and hence, that this loved one's death "must be." Such knowledge "ought logically to make grief worse, not better: not only has my father died, but so will everyone I ever love."[10] The universality of death may nonetheless console; as one able to think about death we stand above it, and thus thinking of the universality of death may distance us from the particular death that we mourn. Time, too, remedies grief in an odd way:

the passage of time, taken by itself, cannot be what dilutes our grief, for the cause of that grief remains untouched by time: the real person whom we really loved is just as dead and gone. Grief must be drowned, rather, by some event that happens in the passage of time.[11]

Bottum suggests that this event is the abandonment of "grief's struggle to maintain the always present absence of the beloved dead person whom we mourn."[12] He considers the guilt we may feel when grief begins to fade and finds that it "reflects a genuine moral impulse." Bottum insists,

unless the dead will stand again before us as themselves—unless death is in fact unreal—grief ought rightly never end.... Short of the immediate opening of the graves—short of resurrection now—there is no consolation: only the vilest of abstractions and the most self-serving of forgettings.[13]

Since ethics ought to identify and disarm beliefs that stunt our capacities to feel, this essay follows Bottum's lead in taking up the question of what it means to sorrow well by inquiring after what consoles sorrow. It compares two literary depictions of grief, found in St. Augustine's *Confessions* and Nicholas Wolterstorff's *Lament for a Son* in order to explore grief as a moral and religious practice. Augustine helps us to distinguish between a consoling sorrow and an unconsoling sorrow. As we will see, consoling sorrow designates the pleasurable indulgence, expressed, say, in self-pity or despair, in a concupiscible love. Such love instrumentalizes what is loved, grasping at it to make it one's own so as to secure one's happiness. A consoling sorrow, then, does not honour the independent value of the dead, but solipsistically wallows in one's own loss. Since this manner of sorrowing expresses a human propensity toward self-serving love, we may further describe it as carnal or worldly. By contrast, an unconsoling sorrow relinquishes creaturely bonds, loving in a manner that avoids inordinate love. For Augustine, this more fitting, spiritual sorrow requires loving the dead in God. What is more, by referring the dead and our loss to God, this sorrow, unconsoling in itself, may be consoled in the belief that in God the dead are not lost to us. In drawing this distinction, I follow William Werpehowski's study of sorrow. With him, I will argue that the helpful distinction between consoling and unconsoling sorrow we can glean from Augustine neglects the risks entailed in such a spiritual consolation. In short, like cultural emphases on "moving on," some religious consolations can undermine the duty to honour the dead, and fail to equip us with the capacity to delight in the goods that are available in and beyond our suffering, inasmuch as they either disorder us in relation to these goods or distance us from them. The belief that our loss will ultimately be consoled should not obscure the present and persistent inconsolability of that loss, nor should it permit a faithlessness that devalues our creaturely attachments in favour of a moral perfectionism that laments these bonds as a sinful bondage. Wolterstorff's *Lament* helps us to appreciate the moral and theological import of a sorrow that is both unconsoling and inconsolable, pointing us to a love that abides. To suffer well, and to be ready for joy, requires learning the art of lament as it enables a proper honouring of the dead, and present solidarity with others in the world.

1.   Consoling Sorrow

Augustine's *Confessions* describe various experiences of sorrow, three of which I will consider: as a child, he read the *Aeneid* and wept sweetly over the death of Dido; as a young man, he wept fearfully over the loss of a friend; years later, he mourned the death of his mother, Monica, and reproached himself for the tears he shed for her. These three experiences, especially as they contrast, approximate, and judge the tears shed by Monica for her wayward son, distinguish a worldly sorrow, which is itself consoling or sweet in its self-pity or despair, from a spiritual sorrow, which more fittingly loves creaturely goods in God and is not itself consoling but is consoled by referring these goods to God.

Augustine's weeping over the death of Dido is presented in the context of an account of his early years. Book I of the *Confessions* describes Augustine's development through infancy and boyhood through the interplay of memory, appeals to authority (e.g., the reports of his parents and nurses, as well as scripture), and a process of understanding oneself "by analogy with others," that is, by learning from the behaviour of other infants.[14] Augustine depicts the emergence and schooling of his love through the development of his communicative skills: tears, gestures, and language.[15] Says Augustine,

> little by little I began to be aware where I was and wanted to manifest my wishes to those who could fulfill them as I could not.... When I did not get my way, either because I was not understood or lest it be harmful to me, I used to be indignant with my seniors for their disobedience, and with free people who were not slaves

to my interests; and I would revenge myself upon them
by weeping.[16]

There is much going on in this little account, for in it Augustine implies
connections among communication, power, desire, and weeping. This
weeping occurs in the absence of power, the power to fulfill his own
wishes (even if what is desired is harmful to himself), to communicate
them clearly, to make others do as he wishes. What is more, this weeping
occurs as an exercise of power, an act of vengeance for the disobedience
of his elders, even if their disobedience involves the prudent avoidance of
Augustine's harm. The interplay of power and desire in attempts to
communicate with other persons, and the tears infants shed in this process
give us a glimpse of our human lot. Granted, Augustine the narrator points
out that neither "custom nor reason" allows reprehension of this sort of
infant behaviour. But this is because an infant would not understand
admonition and because with age such behaviour will pass away, not
because it is innocent.[17] For example, when Augustine considers the good
and providential nourishment that mothers and wet-nurses offer in light of
the greedy suckling of infants, and the jealous glares they direct at their
brothers who share the breast, he finds evidence for the legacy of original
sin, our disordered and selfish response to the goods of creaturely life.[18]
Gradually Augustine becomes better able to "express the intentions" of his
heart to "persuade people to bow to [his] will," but this only intensifies his
predicament, since with the acquisition of language he enters "more
deeply into the stormy society of human life."[19]
    Augustine's weeping as an infant is, indeed, infantile. By it he
endeavours to make others fulfill his wishes, and laments when he does
not get his way. There is an obvious point to grasp concerning sorrow,
namely that it is a response to the absence, or loss, or violation, of
something perceived to be good. Yet from the beginning we see the
ambivalence of our human lot. Augustine depends upon others to get what
he wants, and to teach him what is good for him to want and to have. In
this process he may learn what are worthy objects of sorrow. But the dark
side of desire's dependence on others, and of learning from them what is
good, is that the internal disorder of Augustine's love, due to the legacy of
sin, is reinforced by the disordered love of society. The legacy of sin, as
Augustine understands it through the language of concupiscence, is nicely
described by Peter Brown as the "dark drive to control, to appropriate, and
to turn to one's private ends, all the good things that had been created by
God to be accepted with gratitude and shared with others."[20] Desire, when
sinful rather than rightly ordered, is concupiscible, a grasping and
instrumentalizing mode of relating to the world. It is the urge to wield the

power one has to obtain and use the goods of creaturely life with a view to securing one's happiness. As Augustine's consideration of infant weeping already indicates, sorrow is a natural response to situations in which those goods are lost, or out of reach, or cannot be had on the terms we would set. His movement into the "stormy society of human life" brings greater prospects of manifesting and satisfying his desires, along with the possibility of learning what he ought to desire and how to get it, but this is in large part the problem, since much of what he learns concerning what and how to love is tragically mistaken.

Augustine makes this clear when he describes his schooling, which mixed a worthy education in the fundamentals of reading, writing, and arithmetic, with the follies of competitions and harmful readings, like the tale of Aeneas and Dido. Looking back, Augustine writes

> What is more pitiable than a wretch without pity for himself who weeps over the death of Dido dying for love of Aeneas, but not weeping over himself dying for his lack of love for you, my God.... I had no love for you and "committed fornication against you" (Ps. 72: 27); and in my fornications I heard all round me the cries "Well done, well done" (Ps. 34: 21; 39: 16). "For the friendship of this world is fornication against you" (Jas. 4: 4) and "Well done" is what they say to shame a man who does not go along with them. Over this I wept not a tear. I wept over Dido who "died in pursuing her ultimate end with a sword." I abandoned you to pursue the lowest things of your creation. I was going to dust. Had I been forbidden to read this story, I would have been sad that I could not read what made me sad.[21]

Augustine weeps over the death of Dido, and finds this weeping pleasurable. His confession of this incident serves to make the point that our sorrowing indicates what and how we love. As we will see, loving rightly enables us to sorrow well, and sorrowing well is part of what it means to love rightly. For now, a moment's reflection on this vignette will help us begin to understand the features of a consoling sorrow and the love that operates in it. The story of Dido affords an analogy for Augustine's self-understanding; the reading resonates with and reinforces the worldliness of his love. Augustine weeps for Dido's death but not for his own. Dido dies at her own hand for love of Aeneas. Augustine is dying at his own hand for lack of love for God, against whom Augustine fornicates by lavishing the love owed to God on sensible pleasures and the follies and pretensions of human society. That Augustine weeps for Dido and not for himself indicates that he does not love the right things. What is more, this adulterous conduct is commended by cheers of "Well done!" which are themselves instances of the controlling, selfish dynamic of a worldly, concupiscible love. Finally, Augustine finds this weeping consoling or pleasurable. "While brought to tears by the terms of the world, [Augustine] remains aligned with them, even delights in them."[22] This pleasurable sorrow bespeaks Augustine's delight in the manner of love Dido displays, a love that refuses to relinquish the beloved, and hence a mourning that drives to its cessation in death. Augustine, as a boy, was already being taught to esteem such love; accordingly, as he enters adolescence he longs to be loved, to sorrow and be consoled on the terms the world sets.

The concupiscible character of this love may become clearer by noting how the consoling sorrow Augustine the boy felt over Dido continues as a young man in his love for theatrical shows. He loved the sweetness of suffering over the sufferings depicted on the stage, but, he reports, "not of a kind that pierced me very deeply; for my longing was not to experience myself miseries such as I saw on stage. I wanted only to hear stories and imaginary legends of sufferings which, as it were, scratched me on the surface."[23] Augustine's love for this experience exemplifies the condition of his soul in his days as a student, when he was "miserably avid to be scratched by contact with the world of the senses."[24] Theatrical tears and agonies were objects of love, prompted not by genuine mercy or compassion for the sufferings of others, but some counterfeit. The "neighbour" on the stage is not the object of compassionate love but an instrument for Augustine's own pleasure. As with Dido, Augustine's consoling sorrow over the theatre signals his love for love, his longing to be "captured" in and by worldly love.[25]

We see one picture of such bondage, and its wages, in Augustine's grief over the death of an unnamed friend. Though they had known one another since childhood, it was only as young men that they became "welded by the fervour of...identical interests."[26] The friend is Augustine's "other self"; they are "one soul in two bodies.'"[27] The friendship, says Augustine "was sweet to me beyond all the sweetnesses of life that I had experienced."[28] When his friend dies, Augustine sees death everywhere and finds his home a torture. In the horror and grimness of his life, "only tears were sweet."[29] Indeed, his weeping replaces his friend.[30] Augustine does not relinquish his friend so much as displace him—his own sorrow becomes a substitution for the friend. This grief is ambivalent, inasmuch as Augustine reports that he preferred his life of misery to the prospect of joining his friend in death. Augustine's sorrow turns in on itself. Such solipsism, expressed in Augustine's preference for his misery, tells the character of his love: "Although I wanted it to be otherwise, I was more unwilling to lose my misery than him."[31] As Gerald Schlabach argues, even the best friendships can be adulterous, inasmuch as "we care not about the friend but the friendship that pleases us."[32]

Augustine tells us that "the reason why that grief had penetrated me so easily and deeply was that I had poured out my soul on to the sand by loving a person sure to die as if he would never die."[33] Eventually, grief yields to new delights but the new delights are "causes of new sorrows" because they, too, are transient substitutions for God.[34] Schlabach points out, "the more passionately we enjoy the beauty of earthly goods, which include friendship, the more we hasten their demise, or at least awareness of their demise."[35] Thus, "once jolted by the death of one friend, [Augustine] would always anticipate the death of any friend, grasping a passing friendship ever more tenaciously, sensing the loss ever earlier, descending still further into self-centeredness, and on and on."[36] Such is the futility of concupiscible love. One endeavours tragically to secure happiness in the beloved "for the soul loves to be in them and take its repose among the objects of its love. But in these things there is no point of rest: they lack permanence."[37] Augustine comes to believe that only if one loves others in God, who is eternal and unchanging, does he lose "none dear to him; for all are dear in the one who cannot be lost."[38]

Augustine's grief for his unnamed friend comes closer to genuine love for others than the fellow-feeling that prompted his sweet sorrow over Dido and theatrical tales of suffering. But this sorrow, and its consoling character, testifies to Augustine's continued bondage to the world and its terms. The self-pity of this sorrow speaks Augustine's attachment to his life of misery; its intensity speaks the inevitable despair that comes from loving what is transient as if it were infinite. What is morally and spiritually problematic about this sorrow is the inordinate character of such bonds. The bonds are a bondage. An appropriate counter to them is not insensibility, for this, in a different way, would fail to express proper love of such creatures. But Augustine's grief over his friend should alert us to the way an inordinate love may house an ironic insensibility. Note that the consoling character of Augustine's tears comes from distancing himself from the source of his pain, the loss of his friend. He contrasts this with the consoling prospect of loving others not as though they were infinite, but in God, because in this way we cannot lose them. I will suggest that although Augustine moves beyond the problems of a consoling sorrow, and rightly warns against an inordinate love of others, to love in a way that forecloses sorrow, or grudgingly permits it, is also mistaken. It, too, seeks the safety of distance, loving in a way that wards off loss. This problem appears in the consolation of Augustine's grief for Monica, and by his grieving over the grief that remains.

2.   Sorrow Consoled

William Werpehowski has argued that Monica's tears over her son are the antithesis to the consoling sorrow we have been considering. Monica weeps for Augustine's spiritual fornicating and dying while Augustine does not, and the propriety of her tears is confirmed by visions, dreams, and eventually the reality of Augustine's conversion to the Christian faith. Although Monica, unlike Augustine, sorrows over the right things, her sorrow is not entirely without fault. Book Five of the *Confessions* reports Augustine's departure from Carthage, and Monica, for Rome and says this about Monica's sorrow:

> She was crazed with grief, and with recriminations and
> groans she filled your ears. But you paid no heed to her
> cries. ...[T]he longing she felt for her own flesh and
> blood was justly chastised by the whip of sorrows. As
> mothers do, she loved to have me with her, but much
> more than most mothers; and she did not understand that
> you were to use my absence as a means of bringing her
> joy. She did not know that. So she wept and lamented,
> and these agonies proved that there survived in her the
> remnants of Eve, seeking with groaning for the child she
> had brought forth in sorrow.[39]

Monica follows Augustine to Rome, and upon Augustine's conversion her mourning is changed into joy.[40] Monica and Augustine then taste the more fitting, spiritual love of others in God when they share a mystical vision at Ostia.

> The vision at Ostia reflects the goal of a true friendship
> that was lacking for Augustine in his Manichean days...
> Monica, not so much mother but rather friend and sister
> in Christ, then reports, confirming the freedom from the
> world that the vision attests, that she no longer finds
> pleasure in this life. It is time for her to die.[41]

Monica's attitude toward her own death exhibits the relinquishing of earthly bonds; she indicates, for instance, that she no longer needs to be buried with her husband or in her native country. Monica's tears for Augustine are rightly expended over his spiritual dying. Although her sorrow at Augustine's departure for Rome may have borne the "remnants of Eve," her attitude toward her own death, and the experience at Ostia all signal the spiritual fellowship that fittingly counters carnal, worldly bondage to others.

We can see the difference this ordering of love to God makes in Augustine's sorrow at the death of his mother. Initially, Augustine contains the tears he would weep at her death because he "did not think it right to celebrate the funeral with tearful dirges and lamentations.... My mother's dying meant neither that her state was miserable nor that she was suffering extinction."[42] Beliefs about Monica's good character, and in God, direct the sorrow Augustine feels. But Augustine the narrator asks, "Why then did I suffer sharp pains of inward grief? It must have been the fresh wound caused by the break in the habit formed by our living together, a very affectionate and precious bond suddenly torn apart."[43] Augustine makes arrangements for her funeral, all the while "using truth as a fomentation to alleviate the pain" he felt, thereby concealing that pain from others, if not from God.[44] However, he inwardly reproaches himself for the "softness" of his feelings. Indeed, it caused him displeasure that these "human frailties" had power over him, "though they are a necessary part of the order we have to endure and are the lot of the human condition."[45] So Augustine sorrows with a two-fold grief: grief over his mother, and grief over his grief. This becomes even clearer as Augustine goes on to beseech God to heal his pain. About this he confesses to God, "I believe that you gave me no relief so that by this single admonition I should be made aware of the truth that every habit is a fetter adverse even to the mind that is not fed upon deceit."[46] Eventually, as Augustine recalls Monica, he weeps. He says he was glad to weep for and about her, for and about himself, and that his heart rested upon his tears because God heard them. But then he promptly goes on to note that he wept for only a fraction of an hour, and to beg for mercy from others and from God.[47]

What are we to make of this weeping? Werpehowski argues that "Augustine the mourner is one who would, in his struggle to contain his grief, die to the world, would kill off the residue of worldly habit and a too carnal affection. As he fails, he grieves over his grief."[48] Augustine's grief over his grief signals his attempt to contain his sorrow, lest it pitch toward despair, inordinately love his mother, and betray his faith that she lives in God. This attempt distinguishes his grief for Monica from his grief for his friend and commends the former. "Augustine struggles not to weep over [Monica's] earthly death, attributing the tendency to worldly habit, and not *finally* to the love of a son for his mother."[49] And when he does weep, he does so as one who refers Monica and his loss to God. Hence, "a real sort of resolution does take place, where the worldly and bodily are included and taken up into the eternal and spiritual."[50]

But Werpehowski identifies an important worry concerning the costs of this resolution:

> Grief now seems to be so aligned with inordinate carnal affection that sorrow over any worldly loss falls under suspicion. Augustine's troubling struggle to curb his tears, and his self-reproach for finally having shed them, attests to this; the reader might easily recall Monica's weeping at Carthage, which Augustine blames for an identical reason. The embodied and worldly tie between mother and son gives way to a mode of spiritual friendship that seems to overwhelm the former bond.[51]

Augustine's consoling sorrow rested on mistaken beliefs about the value of human bonds. His unconsoling sorrow may do the same, as it devalues the particular and embodied nature of those bonds in favour of an impersonal, universal fellowship. Moreover, if for Augustine "every habit is a fetter adverse," his sorrow may not only devalue the particularity of special bonds, but human bonds as such. Granted, sorrowing well "expresses a proper love of the creature in its order."[52] But this proper love ought as such to affirm the special and embodied character of creaturely bonds without conflating human bonds simpliciter with carnal bondage.[53]

Perhaps we do Augustine a disservice if we make too much of his grief over his grief. Nicholas Wolterstorff points out that what Augustine confesses here is "not so much the sin of weeping over the death of his mother as the sin of which that weeping was a sign," his concupiscible love.[54] As we have seen, for Augustine the remedy for such misplaced and inordinate love is to love God, our highest good, and everything else in God. We can only be happy if we love God, who is truly good and cannot be lost against our will.[55] But "to reorient oneself toward loving God is to open oneself to a new mode of grief," since

> this newly oriented self never wholly wins out over the old. And over that repetitious reappearance of the old self, the new now grieves. The *passive* grief of negated affection is replaced by the *active* grief of lamenting over the faults of one's religious character—over those persistent habits of the hearts that one now recognizes as sin.[56]

In fact, notes Wolterstorff, for Augustine we are to cultivate sorrow over sin.[57]

To be sure, our imperfection is a fitting object of sorrow. But if sorrowing well entails sorrowing over the right things *and* sorrowing over them fittingly, then sorrow over our sin may go awry. Wolterstorff sees that this sorrow may come at the cost of acknowledging the goodness of creation.

> In the presence of all those griefs which ensue from the destruction of that which we love, Augustine pronounces a "No" to the attachments rather than a "No" to the destruction—not a "No" to death but a "No" to love of what is subject to death. Thereby he also pronounces a "Not much" concerning the worth of the things loved. Nothing in this world has worth enough to merit an attachment which carries the potential of grief—nothing except the religious state of souls. The state of my child's soul is worth suffering love; the child's company is not.[58]
>
> There is another way to go. To some of the things in this world one can pay the tribute of recognizing in them worth sufficient to merit a love which plunges into suffering upon their destruction. In one's love one can say a "Yes" to the worth of persons or things and in one's suffering a "No" to their destruction. To friends and relatives one can pay the tribute of loving them enough to suffer upon their death.[59]

Whether or not Augustine does pronounce a "not much" concerning the worth of creatures, Wolterstorff alerts us to the possibilities that endeavouring to love rightly can become a cover for playing it safe, for loving in a way that wards off loss, and that sorrowing over the imperfection of our love can involve a devaluation of creatures and our bonds with them.[60] Even if we avoid the "not much," sorrow over sin may also go awry if it expresses a moral perfectionism whereby we not only long and hope for the perfect ordering of love in beatitude, but impatiently inhabit this world, grudgingly biding our time, frustrated by our inability to get our loving *just right*. Here, grief co-opts our affirmation of the beloved's value, so that our sorrow serves less to honour him than bemoan our failings. Here we grieve not because we loved one who, as a transient creature, could not secure our happiness, but because our own efforts to love well prove insufficient to secure it for ourselves. Here, too, beliefs we may hold (about God, the world, our goodness) can thwart our capacities to delight in the goods of creation.

Earlier we saw that a consoling, worldly sorrow testifies to a disordered, concupiscible love of our fellow creatures. Here we have seen that a spiritual sorrow testifies to a more fitting, relinquishing love that may nevertheless overcorrect inordinate love for others by devaluing our particular, embodied bonds with them. What is more, both the consoling and unconsoling sorrows sketched thus far may distance us from the beloved. Recall that Augustine's grief for his friend alerted us to the possibility that an inordinate love can house an ironic insensibility, if we love not the friend but the friendship, if in our grief we substitute the friend with our own sorrow. A similar distancing can occur in an unconsoling sorrow, if the object of our sorrow becomes us in our imperfection, rather than the beloved.

Now since our loving and our sorrowing in this world will inevitably be imperfect, the helpful distinction between a worldly, consoling sorrow and a spiritually, unconsoling sorrow, between concupiscible and relinquishing love may be too neat. An unconsoling and inconsolable sorrow fits our creaturely status in a world that is fallen but good as we struggle to abide in love.

3.   **Inconsolable Sorrow**

Wolterstorff's *Lament for a Son* reflects on the death of his child Eric, lost in a mountain-climbing accident. It describes Wolterstorff's struggle to own his grief redemptively, to mourn in a way that properly expresses dying and rising in faith.[61] This means sorrowing in a way that affirms that death is not the last word. But curiously enough, to do this is to refuse the sorts of consolations that would lessen the awfulness of death by skipping ahead to some future, resurrected fellowship, or explain it as a "normal instrument of God's dealing with us."[62] Such consolations fail to honour the particularity of the dead and of our bonds with them. They also problematize attitudes toward suffering more generally by obscuring the relation between suffering and love. We honour the dead and ready ourselves for joy only if we sorrow in a way that does not disorder us in relation to, devalue, or distance us from creaturely goods. To do so, we must enter into the mystery of suffering love.

An unconsoling and inconsolable sorrow affirms the goodness and particularity of creaturely bonds. At the beginning of *Lament*, Wolterstorff asks about Eric, "How can I be thankful, in his gone-ness, for what he was? I find I am. But the pain of the *no more* outweighs the gratitude of the *once was*. Will it always be so?"[63] Wolterstorff's gratitude for Eric distinguishes his affirmation of Eric's value from the inordinate and self-serving grasp of concupiscible love. It implies a proper regard for Eric as a gift. At the same time, Wolterstorff laments that Eric is "no more." He sorrows over the "never again" of Eric's company and the "never will be" of what might have been for and with Eric. Wolterstorff's lament does not amount to despair. His faith in the resurrection enables him to hope he will be with Eric again. Nevertheless, faith and hope do not console the present and persistent grief over the fact that "Eric is gone, *here* and *now* he is gone." Says Wolterstorff, "*That* is my sorrow.... That's my grief. For that grief, what consolation can there be other than having him back?"[64] The inconsolability of his sorrow affirms Eric's irreplaceable value and the goodness of Wolterstorff's particular, embodied bond with him: "grief is existential testimony to the worth of the one loved. That worth abides."[65] To affirm the goodness of creation and of the dead whom we love we must squarely face the awfulness of death. Wolterstorff writes, "I will indeed remind myself that there's more to life than pain. I will accept joy. But I will not look away from Eric dead. Its demonic awfulness I will not ignore. I owe that—to him and to God."[66] The inconsolability of sorrow here honours the particularity of the dead, and thereby refers the dead to God in gratitude and lament.

A cussed affirmation of creation's goodness makes death more difficult to live with.

> When death is no longer seen as release from this miserable materiality into our rightful immateriality, when death is seen rather as the slicing off of what God declared to be, and what all of us feel to be, of great worth, then death is—well, not friend but enemy.[67]

Thus, we rightly ought to resist consolations which suggest that death is anything less. Wolterstorff writes,

> If you think your task as comforter is to tell me that really, all things considered, it's not so bad, you do not sit with me in my grief but place yourself off in the distance away from me. Over there, you are of no help.... To comfort me, you have to come close. Come sit beside me on my mourning bench.
>
> I know: People do sometimes think things are more awful that they really are. Such people need to be corrected—gently, eventually. But no one thinks death

is more awful than it is. It's those who think it's not so
bad that need correcting.[68]

Lest the awfulness of death prompt a consolation that explains it
away, or invite a despairing resignation to death, Wolterstorff also corrects
religious perspectives that would have us believe that God uses death or is
powerless over it. The former perspective suggests that God is the agent of
death: "You there have lived out the years I've planned for you, so I'll just
shake the mountains a bit. All of you there, I'll send some starlings into
the engine of your plane. And as for you there, a stroke while running will
do nicely."[69] This is wrong, says Wolterstorff, for the same reason that
insisting on God's powerlessness over death is wrong. God has overcome
death. Moreover, God remains appalled by it.[70]

To believe that death is not so awful—for us or for God—not
only devalues the goodness of creation, it overlooks what Christian
revelation might teach us about suffering and love.

> To redeem our brokenness and lovelessness the God
> who suffers with us did not strike some mighty blow of
> power but sent his beloved son to suffer *like* us, through
> his suffering to redeem us from suffering and evil.
> Instead of explaining our suffering God shares
> it.[71]

In our suffering we may know something of the heart of God,
who suffers in love. We may also know something of the hearts of our
neighbours, since

> we all suffer. For we all prize and love; and in this
> present existence of ours, prizing and loving yield
> suffering. Love in our world is suffering love. Some do
> not suffer much, though, for they do not love much.
> Suffering is for the loving. ....
> This, said Jesus, is the command of the Holy
> One: "You shall love your neighbour as yourself." In
> commanding us to love, God invites us to suffer.[72]

If we truncate our suffering, say by wallowing in a consoling
sorrow, or taking refuge in cheap consolations, we truncate our love—for
the dead whom we mourn, for others who mourn, for those who live with
us here and now. Rather than play it safe by loving in a way that wards off
loss, we know and love the goodness of creatures by opening ourselves to

suffering over and with them. In short, Christian revelation teaches us that to love is to suffer, and that suffering belongs to the work of love as it protests the destruction or loss or incompletion of what is good.

This insight does not resolve the mystery of why love *without* suffering is not the meaning of life, but an unconsoling and inconsolable sorrow helps us to appreciate that if we struggle so that love for the dead abides, we may abide in love with God and others.[73] How is this so? Consider Wolterstorff's struggle in this regard. As he grieves for Eric, he does not plunge back into work, or put Eric's belongings out of sight, because "if Eric's life was a gift, surely then we are to hold it in remembrance—to resist amnesia, to renounce oblivion."[74] By avoiding practices that would "muffle" sorrow, Wolterstorff endeavours to remember Eric. His love for Eric abides not only in remembering him, but in lamenting that,

> all I can do is *remember* him. I can't *experience* him. The person to whom these memories are attached is no longer here with me, not in my life. Nothing new can happen between us. Everything is sealed tight, shut in the past. I'm still here. I have to go on. I have to start over.[75]

The new start Wolterstorff struggles to make is not that of "moving on," but living authentically and faithfully in Eric's absence. Wolterstorff describes a manner of sorrowing that is unconsoling in itself—remembering Eric is no substitute for him—and is inconsolable— rather than "get over" his loss of Eric, Wolterstorff seeks to live with it. He struggles to love Eric abidingly by resisting beliefs and practices that would soften his sorrow, both because these would amount to failures in honouring Eric and because they would obstruct love for others. This struggle includes the regrets Wolterstorff feels with respect to Eric: "I shall live with them. I shall accept my regrets as part of my life, to be numbered among my self-inflicted wounds. But I will not endlessly gaze at them. I shall allow the memories to prod me into doing better with those still living."[76] The imperfection of our love is a fitting object of sorrow, but should neither encroach upon our honouring of the beloved dead nor distance us from others. Indeed, our sorrow ought to dispose us to know and love the good.

> If sympathy for the world's wounds is not enlarged by our anguish, if love for those around us is not expanded, if gratitude for what is good does not flame up, if insight

is not deepened, if commitment to what is important is not strengthened, if aching for a new day is not intensified, if hope is weakened and faith diminished, if from the experience of death comes nothing good, then death has won.[77]

According to Wolterstorff, "To believe in Christ's rising and death's dying is also to live with the power and the challenge to rise up now from all our dark graves of suffering love."[78] Faith in the ultimate consolation of our sorrow empowers and challenges us here and now to go on sorrowing as we may thereby honour the dead and the particularity of our creaturely bonds with them, affirm the goodness of God's creation and share in God's sorrow for its incompletion and imperfection, endeavour to love others better, and stand in solidarity with those who sorrow. This rising is not "moving on," putting grief to rest, but living with and through it, against death and in openness to others.

In contrast to a worldly, consoling sorrow and a spiritual, unconsoling sorrow, I think it apt to describe an unconsoling and inconsolable sorrow as a creaturely one. In gratitude it affirms that goodness of this world and our embodied lives in it with particular others of irreplaceable value. In lament it protests the loss of these goods by refusing beliefs and practices that would distance us from or soften our loss and thereby devalue the dead and our bonds with them. It describes the struggle to abide in a love that is ready to suffer over creatures. Moreover, an unconsoling and inconsolable sorrow does not betray the belief that our will be ultimately consoled. Instead, it does not permit this belief to divert us from the work of gratefully lamenting the present and persistent character of that loss. This manner of sorrowing sharpens our longing for the day when we might be reunited and reconciled in the fullness of love, but without balking in the face of the inevitable imperfection and incompletion of loving here and now.

At the start I argued that we ought to reject beliefs and practices that stunt our capacities to feel, because they stunt our capacities to know and love the good. I have explored a range of consolations in and of sorrow in order to identify the subtle ways they undermine our capacities to know and love the good by disordering us in relation to, devaluing, or distancing us from our fellow creatures. And finally, I have suggested that an unconsoling and inconsolable sorrow is one that may drive us into the world with others in faith, hope, and love.

Notes

I am grateful to Rob Fisher for inviting me to participate in the *First Global Conference: Making Sense of Death and Dying*, where an earlier version of this essay was presented, and to William Werpehowski and Brett Wilmot for the feedback and conversation they offered during the revision process.

[1] Beverly Wildung Harrison, "The Power of Anger in the Work of Love," *Making the Connections: Essays in Feminist Social Ethics*, ed. Carol S. Robb (Boston: Beacon, 1985), 14.

[2] Ibid., 13.

[3] Ibid., 14.

[4] Ibid.

[5] Ibid.

[6] Ibid.

[7] There is a tension between Harrison's insistence that feelings are not right or wrong, and my claim that we can feel in better and worse ways. But I do not think this tension is ultimately a contradiction. Harrison makes her claim because she wants to counter Christian tradition's identification of anger as wrong. Nonetheless, since Harrison understands feelings, including anger, as signals that alert us to the moral quality of our relationships, her defense of anger against the tradition's condemnation of it is in fact an attempt to show that anger may be a feeling that is fitting for Christians (indeed, for persons in general) to have. Moreover, since our capacity to feel is a condition for our moral agency, it may not be utterly unfaithful to Harrison's project to argue that we ought to cultivate feelings that enable us to know and love the good

[8] See for example Elisabeth Kübler-Ross, M. D., *On Death and Dying* (New York: Scribner Classics, 1997), copyright Elisabeth Kübler-Ross, 1969.

[9] Most of the essay appears in *The Eternal Pity: Reflections on Dying*, ed. Richard John Neuhaus (Notre Dame, IN: University of Notre Dame Press, 2000). For the complete manuscript, see Jody Bottum, "All That Lives Must Die," *First Things* 63 (May 1996): 28-32. Citations are taken from the version published in *Eternal Pity*.

[10] Ibid., 169.

[11] Ibid., 171.

[12] Ibid.

[13] Ibid., 172.

[14] Augustine, *Confessions*, Translated with and Introduction and Notes by Henry Chadwick (Oxford: Oxford University Press, 1991), I.6.10.

[15] See ibid., I.6.7-I.8.13.
[16] Ibid., I.6.8.
[17] Ibid., I.7.11.
[18] Ibid.
[19] Ibid., I.8.13.
[20] Peter Brown, *The Body and Society: Men, Women and Sexual Renunciation in Early Christianity* (New York: Columbia University Press, 1988), 418. See also Oliver O'Donovan *The Problem of Self-Love in St. Augustine* (New Haven: Yale University Press, 1980).
[21] Augustine, *Confessions*, I.13.21.
[22] William Werpehowski, "Weeping at the Death of Dido: Sorrow, Virtue, and Augustine's Confessions," *Journal of Religious Ethics* 19.1 (1991):175-191, 180.
[23] Augustine, *Confessions*, III.2.4.
[24] Ibid., III.1.1.
[25] Ibid.
[26] Ibid., IV.4.7.
[27] Ibid., IV.6.11.
[28] Ibid., IV.4.7.
[29] Ibid., IV.4.9.
[30] Ibid.
[31] Ibid., IV.6.11.
[32] Gerald W. Schlabach, "Friendship as Adultery: Social Reality and Sexual Metaphor in Augustine's Doctrine of Original Sin," *Augustinian Studies* 23 (1992): 125-147, 128.
[33] Augustine, *Confessions*, IV.8.13.
[34] Ibid.
[35] Schlabach, "Friendship as Adultery," 129.
[36] Ibid., 128.
[37] Augustine, *Confessions*, IV.10.15.
[38] Ibid., IV.9.14.
[39] Ibid., V.8.15.
[40] See ibid., VIII.12.
[41] Werpehowski, "Weeping at the Death of Dido," 183. See Augustine, *Confessions*, IX.10.26-IX.11.27.
[42] Augustine, *Confessions*, IX.12.29.
[43] Ibid., IX.12.30.
[44] Ibid., IX.12.31.
[45] Ibid.
[46] Ibid., IX.12.32.
[47] Ibid., IX.12.33.

[48] Werpehowski, "Weeping at the Death of Dido," 184.
[49] Ibid., 185.
[50] Ibid., 185-86.
[51] Ibid., 186.
[52] Ibid., 184.
[53] Ibid.
[54] Nicholas Wolterstorff, "Suffering Love," *Philosophy and the Christian Faith*, ed. Thomas V. Morris (Notre Dame, IN: University of Notre Dame Press, 1988), 197.
[55] See Augustine, *On the Morals of the Catholic Church*, especially chapter X.
[56] Wolterstorff, "Suffering Love," 201.
[57] Ibid., 205.
[58] Ibid., 228.
[59] Ibid., 228-29.
[60] Wolterstorff and Werpehowski both worry that Augustine's grief over his grief may point to a devaluation of particular bonds. Unlike Wolterstorff, however, Werpehowski indicates that the consolation Augustine experiences when he weeps signals an affirmation of his embodied life with Monica in God. See Werpehowski, "Weeping at the Death of Dido," 185.
[61] Nicholas Wolterstorff, *Lament for a Son* (Grand Rapids, MI: William B. Eerdmans, 1987), 6.
[62] Ibid., 66.
[63] Ibid., 13.
[64] Ibid., 31.
[65] Ibid., 5.
[66] Ibid., 54.
[67] Ibid., 31-32.
[68] Ibid., 34-35.
[69] Ibid., 66.
[70] Ibid.
[71] Ibid., 81.
[72] Ibid., 89.
[73] Ibid., 90.
[74] Ibid., 28.
[75] Ibid., 47.
[76] Ibid., 65.
[77] Ibid., 92.
[78] Ibid.

Understanding Our Pain: The Experiences of African American Women Through The Death and Dying Process

Clarice Ford

1   Introduction

Death is such a simple, even sweet sounding word the way its easy rhythm curls the lips, it syllables falling almost hypnotic…DEATH. I have come to hate the word and the idea it conjures up of some romantic notion of noble human drama. There is nothing simple or sweet or evenly remotely romantic about losing a love one. For those left behind, the word itself takes on an aching, overwhelming power and becomes heartache. How can anyone deal with such pain? How do African American women deal with the lost of a loved one? Are they taught or does it have something to do with their development as African American women?

Unfortunately for those interested in studying the experiences of African American women and their mourning process, there is no well known publication that documents their experiences. In a historical view, the experiences of African American women have been examined from a problem perspective such as welfare, single parenting, juvenile delinquency, and teenage pregnancy.

This study will contribute to the body of literature on death and dying where very little has included African American women as contributors to the field. Despite the lack of attention to the needs of African American women, they continue to learn and grow though the experience of the mourning process.

2.   African American Women Development

A focus on the historical role of African American women played in society is essential to understand the development of this group of women. The most useful tool is the original model developed in 1908 by W.E.B. Dubois. He stresses the importance of recognizing the historical relationships of African heritage and tradition of the Black family. When studying African American women, it is "important to contextualize the framework of their perspectives by comprehensively analyzing the historical components which help identifies their thoughts, feelings and experiences" (Gregory, 1995).

Peterson (1992) describes the strength and power of the Black woman. This power she discusses has to do "with God, family, friends, and community."

> "The black female's ability to define herself comes from a belief that no human has the right to define another. Each person is a unique creation of God; and with God, the individual elicits her own becoming....The black female who understands this knows that only she has the responsibility to determine her path. The Black woman knows that she is constantly in a state of becoming as she is moved in different directions." (pgs. 86-87)

To resist in the services of her own liberation, an African American female must learn to identify negating distortions, understand their origins and whose interest they serve, and must ultimately look beyond these demeaning portrayals by embracing the admirable qualities of black womanhood these images obscure, particularly the unique wisdom, strength, and perseverance of African American women (Robinson & Ward, 1991).

For the African American female, the ability to move beyond the internalization of racial denigration to an internalization of racial pride involves a process of confronting and rejecting oppressive negating evaluations of blackness and femaleness, adopting instead a sense of self that is self-affirming and self-valuing (Collins, 1989; Ladner, 1971; Ward, 1990).

The Afrocentric, or African –centered worldview is very different from the Eurocentric-centered worldview. Afrocentrism is centered around the beliefs that the highest value of life lies in the interpersonal relationships between humans; one gains knowledge through symbolic imagery and rhythm; one should live in harmony with nature; there is a oneness between humans and nature; the survival of the group holds the utmost importance; one's self is complementary to others; there's a plethora of deities to worship, and the Afrocentric worldview is a circular one which all events are tied together with one another.

The Eurocentric worldview is quite different. It is centered around the beliefs on gains knowledge through counting and measuring; one should control and dominate nature; the survival of the fittest holds the utmost importance; all men are considered to be individualistic unique, and different; there is only one supreme deity to worship; competition, independence, separateness, and individual rights are the key values to which all should strive to achieve; and the Eurocentric worldview is a linear one, in which all events are separate and there is no togetherness.

Several aspects of African American culture seem particularly relevant in considering African American women's sense of self-in-relation (Collins, 1989). The self-in-relation clearly defines the self in relationship with an intimate other, with the community, the nation and the world. Noting its similarity to a "feminine worldview", Harding (1987) describes an Afrocentric perspective as one in which the self is dependent on others, defined through relationships to others, with self-interest tied to the welfare of the community or relational complex.

In African American families, there tends to be close ties and a reliance on kinship networks. On the other hand, African American women are raised to be strong, independent, and commonly taught skills for survival in and for the African American community (Joseph, Lewis, 1981). This strength has sometimes been misconstrued and stereotyped by the larger society.

Ladner (1971) points out that education was most frequently seen as the means to the end of dependence upon males. Jeffries (1985), exploratory research produced evidence that young Black women were told marriage and children are an important life stage, yet they are also told not to depend on a man; they are told to love, but "don't ever trust a man to take care of you" (Jeffries, 1985).

Hill (1972), identified five major strengths, and maintains they are the means for survival, advancement and stability in the Black community. These characteristics are strong kinship bonds, adaptability of family roles, strong religious orientation, strong work orientation, and strong achievement orientation. These values and ethics, Hill contends, have helped to keep Black women and their families together, and have strengthened their roles as wife and mother.

An essential singular aspect in the African American community, which as richly benefited African American women and their families, are what McAdoo (1980) refers to as extended family support networks. These extended networks "provide emotional support, economic supplements, and most important, to protect the families integrity from assault by eternal forces" (pg. 125). This system of mutual aid is based on the African heritage of communalism and is most likely a consequence of socialization that has traditionally encouraged respect and assistance to elderly family members (Chatters, 1986; Taylor and Chatters, 1986). Unfortunately, these patterns are also typically influenced by socioeconomic conditions (Mutran, 1985). Extended families are important in the Black community because they help provide a source of strength and protection (Hill, 1972) and enable Black families to cope with problems by "banding together to form a network of intimate mutual aid and social interaction with neighbors and kin" (Billingsley, 1968). This network enables women to work while friends, family, or neighbors to assist helping each other. This mutual interdependence is also a means for many Black women to cope with poverty and racism (Stack, 1974). The unspoken words are often "you take care of mine and I'll take care of yours" (Jeffers, 1967, pg. 47).

3.   Understanding Loss/Bereavement
        Death of a love one is the number one stressor of all losses, according to Holmes and Rathe (1967). Because of the bond established within a relationship between parent/child and husband/wife. Sanders (1989) maintain it is difficult to clearly understand what is being grieved because the tasks and needs the mate/child provided could be endless.
        Strobe and Strobe (1987) cited three important functions of the African American community during the loss of a love one: (a) instrumental support-helping with the funeral, household tasks, and so on; (b) emotional support-helping the mourners accept the reality of the death; and (c) validational support-helping the mourners know what to expect during the period of grief and reassuring them that what they are experiencing is normal.
        In addition to providing a place for catharsis, normalizing, and dealing with feelings of anger, guilt, anxiety, helplessness, sadness, and depression, the grieving must address the following specific issues:

(1) Loneliness and aloneness. After the death of a loved one, the mourner loses the daily intimacies of having someone special to share significant events with and the sense of being the most important person in someone else's life. Being single rather than being a couple is also a difficult transition, as is the realization that part of the mourner's "history" died with the mate (Yalom & Vinogradov, 1988).

(2) Sense of deprivation. According to Sanders (1989), the sense of deprivation following the death of a mate/child is particularly acute. Many may feel deprived financially, socially, sexually, physically, and emotionally, in any combination. Role redefinition becomes a major task that is frequently painful and frustrating. To fill roles the mate/child had assumed or to learn to do them oneself is often

overwhelming. Survivors with children have an even greater sense of deprivation and struggle with their own issues of grief in addition to the children's.

(3) Freedom and growth. Despite the negative impact of loss, mourners inevitably find an awareness of freedom and the potential for change. Viorst (1986) emphasizes that losses are linked to gains; loss can result in "creative transformations" (pg.326). Helping the grieve recognize the strength that comes from facing and surviving a loss and coping effectively with adversity is an important step in recovery. Encouraging the griever to look at the potentials of independence and freedom is also essential. Along with this sense of freedom comes a sense of choice and greater awareness of "Who am I?" and "What do I enjoy?" (Yalom & Vinogradov, 1988).

(4) Change. Following the death of a loved one, the survivor usually has to learn new behaviors that result in personal change. A major lifestyle change, such as relocation or starting a job, also may accompany loss. Even though these changes can be positive, stress and readjustment are to be expected.

(5) New relationships. Forming a new relationship may signify readiness to put the past aside and move ahead, but this aspect of change is often difficult. Yalom and Vinogradov (1988) note that many often feel as if they are betraying their marriage or diminishing the love for the deceased by entering into a new relationship.

4.   The Mourning Process

The impact of a loss relates to the degree of attachment one feels about the object or situation that is lost (Bowlby, 1980). Attachment implies the need for security and safety, and when this is threatened, as in a loss, grief-like behavior ensues. Bowlby's theory provides a perspective for assessing the degree of mourning associated with a loss. The greater the attachment or dependency (for safety or security), the greater is the sense of loss.

Engel (1980) notes that mourning is an adaptation to loss, and it involves four basic tasks: accepting the reality of the loss, experiencing the pain of grief, adjusting to a new environment, and withdrawing and reinvesting emotional energy.

Whether the loss involves a person, self-esteem through rejection, ability to function, or relocation, the first task of mourning is to accept the reality of the loss. This is often difficult to do and denial is common; denying the facts of the loss, denying the meaning of the loss is irreversible (Worden, 1982). Working through denial is essential before a person can experience the pain of grief.

Mourning among African American women is as diverse as the multiple hues of skin color and as rich as the brilliance of a rainbow. Many African American women are acculturated to Caucasian tradition in the United States of America. Others integrate ancient African customs with the American potpourri of ethnic blending, uniting these with family tradition, geographic-cultural practices and religion. This is clearly seen at the funerals of African Americans.

It is essential to continually recognize that African American women are of the African Heritage. In many African communities, the newly bereaved shave their heads. This distinction allows the community to offer support and help the bereaved to re-enter the social fabric at the conclusion of the mourning period, when their hair has re-grown. African Americans wear black or white mourning clothes while Africans wear red or black to denote mourning.

5.   The "Living-Dead"

Death the inescapable disrupting factor, signals the great divide between the living that are visible and world of spirits who are invisible. These spirits are an important presence who continue to influence and watch over the living.

Understanding the African American women's respect for the "living-dead" has been a mind-expanding experience for me. This concept has been learned when very young has nothing to do with the stereotypes of "zombies" commonly associated with voodooism. But this refers to the souls of those who have physically died but continue to live on spiritually in the memories and conversations of those left behind. They are invisible. As long as anyone continues to call their names, they are considered the "living-dead" and they continue to influence those who are still alive. They are the ones expected to welcome those who follow them in death into the new rhythm of existence. They may remain in the "living-dead" state for generations, and it is only when their names cease to be known or called that the rhythm ends and they are finally determined to be dead. The six participants in the study consistently spoke of the presence of the "living-dead" in their homes. Lucretia remembers when her daughter was buried and every morning the kitchen light would mysteriously flicker as she sat eating her breakfast. This was their special time together when her daughter was alive. Many of the participants discussed hearing footsteps, imprints on their side of the bed, and other noticeable items suddenly appeared after their loved ones were buried.

6.   Feel My Pain

Studies of African American women have documented the everyday racism and discrimination these women face in their daily lives. For the African American woman, the ability to move beyond the internalization of racial denigration to an internalization of racial pride involves a process of confronting and rejecting oppressive negating evaluations of blackness and femaleness, adopting instead a sense of self that is self-affirming and self-valuing (Collins, 1989; Ladner, 1971; Ward, 1990).

When African American women are unable to adapt to a loss, they may promote their own helplessness with race, economics and other factors that could have made the loss different such as drive by shootings, burglaries, murder, and etc.. These non-adaptations make the outcome of mourning more difficult. As Bowlby (1980) notes, "On how he achieved this third task turns the outcome of mourning- either progress toward a recognition of her goals in life, or else a state of suspended growth in which she is held prisoner by a dilemma she cannot solve" (p.139).

Unfortunately in the United States of America society is often uncomfortable with grieving and may send the message that "you don't need to grieve", manifested by repressing feelings or thinking only pleasant thoughts about the loss as a way to protect oneself from the discomfort. Bowlby (1980) notes that grieving is necessary. He states, "Sooner or later, some of those who avoid all conscious grieving breaks down usually with some form of depression" (pg. 158). When we look at how many days of bereavement we receive at our jobs, the message is quite clear – Learn how to deal with it quickly!

Samantha remembers "I returned to work a week after my teenage son was shot down by gang fire. Everyone tried not to talk about it at the office. The third week at work, I had a major breakdown and had to quit my job when my sick leave ran out. There was no one to talk to about my loss except the pastor. Even I was afraid that he would see me as being weak and not a good mother for allowing my son to be killed. For two years, I tried to find a way to deal with my pain by drinking but it didn't work.

Gwinnett discussed her frustration and pressure to function without her husband of twenty years. He died suddenly and had not prepared a living will. "Everyone criticized my dead husband for not leaving his family with the proper finances to survive and for his burial. I was so angry at him and others around me that I just waddled in my pain for years."

Dr. Darcie D. Sims of Grief Inc. clearly states "Grief is the price we pay for love." The participants dealt with physical and behavioral changes such as sleep irregularities, changes in appetite, gastro-intestinal disturbances, "heart ache", restlessness, spontaneous crying, irritability, sighing or muscle tension during the grieving process.

Depending on the nature of the loss, a sense of unreality and numbness generally help the person temporarily disregard the loss (Worden, 1982). But accepting the loss is important and the person must be encouraged to talk about it and to identify and express feelings commonly associated with most types of loss: anger, guilt, sadness, anxiety, helplessness, frustration, and depression (Stern, 1985; Worden, 1982).

Feeling angry over a loss is normal, but African American women have trouble admitting this anger because they feel ashamed. In the case of death of a mate, survivors may be angry particularly because they are left with many responsibilities and necessary painful changes. At the same time, they may feel guilty because they know their mate suffered and did not want to die. In these instances, the anger may be experiences as depression.

Many of the participants discussed the feeling of emptiness or hollowness that remained for some time during the grieving process. They experienced headaches, muscle aches, and two of the participants became hospitalized after the first month of the lost of a loved one. Marie was hospitalized two weeks after her husband was buried. She had knee surgery and could not take care of herself for a month. There she remained in their bedroom and mourned her loss quietly.

7.   The Strong Black Woman Syndrome

Stereotypes about African American women often can mask the reality of their experiences. For example, African American women are culturally stereotyped as being independent, emotionally strong, and capable of taking care of themselves in some settings. Professionals such as bereavement counselors may be unaware that African American women's "toughness" sometimes masks uncertainty and vulnerability (Moses, 1989).

Lipinski (1980) posits that any type of loss disrupts familiar patterns and relationships. The series of losses we encounter throughout our lives has consequences for our self-esteem, general sense of well-being, and emotional integrity. Whether the change is dreaded or welcomed, accidental or planned, African American women need to adapt to the loss. This often results in anxiety or ambivalence.

Many of these needs resulting from a loss can be effectively addressed within a group setting. Support groups allow people to share common problems and provide mutual aid. When African American women are involved in support groups they are provided with emotional and educational support. In addition they receive encouragement and relief, learning about resources, mastering burdens, and the opportunity to help others gain strength. Zimpfer (1989) identified five purposes for loss groups. They are support, sharing of feelings, developing coping skills, gathering information and education, and considering existential issues.

The participants spoke about their negative experiences with bereavement facilitators/grief counselors. They faced poor treatment from White staff persons. Such treatment included (1) having their intelligence constantly called into question; (2) being excluded from the large support groups; and (3) having White professionals judge them according to negative stereotypes.

Carol discussed the lack of empathy shown by her grief counselor. "She told me to remember my history and how strong Black women are….after all you did survive slavery without complaining!"

One of the participants named Lynne felt because she was "white-skinned" and many of the hospice staff was "unaware" she didn't really experience the bereavement process/counseling as an African American woman. She was the only participant who participated in a support group with the majority being White.

The most important function groups provide is the support that comes from meeting with others who share a similar experience regardless of race. This meeting with people who have a similar experience can create a certain bonding amongst group members who share reactions they all can relate to during the grieving process. Members' support comes through encouragement and helping others mobilize their inner resources to gain strength to heal and to continue life. This setting allows African American women to feel safe to bring up issues without avoidance, disapproval, or patronization.

8.   The End

Hill (1972) identified five major strengths and maintains they are the means for survival, advancement, and stability in the African American community. These characteristics are strong kinship bonds, adaptability of family roles, strong religious orientation, strong work orientation, and strong achievement orientation. These values and ethics that are part of the African American woman's development helped to keep them and their families together, and have strengthened their roles as wife and mother.

Gregory (1995) agrees and found that one of the greatest sources of strength for African American women is the Black church that is also at the center of many in the community. All the participants spoke eloquently about their support from family, friends, social organizations, and the church. These extended networks "provided emotional support, economic supplements, and most important, protected our families integrity from assault by external forces." This was very important to those who lost family members by the means of suicide of HIV/AIDS.

Many African American women are losing their loved ones and becoming quite frustrated with the church. Lying about the cause of death (AIDS vs. Pneumonia) in order for the loved one to have a funeral in the church. According to Sanders (1989), frustration results "when the bereaved is deprived of the things that have been expected, needed, and cherished, and when there is no hope of retrieving these resources (p.66). Renee remembers how much her son enjoyed playing for the church choir and she lied about his cause of death since her was gay. Accompanying the frustration is a sense of disappointment and emptiness that things will not be the same again. Regardless of the type of loss, African American women were frustrated as they attempted to adjust to new situations.

Lucretia learned how to reinvest emotions and energy to another relationship and situation after losing her husband and daughter. She has a group of senior citizens visit once a week to play UNO cards. Three times a week she goes to the gym to work on the lightweights with a group of women from the church. Lucretia has successfully worked through the withdrawal stage to live fully in the here and now.

When the loss involves death, loss often leads to the realization that the present is very temporary. African American women begin to see that ultimately they have responsibility for their lives and happiness. This realization brings several results: recognizing the importance of living each day to the fullest, clarifying, what is important and meaningful in life, and learning the importance of not having things left unsaid (Yalom & Vinogradov, 1988).

Mourning can be a long-term process. Worden (1982) contends that it is impossible to set a date by which mourning should be accomplished. The acute grieving is over only when the tasks of mourning are completed and a person is able to go on with life.

8.   Conclusion

My primary intent was to provide information which supports my assumption there was a connection between the development of African American women, the access to counseling and the educational environment that relates to how African American women learn how to deal with loss.

Although we typically equate loss with death, loss is a prevalent theme throughout our lives as African American women, a theme tied to change and growth. According to Judith Viorst (1986), "we lose not only through death, but also by leaving and being left, by changing and letting go and moving on."

According to Collins (1991), African American women's lives are inextricably linked to a history of racist and sexist oppression that institutionalizes the devaluation of African American women as it idealizes their White counterparts. The issues of gender are always connected to race because the two are inseparable for African American women. While their race and gender make them so visible on the outside, when they are devalued, ignored, and disrespected, they are sometimes left feeling invisible inside (Williams, 2001). Many of the participants in the study were confronted with the stereotypes, overtly and covertly, which suggested to some as being not good mothers and/or wives, lacked financial means to obtain counseling and not worthy of belonging to a support group.

Despite all the obstacles the participants encountered during the mourning process, they self persevered by depending on friends, family, the church, and social organizations to survive. Clearly, there is much work to be done to ensure all African American women will be supported during such a difficult time in one's life.

The six basic principles about African American women and grief:

1.   Grief is a natural reaction to loss. When a person dies, those who are much likely impacted by the loss of a loved one experience grief. This sense of being out of control may be overwhelming or frightening since it cannot be controlled, yet grieving is natural, normal and healthy.

2.   Each woman's experience is unique. While many theories and models of the grieving process may provide a helpful framework for understanding grief, the path itself is a lonely and unique one

for every African American woman. There's no book, article, song, or class to prepare you for this experience.

3. Every death is different. Depending on the nature of the death and the relationship grief is expressed differently. Some of the African American women wanted to be alone, others were afraid to be alone; many cried unexpectedly and most felt sick literally. No matter how they died the participants felt the loss of a loved one.

4. There's no right or wrong ways to grieve a loved one. Coping with a death does not follow a specific set of rules. Some choose destructive behavior such as drinking, prescription drugs, and etc.. Most African American women talk to family, community persons, and church members about their experiences of loss.

5. The grieving process is influenced by a group of impacting issues. There are many issues impacting how African American women react to a death. Some include: the nature of the death; the strength of the community system available (family, friends, church, social organizations); the nature of the relationship with the deceased; and the emotional state of the griever.

6. Grief never ends. Unfortunately this is one of the least understood aspects of grief in our society. When a significant person dies, his or her death leaves a vacuum in the lives of those left behind. Life is never the same again. You cannot live the moment ever except in your mind. No matter how many years go past, the emptiness will be felt over one's lifetime.

It is important to note, African American women are at risk for losing family members and friends through violence, lack of medical attention, disease and still expected to continue holding the household together despite their grief and loss.

Statistics facing African American females in the United States are the following: (1) African American women are nearly twice as likely to be rape victims as white women. In one year, the rate for African American women was 115 per 100,000! (2) African American women are attacked sexually 355 per 100,000 annually vs. White women 196 per 100,000. (3) Loss of African American men in our lives have a 6-7x's greater likelihood of being a murder victim than a white male. The chief victims are our sons, brothers, and nephews between the ages of 17-29

years of age. (4) African American children between the ages of one and four have death rates from homicide, which are four times higher than for white children the same age. Our children are arrested at almost seven times the rates for white children for the most serious violent crimes and are arrested at more than twice the white rates for serious property crimes. (5) Suicide for African American women is 3.5 per 100,000 and rising/African American males 11.4 per 100,000 between the ages of 20-34 years of age. (6) Today,
African American women between the ages of 17-34 are fighting HIV/AIDS in the United States and losing the battle.
  This study suggests implications for future research that investigates grief as a cross-cultural experience and the power to educate counselors and bereavement facilitators to understand and support African American women during the grieving process.

Bibliography

Billingsley Andrew, *Black families in White America.* Englewood Cliffs, NJ: Anchor Books, 1968.

Bowlby John, Attachment and Loss, sadness and depression (Vol.3). New York: Basic Books, 1980,139.

Cebollero, Anthony, Cruise, Kathy, & Stollak, Gary, "The long-term effects of divorce: Mothers and children in concurrent support groups." *Journal of Divorce*, 10(1987), 219-228.

Chatters, James, John Taylor. *Women, girls, and race.* New York: Guilford Press, 1986.

Collins, Patricia. "The social construction of Black feminist thought: Knowledge, consciousness, and the politics of empowerment." *Signs,* 14 (1989), 745-773.

Engel, George. "A group dynamic approach to teaching and learning about grief." *Omega,* 11 (1980-81) 45-59.

Gregory, Sandra. Economic and psychosocial factors which influence career mobility among African American women. Published dissertation, University of Pennsylvania, Philadelphia, 1995,

Harding, Susan. "The curious coincidence of feminine and African modalities: Challenges for feminist theory." In *Women and moral theory*, edited by Elizabeth Kittay & Karen Meyers (Eds.), Totowa, NJ: Rowman & Littlefield Press ,1987, 52-54.

Hill, Robert. *The strength of Black families.* New York: National Urban League, 1972.

Holmes, Charles, John, Rathe. Death and Trauma: The understanding of grieving. Harper Collins, 1967.

Jeffers, Charles. *Living poor.* Ann Arbor, MI: Ann Arbor Publications, 1985, 42.

Joseph, Gloria and Jill Lewis. Common differences: Conflicts in Black and White feminist perspectives. Garden City, NY: Anchor Press, 1981.

Ladner, Joyce. *Tomorrow's tomorrow: The Black woman.* Garden City NY: Anchor Books, 1971.

Lipinski, Mark. *Healing the Dying.* Bantam Books. New York, 1980.

McAdoo, Henry. "Black mothers and the extended family support network." In the *Black woman* edited by La Frances Rodgers-Rose, Newbury Park, CA: Sage Publications,1980, 125-144.

Moses, Yolanda. *Black women in academe: Issues and strategies.* Washington, DC: Association of American Colleges Project on the Status and Education of Women, 1992.

Murphy, Paula, Perry, Karen. "Hidden grievers." *Death Studies* 12 (1988) 451-462.

Norberry, Leon. "A program of support. Journal for Specialists in Group Work" *Journal for Specialists in Group Work,* 11 (1986), 157-162.

Peterson, Elizabeth. African American women: A study of will and success. McFarland, 1992, 86-87

Robinson, Sandra, Ward, John._Racial identity formation and transformation._Cambridge, MA: Harvard University Press, 1991.

Sanders, Charles. The Mourning After: Dealing with Adult Bereavement. New York: John Wiley & Sons, 1989.

Stack, Carol. All our kin: Strategies for survival in a Black community. New York: Harper & Row, 1974

Stern, Allen. Coming Back: Rebuilding Lives After Crisis and Loss. New York: Random House, 1985.

Strobe, Allen, Strobe, Marilyn. *Grieving through personal crisis.* New York: Random House, 1987.

Viorst, Judith. *Necessary Losses.* New York: Simon & Schuster, 1986, 326.

Ward, James. *Racial identity formation and transformation.* Cambridge, MA: Harvard University Press, 1990.

Worden, William. Grief counselling and grief therapy: A handbook for the mental health practitioner. New York: Springer, 1982.

Williams, Julia. " What stymies women's academic careers? It's personal." *The Chronicle of Higher Education,* p. B10, 2001.

Yalom, Irvin, Vinogradov, Sophia. " Bereavement groups: Techniques and themes." *International Journal of Group Psychotheraphy*, 38(1988), 419-446.

Zimpfer, David. *The Art of Support Groups.* New York: Harper Collins, 1989.

Terror of Death in the Wake of September 11th: Is this the End of Death Denial?

Kate Arthur

1. Introduction: Fear of Death

It is not only the sheer horror of the piercing aerial attacks that burns in the mind's eye. It is also the nightmare of the hot billowing cloud of death chasing us through the narrow streets of lower Manhattan, that haunts our memory. Death's dust has caught up with each one of us. In the immediate aftermath of the attacks on the World Trade Center it was impossible to dismiss or deny this calculated, murderous terror.[1] The mental concussion of the impact and its cascade of macabre dust forced a recognition – if only a fleeting recognition – of our own mortality. We too, were vulnerable.[2] Here, in the centre of American commerce, on that sparkling late summer's morn, life's illusion was dissolved.

> This quiet Dust was Gentlemen and Ladies,
> And Lads and Girls;
> Was laughter and ability and sighing,
> And frocks and curls.
> This passive place a Summer's nimble mansion,
>
> Where Bloom and Bees
> Fulfilled their Oriental Circuit,
> Then ceased like these.
>
> (Emily Dickinson, 1924, Part Five: The Single Hound LXXIV)

The stunning coincidence of summer, mansion (the twin towers), and dust in this gentle poet's words are eerily apropos. The dead are dust, the earthly remains of the now deceased adults, who once were children laughing and sighing in the midst of nature's round. In this chapter, I intend to question whether the events of September 11th 2001 fundamentally altered America's 'denial of death.' I conclude, that though the terror attacks fermented much public lamentation, in the end, death denial continues to be operative in American culture. Creeping denial is responsible for a furtive, often contradictory, approach to dying and death in the public realm. Within wider society, death is exploited, demonized and fictionalized yet rarely meaningfully scrutinized.

Fear of death, and its repression, is endemic to contemporary Western culture. An established corpus of scholarly research shows how terror of death is so overwhelming, to our conscious selves, that we repress it.[3] Whether death fear and repression is universal to human experience, historically and culturally, is up for discussion. Few would contest that Western industrialized culture 'banishes' death, as Phillipe Ariès said. Scholars from various fields have attributed our latent anxiety of personal extinction to the following causes: ignorance of the natural process of dying, secularism, rationalism, materialism, medicalization, post-modern or technological alienation and social/economic/political structures. Doubtless, each of these factors contribute to the causes of 'fear of death.' I will show, in the pages to follow, how the events of September the 11th 2001 corroborate theories of the toxicity of repressed death fear. Secondly, I will discuss events subsequent to the World Trade attacks and demonstrate how they vindicate the darkly prescient theories of social anthropologist Ernest Becker. Becker believed that all human vanquishing is rooted in repressed terror of death. Finally, I will illustrate how the human spirit's drive to ultimate value through spiritual expression and aesthetics may offer hope in the face of this dynamic of fear and repression.

2.   Death is THE Source of Terror as it is the End of all Worldly Possibility

And the dust returns to the ground it came from,
and the spirit returns to God who gave it.
Ecclesiastes 12:7

When it approaches too close, sudden death is monstrous and often terrifying. Perhaps fear of death is, indeed, the universal fear.[4] For some people, death fear is expressed as the terror of acquiescence and loss of dignity associated with the dying process itself. Death dread is sometimes articulated as a fear of a possibly premature or especially hideous death. It is significant that most Americans say their preferred way to die, is in their advanced years, while asleep. Most of us though, if we think about it at all, would say any terror is largely attributable to the involuntary surrender to the unknown and our own mutability that death represents. We are horrified by the impossible question of the postmortem enigma and our own inevitable decay. Here is the outrage of the capitulation of our destiny. Especially abhorrent is death caused by human violence and war.

Not everyone dreads death as ultimate annihilation. But even if we trust in some form of postmortem hope, we may, nevertheless, fear extinction of the self. Theologian Michael Simpson expressed it this way: "death marks the end of the possibility of creating one's destiny."[5] Jean Paul Sartre said that dread of death is due to the fact that it prevents the individual from realizing his possibilities. Here is the anticipation of an assault on everything that we have been, all memories and loves extinguished. It is the destruction of the project of living in the world. Older persons often report a lessening of their fear of death, possibly attributable to a reduction of these concerns. Death anxiety seems to be inversely correlated to life satisfaction and the perception of achievement in that life.

In the rationalist and secular world of ideas that we inhabit, what can we possibly hope for after we die? Humanist Thomas Clark said the 'hard-boiled' materialist anticipates nothing but an utter void of darkness and silence following death. Terror of death then, is compounded by an inconceivable permanent extinction of the self, an eternal nothingness. This is Swinburne's abyss of the "eternal night" sucking us into an endless nullity of experience. What is beyond the veil of death is charged with mystery and ineffability. In this life, we know death through proxy only, said commentator Elisabeth Bronfen. It is impossible to experience and analyze the actual death event. Death is the definitive 'in-itself' which cannot be experienced and is beyond communication. Any experience of the moment after death is evidently unverifiable by an observer of that death. Therefore, death is the most solitary and private event of all human experience, and no scientific claim of the subjective experience of death is possible. Death, and any knowledge of it, is truly the sole possession of the person who is actually doing the dying. In "its very essence death is in every case mine, insofar as it is at all" said philosopher Martin Heidegger.[6] He said we cannot grasp our own deaths.

3.   Death Negated, Denied and Repressed

(W)hat is this quintessence of dust?
William Shakespeare

The futility of the familiar methodology leads me to conclude that my personal death is inconceivable. On the other hand, my death is conceivable to my companions, an issue with which we will deal presently. Philosopher Jacques Choron acknowledged this "strange – although by now well established – fact, that no one really believes in his own death."[7] This is so, despite our rational awareness of the inevitability of death. In short, absent proof of my death as my final end, I tend to dismiss or deny it. I must resort to negations, and negations only. Commentator Jonathan Dollimore is correct that we only begin to understand the vital role of death in Western culture when we accept death "as profoundly, compellingly and irreducibly traumatic."[8] Philosopher William James named recognition of our mortality the "worm at the core" that threatens pretensions to happiness. Denial refuses to acknowledge our true attitude, which is one of unconscious fear and dread, hence repression. But as Ernest Becker said, it is only natural that we should repress this dread, to permit normal functioning.

The theme of this trauma, this anxiety, this denial, plays repeatedly throughout 20th Century death commentaries. The psychoanalytic school and many of its philosophic successors agree that death is the basic source of all anxiety, the terror that haunts all human activity. All mortal pursuits are governed by consistent effort to overcome 'the fatality' of death. Herman Feifel, an early contributor to multidisciplinary death studies, felt that fear of death was a powerful factor in exacerbating our denial of reality. Dismissal is not simply the discreet activity of a monad, an inquiring or especially psychologically or philosophically inclined mind. Feifel, Becker and Ariès, among others, developed cogent arguments that denial is an inherent cultural pathology. As we will see, Ernest Becker, a social critic, anthropologist and Pulitzer-Prize winning author of *The Denial of Death*, extended his argument to say that all human achievement in the symbolic world is an attempt to deny and overcome this 'grotesque fate' of ours; death. Society conspires to nourish our sense of immortality, said Becker, through affiliation with socially sanctioned projects.

This is a variation on Sigmund Freud's theme, dating from his essay at the start of 'The War-To-End-All-Wars,' World War 1.[9] Freud said that the cultural and conventional forgetting of the presence of death meant that death was dismissed, put aside and hushed up. This resulted in a toxic effort to eliminate all death from life, he said. He associated anxiety and neurosis to both the terrors of nature and the painful riddle of death. Since we are all convinced of our own immortality, Freud said, conventional, or civilized society typically denies death. Elisabeth Kübler-Ross famously took up Freud's theme of unconscious denial, upon which she premised her study, and the development of her death awareness movement. Geoffrey Gorer, a British anthropologist, developed the theme that death is so obscene and disgusting that it is unmentionable in polite company. The art of embalmers, the sanitized funeral industry, the disdain of lurid mourning and euphemisms for death all prove societal denial of the horror of the reality of death. The public lamentation in America, immediately following September 11th, stands out as a striking exception to this rule, hence, my interest in the social and political implications of death denial.

Denial is a natural human response to the outrage of a sinister and fearful force that cannot be studied, categorized, analyzed or understood by the enlightened intellect. Death's denial is, according to historian Phillipe Ariès, a symptom of industrialization and modernity. Death denial (and the accompanying erotic fascination, he argued) developed in the 18th Century during the Enlightenment, along with the symbolic 'removal' of death from the realm of the living. The "reversal of death" was symbolized by the relocation of cemeteries to the outskirts of town. Death became traumatic, shameful, forbidden and repressed. In our desperation to drive death from life we marginalized it, shrouded it, in a kind of pornography of secret fascination. As death was banished, relegated to tabooed territory, the result was, what commentator Herman Feifel, called profound contradictions in our thinking.

4.   To Die this Death, Knowing that this is All, is to Live

Dust claims dust - and we die too.
Percy Bysshe Shelley

An example of such contradictory thinking is the public scorn of death represented by materialists and nihilists. The abiding influence of nihilism is the commonly expressed opinion that death is all there is.[10] We live in a pluralistic environment in which a shared vision of an afterlife cannot be assumed. The question of meaning in a post-Christian, post-modern and digitally connected globe often seems to be located in the living of life itself, nowhere else. Especially influential is a kind of European thinking, which encourages a secular nihilist proposition in the face of the problem of the finality of death. This defiant stance promotes human finitude as the sole source of meaning. The aim of this philosophy, and certain psychological schools, is to learn how to die this death, my death, knowing that there is nothing else after this death. If God is dead, and we have no postmortem hope, life in the present moment is all that matters. The materialist will not allow the fact of death to poison her enjoyment of life. Here fulfillment is achieved by throwing oneself into some temporal absolute or other, whether politics, sexual fulfillment, mind altering substances, fame, material acquisition, or work.

So the existentialists, like the Stoics of the ancient world, responded to the fear of death and its attendant unpleasant emotional affect by urging a constant mindfulness of death in life. By realizing the threat of non-existence, Martin Heidegger said, we can attain a fuller understanding of our life, its meaning, and free ourselves from fear of death. But if Freud and Becker, and their successors are right, this secular affirmation of life (whether or not in the presence of death) inevitably collapses into the ugly reappearance of repressed unconscious death anxiety.

5.   Death is Turned Away: Life at Full Throttle

Who then to frail mortality shall trust,
But limns the water, or but writes in dust.
Sir Francis Bacon

Phillipe Ariès said the focus on the self and personal fulfilment through passionate attachment to the material world has contributed to resentment of death. Ours is as much a world where death is publicly denied and relegated to the realm of private misery and dread, as ever. Nearly thirty years after Kübler-Ross's contribution, the death event is still a restrained, solitary and middle-of-the-night affair. Most people hope to die at home, surrounded by loved ones. Yet tragically, the majority of Americans actually still die in institutions, out of sight of life and the living. Western culture idolizes youth and ghettoizes the old and decrepit. Where individual autonomy trumps all else, we expect to have control over all choices in life, which includes control over our own dying. We have become so accustomed to think that death can be indefinitely postponed, we routinely expect the medical, priestly class to perform miracles. Physical survival in end-of-life care is often fought for, at all costs including further suffering. Ariès is right, this has not helped to annihilate death, nor fear of death, it has only served to underscore death's savagery. We are habituated to think that science will always bring us back from the brink of destruction. The Human Genome Project, gene therapy, organ transplantation, nano-technology, cloning and artificial hearts all promise hope, however faint, of curing us of our mortality.

In our frenzy of material acquisition, anything that thwarts our individual expression of success is threatening. Death truncates the dream of progress and so is disdained. Ariès's statement still holds: in the most industrialized, urbanized, and technologically advanced areas of the Western world...society has banished death. Everything in town(s) goes on as if nobody died any more.[11]

America's pursuit of life, liberty and the pursuit of happiness 'dream' sometimes manifests as an embarrassment of riches. This feeds an insatiable appetite for gratuitous material existence. 'Shop for America,' was the slogan following the events of September the 11th 2001, a presidential refrain. Bradley Butterfield decried this in his article "The Baudrillardian Symbolic, 9/11 and the War of Good and Evil."[12] He said that America goes to the shopping mall to celebrate national holidays to honour the dead, such as Memorial Day. Inherent in this market-economy solipsism is a ravenous yearning for more possessions, and possessing more life. The 2001 Hollywood movie *Vanilla Sky*, starring Tom Cruise as David Ames, pictures a relentless pursuit of happiness. The Ames character overcomes death to achieve physical immortality, even perhaps, a kind of spiritual resurrection. What is important about this version of the film, based on the 1997 Spanish film *Abre los Ojos*, is the hedonistic values of the main characters. Especially interesting is that the afterlife pictured is a creation of the 'Ames' character's own design, imbued with the people and events of his ego's own creation.

6. Death Confronted

I will show you fear in a handful of dust.
T.S. Eliot

In our private musings on death, as I said earlier, we cannot imagine our own demise. But in our most intimate thoughts each one of us is aware of the distasteful notion that we are equally convinced that other people die. Becker is right, that one of the meaner aspects of our natural human narcissism is that we feel that practically everyone is expendable, except us. Luck is, as Aristotle said, when the guy next to you gets hit with the arrow. When we read about deaths in the media, of people killed in far-off wars, or on holiday weekend highways, said Kübler-Ross, this only supports our unconscious belief in our own immortality. On September 11, 2001, all that suddenly changed, if only very briefly. America's sense of security and way of life was attacked. If the suicide bombers knew that the Twin Towers were vulnerable to such catastrophic destruction, they also knew that the veneer of America's 'denial of death' could be dissolved into so much dust. Their cunning power was partly due to the fact that they knew the West better than we knew ourselves. They turned Western death phobia into a weapon of terror against America. For a time the dark heavens opened wide and it rained death. The particulate matter that spread across Manhattan, in September of 2001, was evidence that death could and did happen in America. We were irretrievably, though involuntarily, involved as witnesses to violent, and unforgiving death. This was real and this was personal. People just like us went to work one day and died. It was not mass death happening in some Godforsaken part of the world, away from the camera's eye.

'The denial of death': was first coined by Freud, in his 1915 essay 'Our Attitude Towards Death' six months into what was then the 'Great War' (World War 1) Freud wrote:

> It is evident that war is bound to sweep away this conventional treatment of death. Death will no longer be denied; we are forced to believe in it. People really die; and no longer one by one, but many, often tens of thousands, in a single day. And death is no longer a chance event.[13]

Here Freud posits the possibility that the horror of this first war of the modern era would be so evident, to all, that repression would be a thing of the past. His hope, evidently, was for an end to the iniquity of war. And of course, the optics of history tragically show how wrong Freud was. The horrific scale of the cumulative daily death toll, of the First World War has yet to be surpassed.[14] Yet there remains an almost universal agreement amongst authors of the classic texts that the way to overcome death anxiety is by confronting it. Herman Feifel, in the early atomic era, affirmed this view:

> ...if we accept death as a necessity...This might possibly mute some of the violence of our times, for energies now bound up in continuing attempts to shelve and repress the concept of death would be available to us for the more constructive aspects of living, perhaps even fortifying man's gift for creative splendor against his genius for destruction.[15]

Clearly, this is what Freud had in mind, and he was woefully mistaken. This said, what would cause me to wonder whether September the 11th marked the end of 'death denial'?

Was it not possible that the unmediated savagery of the World Trade collapse made us face our own mortality? America felt unsafe. For the millions of witnesses on the streets of Lower Manhattan, the uptown Avenues and across the water in New Jersey, this was apocalypse 'live'. Death was unmediated for many, many, people in Manhattan; including the survivors. The horror of the event was not mitigated by the fact that so many people said it had 'the look' of a Hollywood disaster film. Most of us, on the other hand, watched the events unfold in repeated televised video clips. The news videotapes of terror were edited within hours; yet, early television viewing was as close as you could get without being there. The film experience brought to us by documentary filmmakers Jules Naudet, Gideon Naudet and James Hanlon, for instance, was intensely real. The videotape recording continues to run throughout the collapse of one of the towers from the location of an adjoining World Trade lobby. The film is a record of the agonizing few minutes after dust engulfs and blackens the scene, and firefighters make their way through the darkness, not knowing who was dead and who was alive.

The American public, inured as they are by images of grotesque violence in film and entertainment media, broke out in a chorus of lament. The ghastly spectacle of the atrocities, broadcast live, dislodged a cascade of fear, anxiety and public solicitude. The visuals packed such affective punch that no one could have anticipated the fervor of the immediate aftermath. The world witnessed a profound public outpouring of grief. This was a public reversal of a furtive treatment of death. The keening was for the loss of the dead innocents, but also for the brutal loss of innocence. For an instant in time, the American illusion of immortality had vanished. Death announced its ubiquitous nature in a way that could not be ignored or denied. It was a spectacle of hyper-realism. Survivors, yet "we are dust."[16]

Susan Sontag's book *Regarding the Pain of Others* is a meditation on photographic images of human-made violence and war. She points out that in earlier times (Freud's time, especially) people used to believe that if the horror was made vivid enough we would finally 'take in' the outrageousness, the insanity, of war. The question becomes: is it possible to feel the horror and truly empathize with the dead and other victims of war and Holocaust? Sontag lets a survivor of the war in Sarajevo express the essence of this dilemma:

A citizen of Sarajevo, a woman of impeccable adherence
to the Yugoslav ideal, whom I met soon after arriving in
the city the first time in April 1993, told me: "In October
1991 I was here in my nice apartment in peaceful
Sarajevo when the Serbs invaded Croatia, and I
remember when the evening news showed footage of the
destruction of Vukovar, just a couple of hundred
miles away, I thought to myself, 'Oh, how horrible,' and
switched the channel. So how can I be indignant if
someone in France or Italy or Germany sees the killing
taking place here day after day on their evening news
and says, 'Oh, how horrible,' and looks for another
program. It's normal. It's human." Wherever people
feel safe this was her bitter, self-accusing point - they
will be indifferent.[17]

Images, whether video or photographic, are precisely that, only
images. And this is Sontag's point in her extended meditation. No image
can properly convey the sheer terror of death. When you are 'regarding'
an image you are affirmed in your own safety, says Sontag. And as
Sontag's Sarajevo woman tells us, whenever people feel safe they will be
indifferent. What was unprecedented about the attack in Manhattan on
September the 11th, was that so many people actually did personally
experience the event, with all the sharpness of their senses. America felt
vulnerable. The tone of lamentation was a measure of this trauma.

7.   As for Death, it is still un-American.

And you may carve a shrine about my dust.
Tennyson

As September the 11th 2001 fades in time, I have had to
reluctantly revise my naïve notions on matters of death denial. My faith
had been in a peaceful transcendence of this ever-present angst. In earlier
versions of this chapter I betrayed a certain kind of optimism. That
optimism was a hope that the world could now be a safer place. The
American population had experienced what it feels to be vulnerable, just
like the rest of the world. America was subject to death, world events and
forces beyond their control. The majority of the world's population
normally feel unsafe. Americans would now have empathy for the plight
of helpless victims of mass genocide and acts of war in Lebanon,

Srebrenica or Rwanda. Any killing of innocent life is evil. Therefore, any suggestion that the evil of terrorism, war or humanly preventable death and suffering can be redemptive must be strongly repudiated. It should be clear that redemption, per se, is not what I seek. During the days and weeks following the collapse of the towers, Americans lived with a dark unease. It was the realization of worst fears confirmed. Terrorism and death proved that America was but one nation in a vulnerable and interdependent world.

Biblical and classical texts show dust as a metaphor for death. But dust also stands for something of debased or despised condition, by definition. Dust is a synonym for garbage in the United Kingdom, as in 'dustbin,' or garbage can. These are powerfully evocative allusions. Smoke, ashes and dust were visible to the world in the plume of smoke drifting from lower Manhattan. These images were available as NASA space photos in the fall of 2001. Confronted with terror and death, America chose to declare war on terrorism. The unforgivable part of the terrorist attacks, said theologian Stanley Hauerwas, was that America felt vulnerable.[18] Mass homicidal death was mortifying for America.

If we can say anything about evolving events since the attacks on September the 11th 2001 it is this. Death, especially horrendous, violent death, would not be tolerated in America. Death, as Butterfield said, is still un-American.[19] Americans just don't die and certainly Americans don't let any one else do the killing, Hauerwas contended. Tragically, Ernest Becker's treatise on the roots of violence in his book *Escape from Evil* appear to be uncannily apt. Americans, somehow, needed to transcend ignoble death and banish it from American soil.

8. Ernest Becker and 'Denial of Death'

What's become of man's great extent and proportion,
when himself shrinks himself and consumes himself to a
handful of dust
John Donne

Ernest Becker's theories were a revision of Freudian theories of repression, with a special affinity for the thought of Otto Rank. Rank, a psychoanalyst and a protégé of Freud's, introduced a broad humanities perspective to the study of fear of death.[20] Becker believed that what distinguishes the human psyche is not language, nor rational thought, per se, but the ability to reflect and stand outside of time and place and engage the imagination. Hence, we anticipate the mortification of our earthly being. Since we are aware of our inevitable death, we are subject to the power that this knowledge has over us. This knowledge, unharnessed in culturally condoned projects, larger than ourselves, has the capacity to drive us mad. For every human endeavor in the symbolic world is subject to death and time.

Becker reworked the Freudian theme that death awareness and its accompanying overwhelming anxiety encompasses *all* human relations and culture. Human striving, said Becker, was not principally rooted in primal sexual energy, evolutionary selfishness or repressed aggression. Becker clearly located the source of turbid energy in concealed fear of finitude. Terror of death is the principle thing that 'moves' human achievement. Fear of dependence and distrust of our fallible animal nature drives persons to seek some kind of worldly immortality or transcendence. We nourish illusions of immortality through devotion to an ideology of self. "Society itself is a codified hero system," said Becker, "which means that society everywhere is a living myth of the significance of human life, a defiant creation of meaning" in the face of despicable death.[21] At its best, this eminence is embodied in great cathedrals, symphonies, art and works of literature.

Denial of mortality and the illusion of the heroic self-image are the root causes of human evil, said Becker. Social institutions, politics and war are all veiled attempts to transcend fear in a culturally acceptable system of sacrifice, scape-goating and "culturally standardized hero systems and symbols."[22] Death denial is at the source of all acts that serve to dehumanize others. It results in an inevitable tribalism in which people are classified as with us, or agin' us. This theory leads to the conclusion that scape-goating the 'other' helps resolve our niggling death anxiety. In its more rapacious form it is will to power and aggression. The Becker theory is that human beings seek self-aggrandizement and a sense of immortality through derogation of persons or groups who we class as different. Merlyn E. Mowrey expresses this affliction well:

> That human beings tend to respond violently to encounters with different others in defense of their cultural worldviews has ominous implications for the future well-being of humankind. As Becker noted in *Escape from Evil* (1975), this problem is compounded by the fact that even if people did not stumble onto different others, we would be psychologically inclined to designate someone (an individual or group) against whose beliefs to test ours. If we can show their

vulnerability, their inability to stand up to our power, we
are enhanced and they are diminished. We qualify for
continued durability, for life, for eternity; and they, not
fully human, as scapegoat bearers of evil, warrant
domination, banishment, and death.[23]

The difficult fact is that the Arab Muslim terrorists furnished Americans
with the ideal 'other', none had to be manufactured. Here is the source of
the unholy instinctive terror of all living beings, both human and non-
human. It explains human acquisitiveness, destruction, conquest, violence
and dominance. Sam Keen provided a concise summary of the Becker
thesis:

> We so need to be heroic, to be on the side of God, to
> eliminate evil, to clean up the world, to be victorious
> over death, that we visit destruction and death on all
> who stand in the way of our heroic historical destiny.
> We scapegoat and create absolute enemies, not because
> we are intrinsically cruel, but because focusing our
> anger on an outside target, striking at strangers, brings
> our tribe or nation together and allows us to be part of a
> close and loving in-group. [24]

Otto Rank is quoted in Becker's book *Escape from Evil*. Rank
said "(t)he death fear of the ego is lessened by the killing, the sacrifice, of
the other."[25] Events since September the 11th so strikingly and
transparently confirm the worst that Becker could imagine. Certainly,
there are numerous reasons offered for the American-led military
campaigns in Afghanistan (2002) and Iraq (2003). Among the contributing
factors were a genuine concern for security to protect America from
further terrorist attacks, a perceived need to ensure American access to oil
supplies, worries about 'weapons of mass destruction' in the hands of
Saddam Hussein and a need for a new strategic base of military operations
in the area. These factors all seem to have played a part. Yet, the blow to
the American sense of security was probably the most dangerous
repercussion of the events of the World Trade Centers's collapse.
Christian-pacifist Hauerwas explains that President George W. Bush knew
that the American people needed to be comforted after September the
11th. Bush needed to retrieve normalcy and assure Americans they were in
control, once again. Hauerwas has a knack for incendiary remarks. But his
reflections have a ring of truth to them. Americans were assuaged by the

move to declare war on what President Bush termed 'the axis of evil' and world terrorism.

> "We are at war." Magic words necessary to reclaim the everyday. War is such normalizing discourse. Americans know war. This is our Pearl Harbor. Life can return to normal. We are frightened, and ironically war makes us feel safe. The way to go on in the face of September 11, 2001, is to find someone to kill.[26]

President George W. Bush appears to confirm Hauerwas's cynicism in the following remarks made to a Joint Session of Congress September 20, 2001:

> We have suffered great loss. And in our grief and anger we have found our mission and our moment. Freedom and fear are at war. The advance of human freedom - the great achievement of our time, and the great hope of every time - now depends on us. Our nation - this generation - will lift a dark threat of violence from our people and our future.[27]

If further evidence is needed to attest that Ernest Becker's theories have been omininously prophetic it is this. Hauerwas said of Americans "(i)n our battles, only the enemy has to die."[28] Proof of American 'denial of death' and the illusion of the power over life and death are recent developments in the American style of war by technology: precision munitions. We have no dimension of the numbers of Afghanis or Iraqis who died during the American-led campaigns of 2002 and 2003. We certainly know that relatively few Americans died and American casualties, from friendly fire declined, with experience. This is controlled death. This new warfare of precision bombing, to credit the Americans, even controlled the number of enemy casualties.

8. Religion and Life and Death

> Religion opens up the depth of spiritual life which is usually covered by the dust of our daily life and the noise of our secular work. (Paul Tillich)

Ernest Becker, like Sigmund Freud and Otto Rank before him, felt that conscious acknowledgement of the dread of death would serve to ameliorate violence. He placed his hopes in the sway of reason, and the human capacity for transcendence through acknowledgement of the brute fact of death.

Death is the philosopher's muse and most philosophical systems are shaped in accordance with some kind of wisdom derived from death. Jonathan Dollimore describes this reigning paradox that we have been dealing with: "death, which consigns everything to oblivion, is also what gives meaning to everything."[29] But philosophy and reason alone do not suffice. The arts, literature and film have historically been rich resources of this kind of this ineffability of death within life. There is, quite rightly, a sense of deep disquiet to even suggest moving unspeakable horror, such as mass murder - from terror - to witness - to aesthetic - or to religious consolation. We are revolted by the very thought that such atrocities can do anything but stand for what they are. Yet the arts and religiosity have always been integral to healing.

Aesthetics express the value of a spiritual appreciation of death in life. Emily Dickinson was surely acquainted with sacredness of life in the presence of death.

DEATH is a dialogue between
The spirit and the dust.
"Dissolve," says Death. The Spirit, "Sir,
I have another trust."

Death doubts it, argues from the ground.

The Spirit turns away,
Just laying off, for evidence,
An overcoat of clay.

(Emily Dickinson, 1924, Part Four: Time and Eternity
XXXI)

This insight from a simpler time in America is more than a quaint remnant of a pastoral sensibility of the past. It is a truth that the Western world must integrate into daily living. We can think of the dust as the transient things of the world, and the Spirit as that part of us that trusts in the Eternal. For me, the overcoat of clay is the memory of all departed souls. I have argued that direct witness of the terror on the streets of

Manhattan did not seem to change death repression in America. The 'worm at the core' burrowed ever deeper, further from sight, as Americans took their war to distant lands.

For Freud, Marx and, many of their successors, 'spiritual comfort' in the face of death was nothing more than a neurotic support. Such childish illusions, said Freud, were employed as crutches to escape the hard realities of life and death. Faith in immortality, he said, was mere compensation for the reality of death; that is, the harsh reality that death signifies the total annihilation of the person.

What I believe was missing was the illumination of an integral sense of the transcendent in both life and death. The challenge is to find meaning in death, and plumb our innate spiritual resources to move from despair and fear into hope. We can retrieve a sense of living in the presence of death that evokes ultimate meaning, mystery and wonder evoked in the poetry of Emily Dickinson. Change, loss and mutability are present everywhere, in everything we do. Two pioneers in palliative care, Dr. Derek Doyle and Dr. Elisabeth Kübler-Ross, spoke of increased spirituality amongst people who tend to the dying. By being ever mindful of death in life, we can discover or recover a sense of mystery. By being conscious of the natural world of eros and thanatos and the ever present transcendent, we are able to retrieve a conscious awareness of the preciousness of life. Emily Dickenson says that Death argues 'from the ground.' The metaphor of ground suggests the ground of all being, God, or possibly the earth, or nature. Death is the natural end to all mortal life. At the risk of a gross distortion of the poet's sensibilities, I suggest that she is expressing a feeling of death implicit in all things and of the eternal Spirit.

The great religions have urged contemplation of death in life as a means to spiritual wholeness. Instead of being abolished from life, death is integral to religious observance and mystical traditions. If the faithful embrace death in life then they are more able to accept the exigencies of life, death and transcendence. Death in life lends symbolic meaning to the conundrums of human existence. *What man shall live and not see death?* says the Hebrew text Psalm 98:48. *Dying yet we live,* is the central message of the Christian Gospel of St. Paul (2 Corinthians 6:9). The Buddhist *Samyutta Nikaya* says *For the Born, there is no such thing as not dying.* The Muslim Holy Book *The Koran* counsels keeping death in perspective and the materialism of this world in perspective: *Every soul shall have a taste of death* (al-Imran 3:185).

Ernest Becker's work was not explicitly religious. But he cultivated an acquaintance with sacredness of life in the presence of death within the cosmos.

We know that something immense is needed to shock man out of the pathetic yet deadly heroisms to which he has been accustomed. And the first step in this kind of shock is a new openness of perception about the human condition, what it means to have been created on a planet in the sun, why we seem to have been left here to murder and poison ourselves, to wheel and deal in such an idiot frenzy. With the right intensity and scope of shock, we might even ask ourselves what are we to do with our lives. We might then begin to think of how to again give to people a secure feeling that their lives count, that there is a heroic human contribution to be made to cosmic life in a dialogue with a community of one's fellows.[30]

Terror of death repressed 'still rumbles' beneath the ground through cultural dominance, said Becker. See what it has wrought. Religion, he said, rightly transforms culturally sanctioned violence and scape-goating "by expanding awe and terror to the cosmos where they belong."[31] He speaks here for a humble appreciation for the mystery of creation and destruction in the natural world, and a spiritual yearning that for the ultimate Other, God. His uncanny choice of words here, mock the concept underlying the American battle plan in Iraq in March 2003, that is: "Shock and Awe."

Bibliography

Ariès, Phillipe. *Western Attitudes toward Death: From the Middle Ages to the Present*. Baltimore: Johns Hopkins University Press, 1974.

Becker, Ernest. *The Denial of Death*. New York: Free Press, 1973.

———. "The Spectrum of Loneliness." *Humanitas* 10 (1974): 237-46.

———. *Escape from Evil*. New York: Free Press, 1975.

Bronfen, Elisabeth. "Death: A Preface." In *In the Limits of Death: Between Philosophy and Psychoanalysis*, edited by Mark Robson and Marquard Smith Joanne Morra, xv-xxiv. Manchester: Manchester University Press, 2000.

Bush, George W. *Address to a Joint Session of Congress and the American People, September 20, 2001* Office of the Press Secretary, The

White House of the United States of America, 2001. Available from
http://www.whitehouse.gov/news/releases/2001/09/
20010920-8.html.
    Butterfield, Bradley. "The Baudrillardian Symbolic, 9/11, and the
War of Good and Evil." *Postmodern Culture*, no. 13.1 (2002).
    Choron, Jacques. *Death and Western Thought*. New York:
Collier Books, 1963.
    Clark, Thomas W. "Death, Nothingness and Subjectivity." *The
Humanist* 54, no. 6 (1994): 15-21.
    Dillard, Annie. *For the Time Being*. Toronto: Penguin, 1999.
    Dollimore, Jonathan. "Death's Incessant Motion." In *In the Limits
of Death: Between Philosophy and Psychoanalysis*, edited by Mark
Robson and Marquard Smith. Joanne Morra, 79-105. Manchester:
Manchester University Press, 2000.
    Feifel, Herman. *The Meaning of Death*. New York: Blakiston
Division, McGraw-Hill, 1965.
Forman, Tom. "9/11." edited by Gedeon Naudet James Hanlon, Jules
Naudet: Paramount Home Video, 2002.
    Freud, Sigmund. *Reflections on War and Death; Zeitgemässes
Über Krieg Und Tod*. Translated by English translation by A.A. Brill and
Alfred B. Kuttner. New York: Moffat, Yard,, 1918.
Gil, Alejandro and Mateo Amenabar. "Vanilla Sky." edited by Cameron
Crowe: Paramount, 2001.
    Gorer, Geoffrey. *Death, Grief, and Mourning in Contemporary
Britain*. Garden City, New York: Doubleday, 1965.
    Hauerwas, Stanley. "September 11, 2001: A Pacifist Response."
The South Atlantic Quarterly 101.2 (2002): 425-33.
    Heidegger, Martin. *Being and Time*. Translated by John
Macquarrie & Edward Robinson. New York: Harper & Row, 1962.
    James, William. The Varieties of Religious Experience : A Study
in Human Nature, Being the Gifford Lectures on Natural Religion
Delivered at Edinburgh in 1901-1902. New York: Mentor Edition, 1958.
    Keen, Sam. "The Enemy as Enemy of God: Psycho-Spiritual
Processes in the Ritual Transformation of the Enemy." In *Death and
Denial : Interdisciplinary Perspectives on the Legacy of Ernest Becker*,
edited by Daniel Liechty, 231-46. Westport, Conn.: Praeger, 2002.
    Kenel, Sally. "A Heroic Vision." *Zygon, Journal of Religion and
Science* 33, no. 1 (1998).
    Kübler-Ross, Elisabeth. *On Death and Dying*. New York:
MacMillan Publishing Company, 1969.

Lapham, Lewis H. "Shock and Awe." *Harper's Magazine* 306, no. 1836 (2003): 7-9.

Liechty, Daniel. "Reaction to Mortality: An Interdisciplinary Organizing Principle." *Zygon, Journal of Religion and Science* 33, no. 1 (1998).

————. Editor, Death and Denial Interdisciplinary Perspectives on the Legacy of Ernest Becker, Westport, Conn.: Praeger, 2002.

Lifton, Robert Jay. "On Death and Death Symbolism: The Hiroshima Disaster." In *The Phenomenon of Death: Faces of Mortality*, edited by Edith Wyschogrod, 69-112. New York: Harper & Row, 1973.

Mitford, Jessica. *The American Way of Death Revisited*. New York: Alfred A. Knopf, 1998.

Mowrey, Merlyn E. "The Religious Hero and the Escape from Evil: A Feminist Challenge to Ernest Becker's Religious Mystification." In *Death and Denial : Interdisciplinary Perspectives on the Legacy of Ernest Becker*, edited by Daniel Liechty, 269-80. Westport, Conn.: Praeger, 2002.

Neimeyer, Robert A. "Special Article: Death Anxiety Research: The State of the Art." *Omega* 36, no. 2 (1997-1998) (1997): 97-120.

Pieper, Josef. *Death and Immortality: Tod Und Unsterblichkeit*. Translated by Richard and Clara Winston. New York: Herder and Herder, 1969.

Robson, Mark, Marquard Smith. And Joanne Morra, Editors. *The Limits of Death: Between Philosophy and Psychoanalysis*. Manchester: Manchester University Press, 2000.

Simpson, Michael. *The Theology of Death and Eternal Life*. Notre Dame, Ind.: Fides Publishers, 1971.

Solomon, Sheldon. "Tales from the Crypt: On the Role of Death in Life." *Zygon, Journal of Religion and Science* 33, no. 1 (1998).

Sontag, Susan. *Regarding the Pain of Others*. New York: Farrar, Straus and Giroux, 2003.

Webb, Eugene. "Ernest Becker & the Psychology of World Views." *Zygon, Journal of Religion and Science* 33, no. 1 (1998).

Wyschogrod, Edith. *Spirit in Ashes: Hegel, Heidegger, and Man-Made Mass Death*. New Haven: Yale University Press, 1985.

Notes

[1] I chose the collapse of the World Trade Centre as the paradigmatic event of September the 11th 2001, partly because of its awesome scale and also because of its haunting symbolism of death, dust.

[2] I am a Canadian. It is safe to surmise that many citizens of the Western world shared a deep personal unease on September 11th 2001.
[3] Along with Sigmund Freud, Otto Rank and Ernest Becker are Friedrich Nietzsche, Søren Kierkegaard, Franz Rosenzweig, Robert Jay Lifton, Rollo May and Irvin Yalom who made important contributions to theories of fear of death and denial. See Daniel Liechty, "Introduction: Generative Death Anxiety--an Organizing Principle for the Social Sciences and Humanities," in *Death and Denial: Interdisciplinary Perspectives on the Legacy of Ernest Becker*, ed. Daniel Liechty (Westport, Conn.: Praeger, 2002), xi.

[4] Ernest Becker, *The Denial of Death* (New York: The Free Press, 1973), Elisabeth Kübler-Ross, *On Death and Dying* (New York: MacMillan Publishing Company, 1969). Jack Morgan, founder of the Centre For Education About Death and Bereavement, at King's College University of Western Ontario, says that in simpler times when death was more familiar it was less a source of terror.
[5] Michael Simpson, *The Theology of Death and Eternal Life* (Notre Dame, Ind.: Fides Publishers, Inc., 1971), 56-57.
[6] Martin Heidegger, *Being and Time*, trans. John Macquarrie & Edward Robinson (New York: Harper & Row, 1962), 284.
[7] Jacques Choron, *Death and Western Thought* (New York: The MacMillan Company, 1963), 18.
[8] Jonathan Dollimore, "Death's Incessant Motion," in *In the Limits of Death: Between Philosophy and Psychoanalysis*, ed. Mark Robson and Marquard Smith. Joanne Morra (Manchester: Manchester University Press, 2000), 126.
[9] Sigmund Freud, *Reflections on War and Death; Zeitgemässes Über Krieg Und Tod*, trans. Authorized English translation by A.A. Brill and Alfred B. Kuttner (New York: Moffat, Yard, 1918).
[10] Dollimore, "Death's Incessant Motion."
[11] Phillipe Ariès, *Western Attitudes toward Death: From the Middle Ages to the Present.* (Baltimore: Johns Hopkins University Press, 1974), 560.
[12] Bradley Butterfield, "The Baudrillardian Symbolic, 9/11, and the War of Good and Evil," *Postmodern Culture*, no. 13.1 (2002).
[13] Freud, *Reflections on War and Death; Zeitgemässes Über Krieg Und Tod.*, 291.
I am referring throughout this chapter to death caused by human [14] violence, as opposed to natural causes, or preventable death from disease or accident. The dimensions of death by natural cataclysm are sometimes

beyond comprehension, such as the estimated 138,000 souls who perished during a typhoon in Bangladesh on April 30, 1991.
[15] Herman Feifel, *The Meaning of Death* (New York: Blakiston Division, McGraw-Hill, 1965), 12.
[16] Emily Dickinson, 1924, Part Five: The Single Hound CII.
[17] Susan Sontag, *Regarding the Pain of Others* (New York: Farrar, Straus and Giroux, 2003), 98-99.
[18] Stanley Hauerwas, "September 11, 2001: A Pacifist Response," *The South Atlantic Quarterly* 101.2 (2002).
[19] Butterfield, "The Baudrillardian Symbolic, 9/11, and the War of Good and Evil."
[20] Liechty, "Introduction: Generative Death Anxiety--an Organizing Principle for the Social Sciences and Humanities.", xi.
Becker, *The Denial of Death,* 7.[21]
[22] Ernest Becker, *Escape from Evil* (New York: Free Press, 1975), xvii.
[23] Merlyn E. Mowrey, "The Religious Hero and the Escape from Evil: A Feminist Challenge to Ernest Becker's Religious Mystification," in *Death and Denial : Interdisciplinary Perspectives on the Legacy of Ernest Becker*, ed. Daniel Liechty (Westport, Conn.: Praeger, 2002), 273.
[24] Sam Keen, "The Enemy as Enemy of God: Psycho-Spiritual Processes in the Ritual Transformation of the Enemy," in *Death and Denial : Interdisciplinary Perspectives on the Legacy of Ernest Becker*, ed. Daniel Liechty (Westport, Conn.: Praeger, 2002), 232.
[25] Becker, *Escape from Evil,* 108.
[26] Hauerwas, "September 11, 2001: A Pacifist Response," 426.
George W. Bush, *Address to a Joint Session of Congress and the* [27] *American People, September 20, 2001* (Office of the Press Secretary, The White House of the United States of America, 2001 [cited); available from http://www.whitehouse.gov/news/releases/2001/09/20010920-8.html.
[28] Hauerwas, "September 11, 2001: A Pacifist Response."
[29] Dollimore, "Death's Incessant Motion," 82.
[30] Ernest Becker, "The Spectrum of Loneliness," *Humanitas* 10 (1974), 246.
[31] Ernest Becker, "The Spectrum of Loneliness," 246.

University of St. Michael's College,
University of Toronto, April 2003.

Kafka's God Of Suffocation:
The Futility Of 'Facing' Death

David Johnson

A strong philosophical tradition asserts that if people face up to the reality of their future deaths, they will be able to live more authentic lives. Two philosophers who embrace this tradition and take it to an extreme are Martin Heidegger and Georges Bataille, figures whose work is central to the formation of the postmodernist concept of time. For Heidegger, facing death gives us a sense of groundlessness, which frees us from staid conventions, enabling us to live spontaneously. For Bataille, a contemplation of our mortality frees us from the vain and laborious attempt to conserve our lives. Against these philosophers, I argue that it is impossible for human beings to face death directly, given that they are caught up in the urgency of their lives. Moreover, how can a consciousness of death, which is a consciousness of a state radically alien to ongoing life, provide a living being with any relevant information about how to live 'authentically' in ongoing time? How can 'facing death' liberate someone from problems that are intimately tied up with life and living?

I shall argue that the death fixation of philosophers like Heidegger and Bataille is at best obscurantist, at worst morbid and nihilistic. What is most obscured is the irreducible reality of the time lived up to the point of death, and what is most nihilistic is the fastidious evasion of this rich duration.

I will try to sum up these problems in a simple way, asking 'How can we face death if we are still alive?' and 'How can death inform life if death has not been reached?' This involves a certain paradox well dramatised not by a philosopher as such, but by the writer Franz Kafka.

Kafka maintains that it is terrible for someone to experience suffocation without having had some earlier acquaintance with this terror. He suggests that it would be beneficial for someone slipping into respiratory illness to have a meeting with the 'god of suffocation' prior to the final horror of suffocation as such. It would be of benefit to have a kind of pre-meeting meeting. He writes:

For each invalid his household god, for the tubercular the god of suffocation. How can one bear his approach if one does not partake of him in advance of the terrible union?[1]

Yet, if an individual were to experience the terrors of suffocation to be suffered at a future date in only a limited manner, this limited foretaste would not sufficiently arm that individual for the more extensive horrors of the future. On the other hand, if the pre-suffocation meeting with the 'god of suffocation' were to be as terrible as that ultimate meeting to be had in the future, then this meeting would simply double the experience of horror. Either the meeting is too insipid, or it is the gratuitous equivalent of death itself (gratuitous given that one is not yet dead).

When the philosopher contemplates death he or she is in essentially the same paradoxical position as the tubercular man contemplating final suffocation via a symbolic meeting. A prior meeting with the god of suffocation cannot be philosophically authentic; only the final meeting is authentic but this meeting is deadly, leaving no space for a sense of meeting or, indeed, for any form of contemplation at all. In showing the absurd position of the suffering tubercular patient, Kafka is also revealing the absurd position of the philosopher.

Of course Kafka's paradox involves the facing of a god embodying a specific pain allied with death, rather than a more general contemplative facing of death as such. But the similarities are very strong. Kafka, Heidegger and Bataille all wish to meet a disturbing final form, but wish at the same time to avoid fusing with it.

Kafka's god of suffocation is a strange and terrible god. It is difficult to imagine a more ugly deity. Or a more ambiguous deity. This invented deity is probably a unique invention; it does not exist in the religious world as a universal archetype; Kafka knows this. Its non-existence in the world at large dramatises its structural impossibility (and vice-versa). The impossible nature of this god combines paradoxically with its necessity (why is there not such a god? one might ask). And the communion with this god, which Kafka also invents, is both necessary and impossible.

When one considers how any meeting with the god of suffocation must be kept at a certain remove, the god seems vague and mysterious. The only alternative to contemplating this god at a distance is to fuse with it by actually dying. But then this god seems infused with all the physicality of a painful death. When this is considered, the god of suffocation takes on a brutal, stark quality that beggars the imagination (for one thing, a god of localised pain seems almost a contradiction in terms), reflecting the impossibility, the morbid gratuitousness and the grotesque absurdity of deliberately bringing death into life.

However much the tubercular patient may need or desire the god of suffocation, however impossible it may be, even, for this patient to desist from contemplating it, this god remains an illegitimate object of philosophical contemplation. A meeting with such a god is impossible and therefore intellectually fruitless. And so the philosophical project of contemplating death for existential profit is also compromised.

1.   Extreme Physicality

To the extent that Heidegger and Bataille remain philosophers as such, they find little problem in insisting that we *think* of death whilst still physically alive. Although they emphasise the rigours involved in the contemplation of death within life, they nevertheless assume that this is as possible a feat as any other thought manoeuvre. Kafka, however, realises that one must physically feel the rigours of death to truly contemplate death (but this ends up as no contemplation at all; rather, it ends up as a deadly fusion with death itself). Heidegger and Bataille are thus revealed to be superficial in their overestimation of the power of thought. Of course this is complicated by the fact that Heidegger and Bataille see themselves as anti-rational philosophers who actually question the over-estimation of the power of thought. Both demand, in their own different ways, a certain existential fleshing out of the act of contemplation. But then they are as compromised as Kafka's sufferer; in these cases they have swapped one absurdity for another, a physical absurdity for a metaphysical absurdity.

When Heidegger and Bataille limit themselves to demanding a purely meditative contemplation of natural death, they treat death like any other philosophical topic. It is difficult to see how one can relate discussions about death in general to the singularity of one's own death. Even when they demand that one consider one's own death in an intimate manner, there is still no sense that one is being asked to consider a particular kind of individual death. By imagining our own death in general terms, and by imagining our own death to eventually take any one of a number of possible forms, the sense of our own death becomes vague. Death is swathed in unreality by being everything and nothing. But death by suffocation cannot be thought of in terms of a general topic, and this particular death does not have a *vague* future form. This end will not be, indifferently, a quiet death, an easy death, a heroic death. It is the specific end which is suffocation.

The god of suffocation is not easy to meet with, or to talk to, because this horror is specific. Death-by-suffocation involves a specific pain, one that we cannot meet in its extremity through mere contemplation. It could be argued that a pre-meeting meeting with the god of suffocation could be authentically staged through a minor asthma attack. However, this physically traumatic meeting, though more concrete then any mere contemplative meeting, does not necessarily provide a true sense of the intensity of full-blown suffocation. To put it slightly differently, we could imagine an individual reaching suffocation's essence in the mind *by analogy* with his or her own as yet more minor physical difficulties. But this remains a predominately cerebral act; this person does not reach the physical extremity that is suffocation. And so it is with the philosopher, who may reach some kind of intellectual essence of death but does not reach the physical state of death without dying.

Although the tubercular individual cannot fuse with suffocation, one might still insist that this individual is further down the road to the truth of suffocation and death than the relatively healthy philosopher who merely thinks of death. And yet, despite his or her greater essential 'initiation' in pain, the tubercular individual still cannot meet his or her ultimate destroyer (this individual is perhaps as far off from this form of death as the philosopher, or even further off; perhaps a little pain makes the consideration of greater pain all the more difficult).

So, Kafka's god of suffocation is hard to meet because it is so horrifyingly specific. Of course, seemingly in contradiction to this, we have also said that the god of suffocation is hard to meet due to its vagueness. But this is not really a contradiction. This vagueness does not come about because of any lack of this death's specificity (suffocation remains a very specific death) but because this death in all it specificity is yet held at a distance in time. This death is impossible to authentically converse with, to authentically negotiate with, and to authentically meet with in advance of meeting.

2.   The Unreality Of Death, The Reality Of Duration

I do not wish to assert that a concrete experience of death is impossible. What I am insisting on is that one cannot experience death authentically and still live. One cannot have one's cake and eat it. It may indeed be the case that death when reached is a concrete physical experience, replete with terror or joy. My theory still holds here, because however much death can be concretely experienced, it can only be experienced when it actually occurs. It is time which comes between the person who contemplates death and the experience of death itself; it is time which makes the authentic experience of death in advance impossible (one hasn't reached it yet…). And so it is time, the reality of time which must be, and can be, legitimately faced rather than death.

With Kafka we see the contemplation of death made physical. And we sense that a contemplation of death is situated, physically, at a concrete stage in time. What stops us from fusing with death is the physical experience of time; the time, that is, that lies between our abstract contemplation of future death and our actual concrete death. This physical time is irreducible; it cannot be transcended in an act of morbid contemplation. Moreover, we are caught up within the intensities of this ongoing physical time, alien to the static nature of death and, indeed, to any ultimate end. Caught within ongoing time, our very sense of death is also, in truth, caught up within an *economy* of life. We know we cannot grasp the essence of death through contemplation, and so we concentrate on the time to be lived before death. We try to 'get it all in' before death. Death is seen to be the end of ongoing events rather than an event in its own right.

Kafka's paradox has a positive aspect. People know, in a way that philosophers do not, that they cannot have a prior meeting with death, because the time between the living present and death cannot be skipped over. Time is substantial, in a way that a symbolic meeting with death is not, and it is the substantiality of time which makes this prior meeting with death impossible. People therefore concentrate on the time before death rather than on the mystery of death itself as an event that can somehow change the nature of time. People dread (or desire) death only as the eventual annihilation of time; time, that is, which is a rich stake (they want to gain the pleasures of time and to avoid the pains of time; this is more important than the bare fact of living or dying).

3.   Heidegger and Bataille
I have chosen to critique the thought of both Heidegger and Bataille. Although both thinkers are radically individual, and can be easily contrasted with each other, both insist that facing the truth of death enables people to undermine complacent forms of thinking and being, forms which are associated with a utilitarian and bourgeois world-view.

One might argue that there is a flaw in the symmetry that I claim exists between Heidegger and Bataille. Heidegger maintains that we must face death, but for the most part in a meditative rather than physical manner. Bataille, however, often demands that we engage in a far more visceral relationship with death, at times even insisting that we actively bring death into life as a concrete event.

Heidegger and Bataille both claim that by facing the ultimate loss that is death, one can, ironically, make specific gains. For Heidegger, these gains include the chance to live in an authentic manner. For Bataille, these gains include the ability to live in an ecstatic and sovereign manner, free from ideological enslavement. However, drawing on Kafka's paradox we can see that it is impossible to meaningfully engage with death, since death is either too far away in time to be met with in any meaningful physical manner, or it is too close, causing the annihilation of the person who wished to contemplate death. Since death cannot be authentically met with, we can conclude that these forms of reward can never be collected.

There are also strategic reasons for dealing with Heidegger and Bataille together. The theories on time developed by both philosophers have had a strong influence on continental philosophy, an influence that has lasted to the present day. Poststructuralist and postmodernist theories of time have drawn extensively upon Heidegger's and Bataille's work. Importantly, their thought reflects a certain contemporary cultural tendency to view time as a transient phenomenon. Through critiquing Heidegger's and Bataille's ideas we can develop the tools with which to critique this wider cultural nihilism.

4.   Heidegger

In *Being and Time*, Heidegger insists that people rarely experience the raw facts of existence in an authentic way, since their thoughts are for the most part made to conform to those superficial values and notions that are born of the essential compromises needed to produce social cohesion. With individuality totally submerged in the communal life of the masses, a sense of individual mortality is erased, since in this shared realm one has the feeling that another can always die in one's place. The masses demand that one lives and thinks within the ideological boundaries that they have set, holding out in return the false promise that they will shoulder one's own death. But by facing one's future death, which cannot be experienced by another, one can see that one is an individual. By becoming conscious that one cannot be saved from one's individual death, one can escape the blackmail carried out by the masses.

In Heidegger's view, people within society make the mistake of thinking that their being has a hard, object-like essence, like a durable tool or a deep-rooted institution, and that this substantial being can evade the ravages of time. But by facing death, which will eventually negate our being, we can see that being is not a 'thing'. Being is, rather, a precarious structure that must negotiate with the dynamic of time that forms it.

For Heidegger, the mass of people believe that they reside in a secure place within the universe, nestled within social institutions and a shared sense of meaning. But this shared sense of ground and meaning cannot alter the fact that each person is 'thrown' into a world that has no such ultimate ground or meaning. One's chance birth throws one into the world, which remains a kind of alien territory, and one will be thrust out of the world again with equal violence at the time of one's death. Facing the void that follows our death enables one to see life as ungrounded, as does the more detached facing of the void that precedes our birth.

For Heidegger, facing the inevitability of future death can help one to reap rich rewards. By accepting that one will inevitably die, one can focus intensely on the time that one has left, or simply act spontaneously (since one has ultimately nothing to lose by doing so). But as we saw with Kafka's paradox, death lies at a distance in time from the present, and so cannot offer any lessons on how to live life intensely or spontaneously. Death is a future event that when reached annihilates one's material existence; it cannot therefore offer any concrete basis for intense or spontaneous material acts. Intense living or spontaneity can only come about through an exuberance that is allied with one's health, one's material possessions, and one's freedom. One's access to health, to goods, and to freedom comes about through one's position in the world, which is a position immersed within the flow of time. Indeed, health, goods and freedom are things that are literally made of time, since time is everything that happens. All the other rewards that Heidegger believes can be drawn from facing death are likewise dependent upon a successful engagement with lived time. A sense of one's individuality, a sense of freedom from utility, and even a sense of 'thrownness' can only be won through an engagement with living duration.

According to Heidegger, we fool ourselves that death can be forever held at a distance, hoping to ignore the fact that death can happen 'at any time'. But by accepting that death can strike at any moment, we can free ourselves to enjoy spontaneous acts that are equally 'out of the blue'. In my view, Heidegger emphasises the ever-present possibility of death in order to embed the future event of death in the present moment, and to thereby avoid the accusation that he is offering a wearisome philosophy that is focused only on events that are distant in time. However, forever facing the possibility of sudden death in the present is not very different to facing death's eventual occurrence in the future. Death can only come when it does come, even if it comes suddenly. It does not matter whether we concentrate on the possibility of death's irruption into the present, or on its inevitable appearance in the future;

either way, we are foolishly attempting to evade the rich duration of existence in which we are enmeshed. Heidegger suggests that death manifests itself at unpredicted moments in order to make meditation on death seem exciting and awesome. But his shock tactic cannot work; it only generates other paradoxes. How can one prepare for a surprise that by definition undermines all preparation? A surprising event is, by definition, surprising. However much we try to equate death with lived time by stressing the intimacy of sudden death within life, death remains a mere intellectual notion until it actually arrives.

The fact that one is mortal is a prosaic rather than an authentically poetic fact, since one's future death cannot be engaged with in any rich or authentically poetic fashion. As a prosaic fact, the inevitability of one's future death cannot inspire one to generate any kind of authentic exuberance or state of mind. It is even possible that facing death can only ever be a depressing and morbid ritual. Facing one's mortality is morbid, but not because it is an uncanny immersion in death. As we saw, any such authentic immersion in death is impossible. Rather, the facing of death is morbid because it is either a tedious and sterile intellectual act held at some distance from death, or it is a nihilistic and suicidal fusion with death that brings about the end of all experience.

5.   Bataille

For Bataille, one must face the fact of death in order to understand the essential nature of the universe. Through a consciousness of death one can understand that the universe is an excessive phenomenon that constantly generates the deaths of beings through its very exuberance.

According to Bataille, the universe expends its energies as fast and as forcefully as it can, in a process that is at the same time both ecstatic and ruinous. But there is another universal instinct, which is the urge to conserve oneself. This instinct, although as natural as the urge to expend, is less intimate. By facing death one can fuse with the universal dynamic of expenditure, and evade the ignoble and inglorious instinct of self-preservation.

In Bataille's view, facing the reality of death is a crucial political necessity. He claims that the bourgeoisie coercively channel the workers' spontaneous and ruinous energies into industries from which the bourgeoisie can draw profit, through the false promise that these industries and projects can provide security and even a certain form of immortality. By facing the fact that death is inevitable, the workers can come to realise that the bourgeoisies' promise of infinite accumulation and long-term security is completely fraudulent. Thus enlightened, the workers can begin to fight to unleash their energies from those industries and projects in which they are invested. The workers can then expend these energies in a ruinous but ecstatic manner.

Bataille's theory of time is extremely complex. It is therefore necessary to deal with the different elements involved point for point, beginning with a critique of Bataille's notion of the ecstatic 'moment'.

6.   The Moment of Expenditure

In Bataille's view, beings naturally expend their energies to the very limit of their capacity. There is no good reason to delay the launching of expenditures, just as there is no good reason to limit the rate at which one expends one's energies. Beings want to expend their energies all at once, in the ruinous and ecstatic *moment*. But under the bourgeois system, the desire to spontaneously expend energies has to be constantly curtailed in order to maintain the social order necessary to construct and maintain industry, and in order to channel energies into the slow and inglorious toil that is necessary to generate productivity. The ecstatic moment of the expenditure of energies must be forever deferred, though not in order to accumulate energies with a view to enjoying more intense expenditures in the future; rather, energies are accumulated simply in order to maintain and perpetuate the project of accumulation itself. But once fully acquainted with the fact that death is inevitable, one has no reason to perpetually defer the ecstatic release of energies in order to maintain slavish projects that falsely promise perpetual survival.

In my view, the moment of expenditure is a myth, since it is possible to enjoy pleasures that last much longer than what one could call a moment of time. Moreover, it is possible in some cases to extend the duration of pleasures at will. And pleasures are, in reality, rarely fatal.

Rather than simply burning out, a moment of pleasure can be dilated (like a long weekend of pleasure) or quickly reproducible. Indeed, the very category of the moment can be seen to be somewhat artificial, since it suggests that there are segments of time that are isolated in a pristine manner within duration's flow. Rather than burning out in isolation, pleasurable experiences constantly flow into each other to create extended, unbroken periods of pleasure.

Perhaps Bataille puts forward the concept of the ruinous moment of ecstacy because it seems to bring a form of death nearer to us, so that our engagement with death does not seem to be akin to an endless, hopeless vigil. The moment of ecstacy, Bataille might argue, is a way of tasting death in the here and now, in a manner that is not merely contemplative. However, this celebration of the moment of expenditure only doubles those paradoxes that can be found in a prolonged facing of death. Either the moment of ecstacy is merely symbolic of future death and therefore inauthentic, or it is the gratuitous bringing forward of future death into the present.

As with Heidegger's notion that death can arrive 'always at any time', Bataille's moment of expenditure remains a failed attempt to flesh out the contemplation of future death. But this engagement with death in the present remains sterile because death is always held at a distance in time. Bataille tries to answer this by celebrating a far more direct physical irruption of death into the present, maintaining the existential authenticity of human sacrifice, self-immolation, and even bloody revolution. The act of trying to solve those problems that are involved in the contemplation of death, through an insistence on the authority and value of rituals and acts that cause real deaths, is desperate and absurd (it is akin to suffocating oneself in order to gain control over suffocation). We can speculate whether Heidegger was also tempted by this form of existential quick fix when he was drawn towards the sacrificial and violent ideology of the Nazis.

In the following sections, we will see how Bataille's concept of the ecstatic moment of expenditure has decisive consequences for his political philosophy.

7.   The Political Paradox

In my view, it is self evident that the bourgeoisie enjoy a sovereign form of temporality, since they work relatively little and can therefore enjoy vast swathes of free time. Moreover, they can enjoy authentic pleasures, since they have access to luxury goods. It would follow that the workers experience a relatively non-sovereign form of temporality, since they have little free time at their disposal, most of their time being tied up in the performance of slavish tasks. The workers also enjoy few authentic pleasures, since they have little or no access to luxury goods. On the surface, Bataille would appear to concur that authenticity and sovereignty are synonymous with the enjoyment of free time, and that sovereign experiences require a certain access to material surplus. Moreover, Bataille's entire temporal system is built on an acknowledgement that the workers and the bourgeoisie experience radically different states of being, and that this difference is due to the fact that the workers are exploited by the bourgeoisie. But Bataille ultimately ends up making the claim that it is the workers and not the bourgeoisie who enjoy the essence of sovereign time and the essence of material pleasure.

Bataille believes that the bourgeoisie are thoroughly inflected by their own ideology. As the main proselytisers for the work ethic, the bourgeoisie succumb to their own propaganda. More importantly, they know that in order to uphold their own elevated social position they must forever hold back from expending their energies, in order to re-direct their un-spent energies into their various works. They cannot recklessly expend their energies or wealth, for fear of weakening their position and laying themselves open to attack from the workers. They feel obliged to re-invest any surplus gained from their industries back into those self-same industries. The workers, on the other hand, have nothing to lose, and can therefore throw themselves into their pleasures recklessly and to the hilt. So, in a very real sense, the bourgeoisie are more enslaved by their factories and industries than the workers.

The bourgeoisie have access to vast swathes of time and extended pleasures. But for Bataille, authentic pleasures are never extended; they are brief and ruinous, and because they are ruinous, the bourgeoisie must hold back from indulging in them. The workers, on the other hand, have little access to free time, enjoying pleasure only those brief moments that they have access to, but this works in their favour, since pleasure's essence takes the form of a quick, reckless moment of abandonment. The costive bourgeoisie cannot enjoy pleasure-time authentically, whereas the feckless workers can, even though the bourgeoisie have more free time to expend in pleasures than the workers. Similarly, due to their costive nature and their inauthentic experience of time, the bourgeoisie cannot enjoy the expending of goods, whereas the feckless workers can, even though the bourgeoisie have more goods to expend than the workers.

Bataille's political thought clearly involves serious paradoxes. By affirming the authenticity of the workers' mere moments of ecstacy over the bourgeoisie's extended pleasures, we have a situation in which the workers are more essentially sovereign than their overlords, even though they clearly remain subservient to their masters in the workplace. If this is not paradoxical enough, we can note that this celebration of the moment of expenditure and its authenticity is meant to stir the workers into revolt. If the workers' brief pleasures are more intoxicating than the bourgeoisies' extended pleasures, how can the workers become motivated to grasp substantial amounts of sovereign time? Sovereign time is surely a crucial stake in any revolution, since time is everything that happens. If the workers enjoy more authentic pleasures in their poverty than the bourgeoisie with their riches, why would they want to grasp luxurious goods? Where, ultimately, can the workers find the motivation to throw off the shackles of slavery if they find themselves in essence in a more sovereign position than their masters?

8.   Dualism

The dualist nature of Bataille's temporal structure helps him to generate the concept of the moment of expenditure. Although Bataille insists that peoples' most profound and intimate desire is to expend their force recklessly, he also states that people are also partially programmed by a certain conservative instinct, an instinct that the bourgeoisie exploit. Pleasures are not enjoyed in a pure way, since they involve a transgression of the realm of conservativism. This transgression is like any invasion; it is naturally violent and ruinous. As we saw, the moment of expenditure is mortal because it is naturally reckless and goes to the end of what it can do. But the moment of expenditure is also mortal because it crashes headlong into the conservative order, partly burning itself out in the explosive irruption. Moreover, the order of conservativism soon re-asserts itself after the irruption of expenditure. The conservative realm itself thus contributes to the mortality of the moment of expenditure.

In my view, Bataille installs this dualist vision of time as an enabling device. The realms of expenditure and conservativism are placed in an antagonistic relationship in order to split time into two, thereby undermining any belief in the possibility that the bourgeoisie can enjoy extended pleasures within a single linear order of time. We are encouraged instead to believe in the authenticity of the discontinuous violent pleasures of the workers. We can also say that Bataille has created two opposite forms of time in order to create the friction necessary to create the explosive ecstatic moment which the slaves have more access to than the bourgeoisie.

The moment of expenditure breaks the taboos that guard the realm of conservativism, in a movement of transgression. The taboos that guard the realm of conservativism generate tensions and also a kind of perverse attraction, and so transgression, when it occurs, is aggravated. Human transgression takes on a serious, ritualistic and self-consciously criminal form, that heightens the violence of transgression at the same time as it limits the direction of its application.

For Bataille, human sacrifice remains the most radical and the most revealing ritual of transgression. Bataille sees human sacrifice as important because it is a celebration of the inevitability of death. We must admit that he also interprets the ritual of sacrifice, human or otherwise, as a celebration of a destruction of utility and future-orientated projects (a man or animal that is killed can no longer be 'used' for work purposes to secure future survival). With this in mind, ritual sacrifice could be seen to be a ritual that liberates energy in the present. But we can say that this liberation of energy in the moment ultimately relates to death, since the liberation of energy is also an *expenditure* of energy, and the moment, as a brief, ruinous period, is profoundly mortal.

Bataille does not demand a physical re-introduction of the archaic tradition of human sacrifice into present day practices, at least not directly. For the most part, Bataille simply acknowledges the integrity of human sacrifice as a ritual that reveals the universal urge to expend. But this scholarly approach to human sacrifice is no more than a meditation on what is already essentially a meditation. No authentic physical engagement with death can be gained through a detached, philosophical consideration of the mere spectacle of death; a spectacle which illegitimately uses the death of another in the present in order to promote a contemplation of the death of oneself in the distant future.

Perhaps in order to avoid affirming a sterile intellectual facing of death, Bataille sometimes comes close to encouraging human sacrifice as a physical act. In an early work, he demands the actual bloody annihilation of the bourgeoisie; an act which he implies would be akin to ritual human sacrifice[2]. On a more speculative level, we can note the rumour that he planned to carry out a real human sacrifice when part of the 'Acéphale' secret society.

A scholarly use of the ritual of human sacrifice reflects one half of Kafka's paradox, since it involves a mere meditation on death. An affirmation of real death involves the other half of Kafka's paradox. The death of a sacrificial victim represents a gratuitous physical insertion of death into the present in an attempt to generate the illusion that facing death as a future event is an authentic act.

Bataille often insists that the ritual of human sacrifice does not essentially involve a mere meditation on death for the sacrificers and witnesses but, rather, an identification with the victim's death. For Bataille, there is a sense in which the sacrificers and witnesses die along with the victim. For me, however, the authenticity of such a fusion of killers, witnesses and victims is impossible to prove. Such a fusion would require not only a mysterious physical equation of killers, witnesses and persons sacrificed, but also an equation of radically different temporalities (the sacrificers and witnesses leave the ritual unharmed, the victims do not).

Bataille often stresses the active role of the sacrificial priest, perhaps in order to gloss over the passive nature of the spectators' role. But the mere fact that the sacrificial priest is able to wield the killing blow or strike does not mean that an identity is reached between the sacrificer's eventual death in the future and the victim's death in the present. However physically intoxicating the act of killing may appear to be to the one who is dealing out death, this intoxication cannot reveal anything about how death actually feels. Similarly, the intense and perhaps alarming experience of witnessing the spectacle of human sacrifice may indeed feel like something concrete and substantial, but it does not enable these witnesses to authentically taste their own future deaths. Bataille is in effect making the assumption that a ritual can heave us out of the continuity of time. If we attempt to look at the act of sacrifice from the anguished point of view of the victim, we can see the gratuitous nature of human sacrifice amplified; the victim can clearly taste future death, but only because it has been forcefully moved into the present by the power of the sacrificial priest.

9.   **The Ruinous Nature of Pleasure**
       We have seen the different ways in which Bataille tries to prove his equation of pleasure and time's transience. He states that pleasures are the result of the exuberance of energy, and that pleasures burn themselves out via their intensity. He states that pleasures generate recklessness and are therefore ultimately ruinous. And pleasures are ruinous because they violently collide with the order of conservativism. But Bataille does not always feel that he needs recourse to these arguments in order to prove his equation of pleasure and transience. In some passages Bataille simply insists, bluntly, that ecstasies are ruinous, subversive and transient at their very core. Such a simple equation of pleasure and ruin is perhaps crucial in providing some kind of basic support structure upon which Bataille can build his complex, and I would say fragile, system of temporality. For if ecstacy is not ruinous in its essence, it cannot really be ruinous in its expression or ultimate effects.
       One of the pleasures that Bataille feels is inherently ruinous is the orgasm, which he likens to a 'little death'. Bataille offers many reasons for his equation of the orgasm with ruinous expenditure. For the most part, he is content to stress that the orgasm can be equated with expenditure and ruination because of the orgasm's effects, rather than because of its inner nature. The orgasm burns up energy in the moment, energy that could otherwise be used to help secure future survival. The intimacy generated by eroticism represents a death of individuality, and therefore encourages a ruinous dismantlement of the conservative instinct, associated as it is with the urge to preserve finite, individual human life. The orgasm can result in reproduction, involving the birth of a being

whose life transcends one's own. On a general level, desire's recklessness carries beings towards ruination. But this insistence that the orgasm is ruinous because of its ultimate effects is based upon the more basic premise that the orgasm is physically ruinous in itself. Bataille points to the example of a certain drone that destroys itself in reproduction, in order to illustrate the orgasm's volatile, almost poisonous nature.

Bataille's direct equation of the orgasm with physical ruin is absurd. To begin with, the orgasm can be seen to be a form of exercise, that can result, for example, in healthy weight loss. As an intense physical activity, the orgasm cannot be regarded as much more ruinous than, say, the act of running. Of course, the orgasm can in some cases have a degenerative effect upon someone who is already suffering from ill health. But it must then be said that the otherwise healthy act of running at full pelt can also have disastrous consequences for someone who is already in fragile health. And we must add that the orgasm would have to be dangerous in the extreme to justify Bataille's claim that it is a phenomenon that effectively breaks the back of time. What we have said here about the orgasm goes for other pleasures. Alcohol abuse, for example, may be more obviously dangerous for the health of the individual than the orgasm, but is it so very damaging that it represents a pure form of expenditure that speeds us towards death?

If pleasure is not inherently ruinous, then we can surely enjoy it in extended forms. Indeed, it would be slavish to want anything other than extended pleasures. It is no doubt the case that pleasure can be extended due to its very nature. Bataille implies that pleasure can only take on extended forms through a dilution of its intensity, but we must see pleasure as being extendable in its duration due to its inherent richness and excess. Bataille is right to insist that beings ultimately destroy themselves via the expression of their energies. But he is wrong in the way that he characterises this journey towards ultimate ruination. For the expenditure of one's energies takes time; it takes in fact an entire lifetime. Time is not destroyed by the expenditure of energies; rather; time is a crucial stake in the expenditure of energies. Pleasurable expenditures can only take place in time.

As we have seen through a reading of Kafka's paradox, pleasure is immersed in the flow of time, and so pleasure's annihilation has no meaning for the experience of pleasure. From the perspective of one who is in the midst of ongoing pleasures, death at the end of life is an irrelevance. Just as it is the duration of life that is more important than its end, we must insist that it is the duration of pleasure that is more important to beings than pleasure's end.

Moreover, it is ludicrous for Bataille to think that we have an erotic bond with death, since death cannot be reached until the end of all erotic experience. Death is not some kind of hyper-intense pleasure to which all living pleasures aspire, since this form of pleasure, if it exists, can only be experienced when reached, and then the being that might enjoy such a rarefied pleasure is annihilated.

10.   The Impossibility of Deriving Gain from Loss
     One cannot gain intellectual or ideological truths that will benefit life in the present from facing death that can only come about in the future. And one cannot gain intellectual or ideological truths that will benefit life from facing the moment when life itself is extinguished. In Kafka's terms, one cannot gain anything from a mere intellectual meeting with death, but even less by a physical meeting that wipes out one's very life.
     Regarding political gains, we must seriously question Bataille's view that facing the fact of death can free workers from coercive systems. For example, a sense of mortality cannot get a person out of his or her prison cell; death can only get that person out as a corpse. It might be argued that through facing the fact of mortality, a person can gain a sense of devil-may-care, which can give that person a certain edge, enabling him or her to break free from prison. But this would be a rather exceptional form of jailbreak, and the exception that proves the rule. It can be said that Bataille never claims that an openness to death can change the laws of physics; rather, he is saying that an openness to death represents an ideological victory, one that could free the workers en masse if they were to appreciate its radical nature. However, even here we must question whether a philosophy based around a facing of death – death which does not come until it does come, and then at a price – can provide any kind of ideological support for the living. The only way to authentically access death on a physical level is through the gratuitous doubling of death in suicidal or murderous acts, which by themselves cannot provide inspiration for political acts or generate the installation of progressive political programs. How can an annihilation of time enliven those whose joys and pains are tied up with the flow of time in which they are immersed.
     Bataille claims that facing death helps to free peoples' energies from the constraints of the bourgeoisies' future-orientated projects, but facing death is a future-orientated obsession. Bataille claims that facing death frees peoples' energies from a bourgeois system that perpetually

defers spontaneous outbursts of ecstacy, but death is a consummation that is either forever deferred or deadly. Such are the joys of facing death. What makes a prior meeting with future death inauthentic is the physical time between this pseudo-meeting and actual death. And what makes a contemplation of future death inauthentic is the physical time between this contemplation and actual death.

It is time, then, rather than death which is the great philosophical mystery and the great political stake. And if we must face death, if we must think of death as an object of philosophical contemplation, then we must think of this death always in relation to lived time.

Notes

[1] Franz Kafka, *The Diaries of Franz Kafka* (Harmondsworth: Penguin Books, 1948/1988), 410.
[2] Georges Bataille, 'The Notion of Expenditure', *Visions of Excess: Selected Writings, 1927-1939* (Minneapolis: University of Minnesota Press, 1985/2001, 1927-1939), 125-129.

Bibliography

Bataille, Georges. *The Accursed Share, Volume I.* New York: Zone Books, 1967/1991.
Bataille. *The Accursed Share, Volumes II & III.* New York: Zone Books, 1976/1991.
Bataille. *Visions of Excess: Selected Writings, 1927-1939.* Minneapolis: University of Minnesota Press, 1985/2001, 1927-1939.
Bergson, Henri. *Creative Evolution.* London: Macmillan & Co., 1907/1911.
Heidegger, Martin. *Being and Time.* Oxford: Blackwell Publishers Ltd., 1926/2001.
Johnson, David. *The Time of the Lords: An Attack on Bataille's Slave Aesthetic of Transience.* Ephemera Books, 2001.
Kafka, Franz. *The Diaries of Franz Kafka.* London: Penguin Books, 1948/1988.

Author Affiliation

David Johnson has a D.Phil. in English and Related Literature from York University, an MA (Distinction) in Continental Philosophy from Warwick University and a BA in Literature and Philosophy from Middlesex University. He is a freelance writer, and has published reviews in various journals. He has published *The Time of the Lords: An Attack on Bataille's Slave Aesthetic of Transience* (2001) and is currently working on a second book dealing with the philosophy of time: *The Myth of Transience.*

Personal and Collective Fears of Death: A Complex Intersection for Cancer Survivors

Heather McKenzie

1. Introduction

For she [Nikidion] might, as often happens, take a walk at dawn in the early spring. She might feel the knifelike beauty of the morning. See leaves half unrolled, translucent, their sharp green still untouched by life; the sun striking sparkles on the moving surface of a stream. And she would listen, then, in the silence to the sweet and deadly music of time.[1]

Drawing on a study of cancer survivors,[2] in which the fear of the recurrence of disease is identified as a significant dimension of experience, I argue here that there is an important relationship between this personal fear of death and the collective fear of cancer. This widely shared emotional response envelops the communal experience of cancer and constitutes a "climate of fear", which is, in turn, reflected in the responses of those who are "healthy" to cancer survivors. These responses are underpinned by the communal need to preserve the everyday practical consciousness in which the intersubjectively understood guidelines for most social action are embedded. A key dimension of contemporary practical consciousness is the collective frame of reference that takes "the future" for granted. In practice, this future-oriented stance involves the "bracketing out", as it were, of the naked fear of death. It is argued here that cancer survivors' fear of untimely death represents a profound threat to this shared understanding of reality. The implications of this for cancer survivors are explored here in some detail.

Every subjective experience of cancer induces an acute emotional response signalling a heightened awareness of human vulnerability. Although for many cancer survivors the initial overwhelming, gut-wrenching feelings gradually give way to a range of less destabilising affects, the fear that one's vulnerability might again be so painfully emphasised is never far from the surface. Perhaps surprisingly, the fear of the recurrence of cancer persists for many years,[3] ensuring that the spectre of cancer retains its "*master status* in relation to other aspects of the person's identity".[4]

However, the data for the study referred to here reveal that once the initial treatment phase of the illness trajectory is over, and contact with health care professionals reduced to a minimum, there is little social support available for cancer survivors as they struggle to cope with this fear. In a practical sense, this means that there are few opportunities in the everyday social world for the expression of distressing fears about cancer recurrence.

I argue here that it is the collective fear of cancer as a social phenomenon that underpins both the lack of acknowledgement of the ongoing suffering of cancer survivors as valid and meaningful, and also the related, continuing stigmatisation of the disease. With reference to a study concerned with the experiences of fifteen cancer survivors[5], I examine, firstly, the "climate of fear" that envelops the social experience of cancer; secondly, the ways in which this climate of fear is reflected in the responses of those who are "healthy" to cancer survivors; and, thirdly, the relationship between cancer and compassion in contemporary social life.

2.   Climate of Fear

In her philosophical discussion of human attempts to transcend the fear of death, Martha Nussbaum points to the very deep and fundamental nature of that fear. The desire to carry out, uninterrupted, the "project of living a complete human life'" is one we all share at the most profound level.[6] Therefore, as Nussbaum suggests, although "Nikidion may confront the fear of death on a certain sort of spring day ... she will be unlikely to admit that it is with her in most of her actions".[7] She is protected from the fear of death in her ordinary daily life by that shared sense of "practical consciousness", which, in Giddens' terms, "is the cognitive and emotive anchor of the feelings of *ontological security* characteristic of large segments of human activity in all cultures".[8] Schütz alerts us to the intersubjective nature of this "natural attitude":

> To it [the natural attitude] the world is from the outset not the private world of the single individual, but an intersubjective world, common to all of us, in which we have not a theoretical but an eminently practical interest ... a pragmatic motive governs our natural attitude toward the world of daily life.[9]

"Practical consciousness", then, is an intersubjectively created resource which is lodged in the thoughts and actions of individuals and maintained through their shared dependence on it. It is not necessarily the same experience, in a qualitative sense, for all cultures. In traditional societies, for instance, it may reflect the generally more precarious nature of individual life. In modern societies, though, the expectation of a long and safe life is realistic for the majority of people, and the degree to which "practical consciousness" shields individuals from existential fears perhaps reflects this general, shared expectation. It may also reflect the "de-metaphysicisation" of mortality — the rationalisation of death, which Bauman argues is a striking feature of modernity. Death

> has been given its own location in social space, a segregated location; it has been put in custody of selected specialists ... [and] linked to a network of techniques and practices of measurable efficiency and effectiveness.[10]

In other words, death is dealt with in the peculiarly modern way, and those for whom it is not an immediate issue can ignore it, secure in the knowledge that it (i.e. other people's death) is safely in the hands of experts authorised to deal with it. The "ordinary" world of daily life is thus not disturbed or disrupted by the naked fear of death, and the "practical interest" is well served by this arrangement.

Not surprisingly, practical consciousness is profoundly threatened by the spectre of a life-threatening disease that is resisting control. Cancer has always been a frightening disease,[11] but it does seem that the collective fear has become more widespread and intense in recent times. It is argued here that the social experience of cancer is increasingly enveloped in a "climate of fear".[12] This may be a reflection of the general feeling that, despite the money, time and effort expended on the "war against cancer", the overall picture remains grim.[13]

Perhaps fuelled by fear, the "war" has recently expanded on to new fronts. Press, Fishman and Koenig argue that the cultural background of fear about breast cancer in the US underpins recent government policy developments in relation to genetic testing for breast cancer, and the authors suggest that these initiatives may be contributing to unrealistic expectations for this evolving technology.[14] Such initiatives notwithstanding, collective hopes of success remain largely unfulfilled, and the disease seems still as aggressive and threatening as ever – perhaps even more so, given the constant flow of information about screening, "anti-cancer" diets and other such measures.

Arguably, though, there are still deeper sources for our collective fear of cancer. Radley has identified the notion of "abhorrence" as crucial to an understanding of responses of the 'putatively healthy' to those who are less fortunate.[15] In line with Sontag,[16] Radley argues that abhorrence is aroused when an illness "evokes a psychological (if not physical) shudder", especially where "the prospect of future mutations and a difficult death are envisaged".[17] In that it subsumes fear, loathing and disgust, all of which are implicated in widespread feelings about cancer, the concept of abhorrence encompasses the range of feelings involved in the emotional climate referred to here. The disease is feared because it appears uncontrollable, but the fear is intensified by feelings of disgust evoked by images of malignant decay, and inevitable and painful death.

3.   Social Responses to Cancer Survivors

The data for this study show that, even many years post-diagnosis, this climate of fear is reflected in the responses of those who are "healthy" to cancer survivors. Feelings of abhorrence and the desire to maintain practical consciousness preclude open communication in the social environment about the personal fear of the recurrence of cancer. This fear – in essence the fear of death – represents a profound threat to the shared understanding of reality. Thus, as with all such existential threats, it is bracketed out of, rather than absorbed into, the everyday practical consciousness. A compassionate social response to the ongoing suffering of cancer survivors is therefore not able to be accommodated within routine social practices. Thus cancer survivors are isolated in their pain, unable to feel re-integrated into the everyday world of common sense understandings.

In part, this isolation is related to feelings of stigmatisation.[18] In spite of their post-patient status, the lives of cancer survivors continue to be deeply affected by their "undesired differentness".[19] This study shows that social attitudes to cancer which were the subject of Sontag's original essay of twenty years ago still seem familiar today, even though Sontag herself has more recently suggested that "attitudes about cancer have evolved".[20] As Stacey points out, although "cancer has a ubiquitous presence in everyday life … the person with cancer is nevertheless confronted by a striking silence that reminds them they have entered stigmatised territory".[21]

A. The conspiracy of silence

It is still the case that for some people the word "cancer" itself can be a stumbling block. Prior to her diagnosis of cancer, Felicity, a nurse, and one of the respondents for this study, had thought of the disease as "the big C totally. I just thought it was the most hideous thing". Prior to her own experience of cancer, Margaret was "terrified at the mere thought of it. I actually couldn't even say the word cancer". When her sister was diagnosed with bowel cancer, Margaret "couldn't even look at her ... In those days it was a word that struck fear in everybody and it was something you didn't discuss". Around the time of her own diagnosis, one of Margaret's brothers was also found to have bowel cancer. Although they were suffering from the same illness, he could not discuss his diagnosis with her:

> *He could not use the word cancer. ... Even when he was sitting there having ray treatment he would say 'that', he would call it 'that'. ... Not once in two years did he ever use the word cancer.*

Molly realised soon after her diagnosis that many of her friends and acquaintances   avoided using the word whenever possible. "Sometimes people say to me, 'How are you?' They really meant to ask 'How's your cancer? How's your check up?' But they couldn't ask it, they just couldn't say the word". Max usually tells the people he meets regularly that he has had cancer, but he finds that, in response, "some people are very stand-offish and don't want to know". Andy explains that "because of the taboo ... on the name ... and the feelings that cancer brings up, people just sort of stay away from you".

Following her own cancer diagnosis, Stacey was shocked by the censorship of the word "cancer", even by medical staff. She interpreted their refusal to use the actual word as a symptom of the profound cultural anxiety surrounding the social experience of cancer. Embarrassed and sometimes shamed by this response, Stacey recognised that the "cultural imperatives of secrecy and disguise" infiltrate the lives of cancer patients from the moment of diagnosis.[22] As a result, many people with cancer – already feeling vulnerable and afraid – experience a real sense of social isolation, which is increasingly pronounced as the imminent danger posed by the initial diagnosis appears to recede.

B. Abhorrence

These are practical matters concerning the realm of interaction. However, without an account of the feelings which underpin such interaction, they can only ever reveal but a fragment of the whole picture. When a person receives a diagnosis of cancer, she does so in the light of contemporary cultural interpretations of the disease. As argued above, collectively we share a fear – or, indeed, abhorrence – of this disease, and it is therefore the case that individual sufferers will be aware of such shared feelings about cancer as a social phenomenon. While the collective fear and its discourses exist independently and in different modalities from agents' anxieties, they profoundly affect individual experiences.

Arguing for the need to account for the emotional dimensions of interaction in analyses of stigma and illness, Radley points out that "the grounds for exclusionary behaviour extend to features of the stigmatised condition that evoke disgust or fear in members of the privileged majority".[23] He suggests that abhorrence and compassion, while in one sense opposites, "lie together on a different plane of experience from that of identity and difference".[24] Both are significant in the social lives of people who have been diagnosed with cancer, and abhorrence especially so for the association of stigma and cancer.

The data for this study reveal that cancer survivors do sense fear and disgust in the responses of others to their plight. They clearly feel that at times others shrink from them when information about their situation is made available. Carol, one of the respondents for this study, was in a stable relationship when she was diagnosed with endometrial cancer. She now lives alone and is "contemplating new relationships". However, perhaps because she feels there is a connection between her illness and the breakdown of her long term relationship, she suspects that simply the fact that she has had cancer may be enough to deter others from wanting to get to know her.

> One of the things I think is, are people going to be
> scared to take me on? ... I know that cancer has very
> strong meanings ... they might be too frightened of me ...
> not even necessarily because they think I'm going to die,
> it's just too freaky or something.

Following her breast cancer diagnosis in her early thirties, Nancy had a mastectomy. She is very sensitive about her single breasted state and worries about people finding out about it. At the time of diagnosis Nancy was married and had a baby daughter. Her husband found it very difficult to cope with her illness, partly because of her altered physical appearance, and she explained that she regretted having shown her mastectomy scar to her husband.

> *One day he turned around and said to me that I made him physically sick when he saw me.... So when he said that to me I felt more depressed than before. So then I made a point of making sure I bolted the bathroom door. ... so if I got changed there'd be no chance of anyone coming in ... That really made me feel like my life was totally destroyed.*

Nancy and her husband later separated and she now lives alone with her young daughter. To date a breast reconstruction has not been an option for Nancy and she uses a breast prosthesis to hide her "undesired differentness". Learning to deal with new intimate relationships has been a very difficult process for Nancy. Emotionally wounded by her husband's attitude to her marred body, she feels "less of a person" because of a perceived loss of femininity, and has to summon great courage in intimate situations:

> *When it comes to the crunch of actually telling them ... you make sure it's very dark ... you don't want to take your top off ... a lot of the time it's very hard for them to accept ... And sometimes you just think to yourself it's not really worth it. ... It's like you have to disclose something about you that you don't want to disclose.*

C.   Disclosure

Because cancer remains a stigmatised illness, the issue of disclosure is an important one for cancer sufferers. Beyond the initial diagnosis and treatment phase of the illness trajectory, most survivors are generally able to keep their cancer history a secret, at least in public. Describing such behaviour as "passing", Goffman suggests that, in relation to stigmatised conditions, "because of the great rewards in being considered normal, almost all persons who are in a position to pass will do so on some occasion by intent".[25] He points out that in some social situations it may not be seen as appropriate to divulge information which may be considered personal, and thus "a conflict between candour and seemliness will often be resolved in favour of the latter".[26] However, the fact that cancer sufferers can – and frequently do – keep their differentness a secret does not free them from being "discreditable". That is, while "the stigma is neither known about by those present nor immediately perceivable by them",[27] the individual remains burdened by the potential for it to become known.

This situation adds yet another dimension to the distress already experienced by cancer survivors. The usual difficulties of negotiating the quicksands of social relationships are compounded, as Stacey notes: "Don't upset this friend or relative, hide it at work, keep it from your children".[28] Goffman points out that it is very common for potentially discreditable persons to divide the world into those people to whom they confide nothing and those to whom they confide all.[29] This is a strategy employed by many of those interviewed for this study.

As noted above, Nancy is very reluctant to disclose her cancer history to other people. Goffman suggests that a woman who has had a mastectomy has no option but to "present ... falsely in almost all situations".[30] Seemly "frontstage" general behaviour is expected if she is to present herself as conventionally "normal", just as everybody else is trying to do. Of course a woman may, in fact, choose not to use a prosthesis, thus declaring her undesired differentness, but it does seem that for most women in this situation, the use of a prosthesis – at least in public – is the preferred option.[31] Nancy does take up this option, but she still feels anxious about her discreditable state:

> Sometimes I worry that people will think I'm a man.
> Because with it being a prosthesis ... sometimes it sticks
> out ... maybe they think I'm a man cross dressing ...
> especially living where I do and going out dancing ...
> Because I've put on a lot more weight ... I feel like I'm
> not as feminine.

Jean was diagnosed with breast cancer thirty-five years ago when she was in her early thirties. She had not heard of a mastectomy when the surgeon told her that she needed to have one. Jean looks back on the experience as a time when she was "on her own". With the exception of her husband, Jean did not disclose her situation to anyone; cancer was never discussed in her circle of family and friends:

> All the years that passed by, I never discussed my health or
> my operation. ... It's not the sort of thing that I would

openly discuss to this day. ... You've had your operation,
you've survived, so you should just get on with your life. ...
It has just made me all the more withdrawn.

Jean has always feared that her secret could become known. Breast reconstruction was not available to her at the time of her diagnosis, and, until recently, she has always worn a prosthesis of some kind. Several years ago, almost thirty years after her mastectomy, Jean was finally able to have a breast reconstruction and did so.

Several respondents also explained that they felt reluctant to disclose information about their cancer history in the workplace. Because she needed leave from work to have treatment for her illness, Carol had no option but to disclose her cancer diagnosis to her employer. When she returned to work she felt she was discriminated against because of her illness. One staff member began behaving towards her in an antagonistic way; her employer then suggested that she was not coping with the work any more because she had cancer, and, although he was not able to dismiss her, Carol eventually resigned as she felt very uncomfortable in this environment.

The issue of disclosure was not a problem for David because he worked for a cancer organisation. However, he explained that for many cancer sufferers:

It's a disadvantage ... because they have to explain a lengthy
absence from work. ... There's also a fear that referees will
disclose that information. ... There's a fear among employers
that someone who's had cancer won't be able to work, they'll
be wanting sick leave all the time. They'll cause too much
problem in the office ... people won't know how to deal with
it. In most employment situations it's a disadvantage.

Although Ralph felt comfortable telling work associates about his experience of cancer twenty years after the event, he advised against disclosure in the early stages. He explained that an episode of cancer is seen as an obstacle by some employers: "We shouldn't actually spend too much time or effort thinking about his career options ... he may not be there".

Many people experience cancer as "a diminution of the self".[32] They *feel* stigmatised – often even before such feelings are confirmed by the responses of others – and so take steps to limit opportunities for rejection. The resulting reduction in sociability, in turn, deprives and thus further diminishes the self – only one part of the spiral of losses associated with a cancer diagnosis. Sometimes unease or embarrassment on the part of others (e.g. being worried about appropriate social responses) is interpreted by the sufferer as a stigmatising response simply because the latter already feels herself to be "less of a person" and hence potentially "discreditable".

D.   Contagion

Some respondents in the study had experienced exclusion or felt they were regarded with suspicion because of a belief on the part of others that cancer may be contagious. Levin suggests that it is very easy to imagine cancer as "the pestilence of our time", so prevalent is the disease today.[33] Perhaps this imagined epidemic status contributes to perceptions of cancer as contagious,[34] as that is our understanding of other serious diseases which tend to be epidemic.

But the connection may be more complex. Crawford argues that in those societies which are preoccupied with issues of control, "contagion carries a symbolic load. ... If the symbolic logic of health suggests purification, locating threatening elements to the outside, then disease, along with all images of contagion, provides a model for all feared threats".[35] Thus the concept of contagion can linked with that of stigma because it strongly suggests the impure and untouchable.

Nancy found it surprising that some of her friends thought her illness might be contagious. "It's weird how people think, 'Can you catch this?' ". Trained as a nurse herself, Nancy was puzzled that some of her friends outside the profession worried about the possibility of infection — particularly from intimate contact. "Specially if they're lay people, they're not medically oriented. They think, 'Oh it's contagious, I'm going to catch it or something like that.' "

For Max the issue was a very personal one. Because he had testicular cancer, his partner was concerned about whether the disease might be sexually transmissible:

> *She thought that if they could detect my cancer in my blood and sperm has blood in it, why can't you get cancer. ... She actually had to ask my GP whether it was possible that she could get it, especially from having sex. ... I found out she'd rung all sorts of people, my GP, my oncologist. ... She wanted to know if I was getting the facts right.*

Max also felt that some of his other friends thought his cancer might be infectious. "Some of them treat you ... as if you do have leprosy and maybe I could catch this cancer ... I think a lot of people think that way, just from touching them. ... That tends to make ... us feel like lepers." And thus we find cancer associated with leprosy, perhaps the most stigmatised disease of all, and the disease which has for centuries been identified with the notion of social death.

E.   Cancer – a death sentence

It may be, as Mellor and Shilling suggest, that we are afraid that death itself is somehow contagious. As noted earlier, we keep the dying at arms length in contemporary life, thus "increasing the boundaries surrounding the bodies of the living and the dying".[36] We tend to shrink from touching the dying in our society, perhaps from the fear of contagion. Clearly the basis for the fear of 'catching' death is the fear of death itself.

Before his own illness, Max thought that a diagnosis of cancer was inevitably a death sentence. When it happened to him he was very frightened by the stories of death which seemed to surround this disease. He was surprised to learn some time later that about fifty percent of people diagnosed with cancer survive. Some years before her own illness episode, Amy's brother died of cancer. She was very distressed by his suffering as she watched him "fall away to skin and bone". It is only very recently — several years after her own cancer diagnosis — that Amy has been able to accept that "cancer isn't a death sentence in all cases". Carol often feels angry by media portrayals of cancer as a deathly disease.

> The other night I got a video out. ... At the beginning it
> revealed that Michelle Pfeiffer had had breast cancer. ...
> The film goes on and then suddenly in the last five
> minutes it's the ... death bed scene. ... It's a very
> common plot device in films and the person always dies
> and there's always a horrible deathbed scene. I think
> this is cheapening what happened to me ... undermining
> me.

Nancy also feels distressed when people assume that she will die of the disease. "A lot of people don't understand about cancer. They think it's a one way ticket out of here, that you're going to get it again and you're going to die. ... This is what everyone thinks."

Ralph remembered that when he was being treated for cancer the people who knew him at the time seemed afraid, both because they feared his disease might be contagious, and also because they assumed that he would die. "I don't see it as contagious but others do ... they see it as a death sentence, as the walking dead. ... People would look at you and you could see that look." Ralph also recognised that, in a society preoccupied with health, beauty and longevity, any illness so closely associated with suffering, mutilation and death is inevitably stigmatised. He compared his cancer experience with his experience of heart disease:

> With the coronary the people around me tended to be
> matter of fact. Oh, he's had a heart attack ... he's had a
> bypass. ... It didn't have the same mystery ... people's
> experience generally with someone that's got cancer is
> that they die. Now there's a stigma attached to that.

Following her own diagnosis with cancer, Sontag was somewhat surprised to discover that this was a disease regarded variously as a curse, an embarrassment, a punishment, and always as a death sentence. "One of the mystifications", she argues, "is that cancer = death".[37] It seems synonymous with untimely death, and with a preliminary social death which strongly implies a degree of separation for the sufferer from the mainstream of society. Therefore, as with Max (above), the concept of "leper" may be used as a stigmatising metaphor for the cancer sufferer because of the perception that death is inevitable. It is painful, physically debilitating and frequently disfiguring, and those affected may take some time to die.

Broadly speaking, an individual may feel stigmatised simply by being associated with the disease perhaps most feared in western societies. In addition, feelings of stigmatisation may be connected with the consequences of particular treatments – because of a colostomy, for instance, or the loss of a breast. A single breasted woman bears a stigma of disfigurement in a society which idolises the symmetrical female form; but she also bears the stigma of potentially terminal disease in a society committed to the pursuit of health, fitness and longevity. The continuing stigmatisation of people with cancer underpins the sense of social isolation experienced by cancer survivors and their related suspicion that generalised compassion is hard to come by in contemporary society.

4.   Cancer and Compassion

Martha Nussbaum argues that compassion is a basic social emotion.[38] Far from being an irrational force in human affairs, compassion, she holds, is "based on thought and evaluation". She goes on to point out that compassion is

> a central bridge between the individual and the community. ... The friend of pity should argue, I think, that pity is our species' way of connecting the good of others to the fundamentally eudaimonistic (though not egoistic) structure of our imaginations and our most intense cares".[39]

Conceptualising compassion as a "certain sort of reasoning",[40] Nussbaum suggests that, in the face of another's suffering, this reasoning involves the recognition that one is not immune from such pain, although one's present situation is indeed qualitatively different from that of the sufferer. Sense is made of the other's suffering by "thinking about what it would mean to encounter that [oneself, and seeing oneself], in the process, as one to whom such things might happen".41

From this perspective, then, a compassionate response to cancer survivors' expressions of pain requires an acknowledgment of some sort of community between self and other; in other words "an understanding of what it might be for me to face such pain".[42] To feel, and express, compassion for those who are fearful of untimely death involves facing one's own mortality, a stance that is usually avoided in the late modern world. Contemporary practical consciousness sanctions the sequestration of death and all its mess and disorder and pain and trouble from public view. Individuals are thus protected from the need to feel pity and empathy in face-to-face encounters (though such sentiments may be expressed in a "staged" way if that is seen to be appropriate).

In a "postemotional" world,[43] a pitying response may be deemed appropriate from a distance, but in the realm of social interaction considerable effort is made to limit one's exposure to the suffering of others, and, therefore, the need to offer an intimate response to such suffering. That most feared thing — fear itself — is thereby diverted, so that there is no place for the pitying response that is unacceptable in a society where individuals are encouraged to avert their eyes from each other's privacies and privations.[44]

This is not necessarily to deny altogether the presence of compassion in contemporary social life. The expression of compassion is, like fear, diverted — in the case of serious illness to designated realms of informal care and the caring professions. However, its very existence within profoundly individualistic societies does signal at least an indirect acknowledgment of the frailty and dependence of the human condition,[45] and perhaps supports Nussbaum's argument about the importance of compassion in human life.

Nevertheless, much of this study's data point to the suspicion of cancer survivors that their suffering is unlikely to be compassionately acknowledged in the context of routine social interactions. Although compassion may be offered under some circumstances, as Radley argues, "it is impossible to offer a compassionate response without acknowledging the suffering of the patient ... [and this] can often involve a recognition of features that are regarded as abhorrent or the source of fear".[46] Because compassion inherently involves an awareness of one's own weakness and vulnerability, it is, indeed, closely linked to fear.[47] Feeling and expressing compassion for cancer survivors entails confronting one's own mortality. The modern urge to defy death[48] leaves us ill equipped to do this; we are unaccustomed to facing our own fears of death, and thus attempt to limit our exposure to the immediate suffering of others.

Cancer survivors are therefore forced to rely on their own resources as they struggle to cope with their distressing feelings. As Nancy explains:

> *Because a lot of people are very scared to talk about it ... they can't cope with the fact that in the back of their mind they think, well you've had cancer, you're going to die from it eventually. ... Or will it happen to me? ... You have to put this brave front on for people ... They don't want to hear you say you're sad or upset ... I cried myself to sleep last night.*

5.   Conclusion

I have argued here that there is a relationship between cancer survivors' experience of the fear of the recurrence of disease and the climate of fear that envelops the social experience of cancer. On the face of it, cancer survivors have become "ordinary" participants in the commonplace social world. However, they do not necessarily *feel* re-integrated into every-day society. Unable to share in the commonplace, taken-for-granted, future-oriented world view, they continue to feel at odds with those around them, and to fear that their 'survivor' status will be undermined by a recurrence of disease.

Cancer is a powerful reminder of the inevitability of human frailty. In the contemporary social world, though, our secular, postemotional sensibility rules out a compassionate response to the raw, painful emotions of cancer survivors. They are thus isolated in their pain, firstly because they cannot share in the practical consciousness of "ordinary" others, and, secondly, because they sense that their suffering will receive no meaningful response in their social world.

Notes

[1] Martha Nussbaum, *The Therapy of Desire: Theory and Practice in Hellenistic Ethics* (Princeton: Princeton University Press, 1994), 192.

[2] The term 'cancer survivors' is used here to describe persons who have experienced an episode of cancer, have undergone treatment and have been symptom-free for at least two years thereafter.

[3] See Mira Crouch & Heather McKenzie "Social Realities of Loss and Suffering Following Mastectomy," *Health*, 4:2 (2000): 196-215. See also Heather McKenzie, *In sickness or in health? The ruptured, suffering selves of cancer persons*. Unpublished thesis: University of New South Wales (2000).

[4] Alan Radley, *Making Sense of Illness: The Social Psychology of Health and Disease* (London: Sage, 1994), 155.

[5] The study referred to here involved nine women and six men. Time since diagnosis varied from two to 35 years, and, as it happened, a wide range of site-specific cancers was represented, including bowel, breast, testicular, prostate and endometrial cancers, and Ewing's sarcoma.

[6] Nussbaum, 1994: 210.

[7] Nussbaum, 1994: 195.

[8] Anthony Giddens, *Modernity and Self-Identity*, (Cambridge: Polity Press, 1991), 36.

[9] A. Schutz, *On Phenomenology and Social Relations*, Helmut Wagner (ed), (Chicago: University of Chicago Press, 1970), 73.

[10] Zygmunt Bauman, *Mortality, Immortality and Other Life Strategies*, (Cambridge: Polity Press, 1992), 152.

[11] See R. McGrew, *Encyclopaedia of Medical History*, (London: Macmillan Press, 1985).

[12] Jack Barbalet, *Emotion, Social Theory and Social Structure: A Macrosociological Approach*, (Cambridge: Cambridge University Press, 1998).

[13] See J. Bailar and H. Gornik, "Cancer Undefeated", *The New England Journal of Medicine*, 336: 22 (1997): 1569-74. See also T. Beardsley, "A War Not Won", *Scientific American*, (January 1994): 118-26.

[14] N Press, JR Fishman & B Koenig, "Collective fear, individualized risk: the social and cultural context of genetic testing for breast cancer", *Nursing Ethics*, 7 (2000): 237-49.

[15] Alan Radley, "Abhorrence, compassion and the social response to suffering", *Health*, 3:2 (1999): 167-87.

[16] Susan Sontag, *Illness as Metaphor*, (London: Allen Lane, 1979). See also Susan Sontag, *Aids and Its Metaphors*, (New York: Farrar, Straus and Giroux 1989).

[17] Radley, 1999: 169.

[18] Erving Goffman, Stigma: Notes on the Management of Spoiled Identity, (Middlesex: Penguin, 1963).

[19] Goffman, 1963.

[20] Sontag, 1989: 15.

[21] Jackie Stacey, *Terratologies: A cultural study of cancer*, (London: Routledge, 1997), 70.

[22] Stacey, 1997: 66-7

[23] Radley, 1999: 168-9.

[24] Radley, 1999: 172.

[25] Goffman, 1963: 74.

[26] Goffman, 1963: 75.

[27] Goffman, 1963: 14.

[28] Stacey, 1997: 67.

[29] Goffman, 1963: 95.

[30] Goffman, 1963: 75.

[31] Audre Lorde, *The Cancer Journals*, (London: Sheba Feminist Publishers, 1985); also see Crouch & McKenzie, 2000.

[32] Sontag, 1989: 12.

[33] R. Levin, "Cancer and the Self: How Illness Constellates Meaning", in *Postmodern Studies on Narcissism, Schizophrenia and Depression*, ed. D. Levin (New York: New York University, 1987): 163-97.

[34] See Deborah Gordon, "Embodying Illness, Embodying Cancer", *Culture, Medicine and Psychiatry*, 14 (1990): 275-97. See also M. Weiss,

"Cancer and imputed infection: images of 'the disease' among patients' relatives", *The Sociological Review,* 43: 1 (1995): 1-35.

[35] Robert Crawford, "The Boundaries of the Self and the Unhealthy Other: Reflections on Health, Culture and AIDS", *Social Science and Medicine,* 38: 10 (1994): 1347-65.

[36] Phillip Mellor and Chris Shilling, "Modernity, Self-Identity and the Sequestration of Death", *Sociology,* 27: 3 (1993): 411-31.

[37] Sontag, 1989: 14.

[38] Martha Nussbaum, "Compassion: The Basic Social Emotion", *Social Philosophy and Policy,* 13: 1 (1996): 27-58.

[39] Nussbaum, 1996: 28, 48.

[40] Nussbaum, 1996: 28.

[41] Nussbaum, 1996: 35.

[42] Nussbaum, 1996: 35.

[43] Stjepan Mestrovic, *Postemotional Society,* (London: Sage, 1997).

[44] Radley, 1999: 171.

[45] Radley, 1999.

[46] Radley, 1999: 172.

[47] Nussbaum, 1996: 34-5.

[48] See Christine Sypnowich, "Fear of Death: Mortality and Modernity in Political Philosophy", *Queen's Quarterly,* 98: 3 (1991): 618-636.

Heather McKenzie
Department of Family and Community Nursing
The University of Sydney
New South Wales
Australia

Last Matters: The Latent Meanings of Contemporary Funeral Rites

Mira Crouch

1.   Prologue

A dead body is an ambiguous object. It is the material remnant of what was once a person – and, for some, a vessel for a soul now departed from the world, though possibly still viable in another realm. Yet the body also points to, and often portrays, death and its anguish of suffering, pain, decay, and, perhaps, uncertainty about what may lie ahead, for the dead and survivors alike. Thus while one may stand in awe of it, one may also be frightened and repelled by it, since it is a powerful marker of ambiguities and perilous passages, both for the deceased and those who are facing what has come to pass. In all human groups, therefore, the disposal of the body is hedged about with ritual, so that the dangers which it signifies may be fenced in. For any given social collectivity, the rituals by which death is managed will reflect the group's moral precepts, as these will offer maximum support during the dangerous journeys to be undertaken.

In societies of the so-called "Western culture", there has prevailed, for some considerable time, a broadly unified frame of reference, hinged to the ideology of emancipation and progress but embracing, too, aspects of Judeo-Christian ethics. Traditional mortuary rituals have been situated in this frame, though somewhat uneasily, since their origin lies not only in religion, but also in superstitions which flow from ancient pagan beliefs regarding, especially, the powers of the dead and their bodies.[1] In the Western tradition, funerals have customarily consisted of three parts: the procession, the service and the committal. During earlier times of high mortality rates across all age groups, this funeral form has served well, and thus endured in, the small face-to-face communities of the past where a necessarily extensive, though perhaps not particularly intensive, social life prevailed. Indeed, all funerals used to be meaningful and important social events in the smaller towns and agrarian communities of Europe and North America several generations ago.[2] Keeping the dead body company, viewing it in state and witnessing its last passage from home to church and, finally, into the grave, were all parts of that social life – in which, in any case, death was a socially visible and ubiquitous event. Community participation in funeral rites was then a matter of course, embedded as it was in the interface of seemly conduct and a belief system unequivocally assumed to be shared.

2.   From Tradition to Diversity

In our very much altered present circumstances, both practical and ideological, funerals are situated in quite a different set of social conditions. Belief, where it still exists, does not any longer guide much of social practice. When it comes to death, there is little evidence now of a conviction that trials of initiation to the spirit world await the deceased, and that ghosts exist and may be malignant; the loss of such convictions lessens the demand for both magical precautions and religious ritual.[3] The attenuation of the funeral's classic form results in part from this attrition of belief; however, practical factors have also exercised considerable influence.

The funeral procession has been almost completely pushed out of the sprawling and congested cities in which most of us now live. (This, in turn, has obliterated the cultural memory of its social meaning, the slow rate of its progress having been originally established by the pace of the erstwhile bearers – community members all – "who *carried* the bier".[4] In addition, the increasing acceptance of cremation during the last century,[5] especially in Australia[6]– certainly on rational rather than traditional grounds - has undermined the distinction between the service and the committal.   Generalising somewhat, the "single service"[7] – frequently shortened as well – is all that is left of what once was a complex and protracted ritual.[8]

Yet tradition may still carry sway in modern funerals of public figures (a description once valid for all persons), certainly for those eligible for State funerals, but also for otherwise well-known and deserving persons. For example, the Australian writer and rebel Frank Hardy was carried to his grave "beneath the Eureka flag with the words of the 'Internationale' …ringing from the [Melbourne] Trades Hall Council choir".[9] Significantly, though, this implies that greater contrast can now obtain between "ordinary" funerals and those of persons who are in some respects extraordinary, either in themselves, or by virtue of their deaths having been caught up in important events (for instance, in recent years, September 11 or the Bali explosions).

Perhaps precisely because in death everyone is equal, funerals, organised by the (still) living, have always lent themselves to expressing social distinctions. But the complexities of contemporary society provide greater scope for status differentiation than has been the case in the past. A case in point is the ethnic heterogeneity of contemporary society. Paradoxically, almost, present-day cultural diversity has both undermined and maintained the established funeral forms. On the one hand, it has unsettled their across-the-board validity; but, on the other, diversity has also established the right of various groups and persons to adhere to their own specific traditional funerary forms, should they wish to do so. Funerals have thus become important strategies in the practice of "identity politics" of our era, for both collectivities and individuals.

In this connection, it may be relevant to consider that these days it is mostly the elderly who die. In most cases, the aged are persons whose deaths have little disruptive effects on social and community life. They matter – if at all – to family and friends only. When they die, mourning, bereavement and re-adjustment will, in all probability, be private, individual concerns of little interest in the larger social context which now supplies no established mourning conventions that need to be observed regardless of how one actually feels about a given death. Thus the elderly may have less elaborate funerals, and the decreased visibility of these may confirm, yet again, the social distance of the old from the rest of society. But since the elderly are so numerous, the *comparatively* expedient manner in which some of them are dispatched may also influence, in turn, the perception of the role of funerals more generally. Arguably, also, as increasing social and geographical mobility and the pace of social change overall keep widening the "generation gap", grief of the younger for the older grows less intense, and thus also their engagement in rituals associated with death.

Another important factor in the attrition of the traditional funeral form has been consumerism, with its drive towards excess (much larger and more highly polished caskets, lavish floral tributes, etc). Extravagance, of course, is within the means of only some (who, perhaps, seek distinction), but it may tempt vulnerable others who may not wish to appear mean (or may be moved to appease the memory of the deceased). Either way, the profit motive continually pushes up expenses associated with traditional funerals, especially those involving a burial, beyond tolerable limits for many people (G. Ryle "The dying game" in *The Sydney Morning Herald*, Monday 30 September, 2002: 11). (Throughout the last century also, escalating costs have played a part in the development and increased usage of cremation services as a way of simplifying funeral ceremonies and reducing the then widespread ostentation[10]). Alternatives have therefore been sought, and the market, as always, has responded to consumer demand by providing a variety of services for what is now a culturally and socially quite diverse clientele.

3.   **The Advent of the Personal**

Simplification is not the only trend that differentiates contemporary funerals from the fully blown traditional model. Of greater importance for this discussion is the changed social context, and therefore also the atmosphere, of many funeral services today. Like funerals in the past, contemporary ceremonies, too, are sometimes attended by neighbours, acquaintances, and relations and friends of the deceased; yet present-day funeral services are also much more likely to be private, even personal, occasions.[11] But the personal does not necessarily overlap with the private. While the latter is a matter of structure, the former is largely a question of content: a private funeral means that the event is attended only by closest kin (and/or other intimate associates), whereas the personal, tailor-made aspect of a funeral service can be prominent even in a very public ceremony. It is to this individualised dimension of funerals that our attention now turns.

Presently funerals can be arranged to suit individual preferences, with non-ritual elements of poetry, music and personal statements by family and friends introduced into the service – or even taking its place. Often, though by no means always, such funerals are secular (e.g. in 1997 up to 25% of all funerals in Victoria were in this category[12]). As such, these represent a radical departure from the traditional model, at its height in the elaborate and rigidly prescriptive mortuary rituals of the Victorian era.[13] Secular funerals can be conducted by a friend, colleague etc, or by a civil celebrant (possibly a woman) who directs the ceremony, announces the various tributes that constitute the service, and/or reads out various texts chosen for the occasion. By their very nature, secular funerals are tailor-made to the dispositions and desires of the persons concerned.

Individually chosen elements can also appear in the traditional funeral form. While once this was feasible only in the form of the selection of readings from sacred texts and the choice of the eulogist (always a man), now poetry, music, video-clips and personal tributes can also be included. The customised funeral service, be it secular or not, emphasises the individuality of the deceased and represents personal wishes of family members with respect to ways of parting from their dead. Sometimes, too, the deceased themselves have left instructions regarding the form and even details of the service, perhaps in an effort to exercise control over the persona projected during the ceremony.[14] (Some anecdotal examples spring to mind: an acquaintance who had dabbled in various Eastern forms of spirituality and specified that a representative text from each be read out at the funeral; and another, whose adult children were instructed to read out, instead of a standard service, personal tributes to their parent.) The funeral industry – increasingly corporatised and globalised[15] - has capitalised on, and, in turn, furthered, this individualising impulse through heightened product differentiation: a range of funeral options is now on offer, including, for example, burials at sea (as advertised in the Sydney Telephone Directory).[16]

4.   The Corpse Exits

The dead body itself is, of course, of considerable significance. Its presence at a funeral is a powerful reminder that the ceremony is, above all, about death. From an anthropological viewpoint, the function of mortuary practices is to delineate the crucial transitional phase of the rite of passage from life to death; cross-cultural studies have consistently shown that these rituals, centred on the body as they are, both release and generate powerful emotions.[17] But funeral rites also set conventions for demeanour which protect valuable routine sociability in emotionally charged situations.[18] At funerals (and other rites of passage, eg weddings) emotions are thus both contained and selectively permitted, and by virtue of this are channelled, it has been argued, into a collective "effervescence".[19] This communal spirit uplifts and comforts the individual just as much as it mends the temporarily damaged social fabric and underwrites – again and again, as Nature will have her way with us – the solidarity of the community.

Certainly traditional religious ceremonies emphasise both the transcendental and social aspects of death, seeking to enlighten as well as to comfort a congregation presumed to be united as much in a common spiritual frame of reference as it is in grief and mourning. The body – not to mince words here, the corpse – is the sacred object of the occasion and therefore also its dramatic subject through which the ceremony is focused unequivocally on death.

Now, however, the bereaved have largely lost contact with the corpse.   No longer is personal care of the dead body the prime responsibility of family and friends, as it once was,[20] nor is the home the typical location of any communal gathering associated with death, holding vigil over the dying or sitting with the body. Increasingly, too, death rituals can be performed in the absence of the body: now there is often a memorial service gathering that follows a private funeral which may be - though is by no means always - quite cursory. (It is to be noted that this is not always a question of choice. In many funeral venues, especially those accommodating cremations, strict time limits are usually imposed on individual events.)

5.   Celebration of Life

A memorial service may be either religious or secular, or an eclectic combination.[21] It is common to cast such ceremonies as "celebrations of life". This term expresses a sentiment that is much easier to project in the absence of the corpse, perhaps with only photographs (or screen images, these days) to remind the mourners of the deceased in whose honour the tributes of speeches, poetry and music are presented. The disembodied and choreographed nature of such a rite does seem to befit a society in which human association increasingly relies on communication rather than on physical presence, thus rendering sociability more virtual than actual. As social practices, celebration of life events are also notably different from the visceral assertions of survival associated with old-fashioned wakes (and also funerals in other cultures), where sorrow and fear are mixed with a desire to give intensity to present life, in lively talk, great quantities of food and drink, and even sexual display .[22]

The principal feature of a "celebration of life" ceremony is the presentation of carefully selected, usually positive and even elevated, but always clearly portrayed as typical, facets of an individual's life. Sentimentality tends to abound, even where some humour is allowed. Often a funeral (where the corpse is present), too, assumes a "celebration of life" character because of the spirit of what is said and done during the service. Be it secular or religious, this type of service - like all "celebration of life" ceremonies - has as its main de facto objective the valorisation of the deceased. (A comment on "themed" funerals in the US seems to bear this out: "People are looking for an experience. They want their lives to end with an exclamation mark, not just a full stop" [M. Musgrove, spokesman for the National Funeral Directors Association, USA, quoted in L. Broadbent "Six feet wonder", The Weekend Australian Magazine, February 1-2, 2003: 9]).

Through their emphasis on individual biographies, these contemporary funerals glorify life itself and leave little room for a contemplation of death and demise as universal aspects of the human condition. Anecdotal evidence indicates that the deaths of elderly people are less likely to be honoured by a "celebration of life" ceremony than are those of younger persons who die "before their time". But chronologically old, "past their prime", individuals, can still die "before their time" if so adjudged by virtue of their social functions and positions at the time of death - in which case their funerals may do more (may also celebrate their lives) than merely dispatch their bodies without much fuss. This, too, tells us that contemporary funerals have much to do with the pervasive individualism of contemporary society, and very little with the meaning of death as such.

A somewhat jaded analytic eye can read a "celebration of life" service as an attempt to deny death in its full, let us face it, horror: the pain, suffering and fear that usually precede it, and the grief – often abject – and guilt and regrets that can follow in its wake. On these occasions, especially where the corpse is absent, death itself is spirited away through a smokescreen of re-enactments of life. Arguably, the mendacity that inheres in such scenarios represents the culmination of the more general trend to sequester death from public view, in a technical/rational society which does not easily own up to defeat. And, of course, death must be fought in a culture where the belief in the afterlife has been lost and natural death therefore becomes frightening to contemplate and impossible to accept [23]

The complexities of the modern denial of death have been noted and extensively discussed since the end of WWII, and works such as Philippe Ariès' *Western Attitudes toward Death*[24] have become classics of cultural critique. Nevertheless it has taken the escalation of individualism during the last two to three decades of the 20th century for that denial to be made to flow into new funeral forms. These do not permit much dwelling on the precariousness of life and the finality of death through which grief, loss and anxiety may be validated in equal measure; instead, "celebrations of life" and other customised ceremonies foreground the uniqueness of the deceased and personal sentiments of the survivors. As a consequence, witnesses to such tailor-made and self-referential displays cease to constitute a congregation; instead, they become an audience. Today we are so accustomed to spectacle that this transformation may pass unnoticed. In fact, some of us may even think that a "good show" at a funeral - or a memorial service - is entirely appropriate for the occasion.

6.   Self to the Fore

Personal revelations during the funeral service can also serve to enhance images of lives other than those that have ceased to be. The production – indeed, the staging – of the various performances which make up the memorial service often project the self-understanding and aspirations of those arranging the service. This is not necessarily a deliberate post-modern "self-production"[25] strategy. On the contrary, it is much more likely to be a subconscious, spontaneously emerging, process: just part of the flow-off, common in many areas of our social landscape, from banked-up individualism towards normative fields flattened through the withering of custom.

The rise of the self as the vantage point of moral life[26] has come about in the context of broad attitudinal changes of modernity: the inexorable march of secularisation, seemingly oddly allied to a variety of "New Age" attitudes to spiritualism, increasing cultural diversity and consumerist sensitivities. All of these have challenged significantly the validity of traditional funerals. Not that there ever was inherent stability in those ceremonies; in fluid Western societies, funerary rites have always been fragile constructions "vulnerable to conflict, avarice, and disbelief".[27] But it was not until well into the 20th century that these factors could hitch a ride on the swell of social change and begin to threaten the basic structure and, through this, the communal spirit of funerals. In this way, the individualistic moments of contemporary funeral ceremonies have not only come to accommodate the currently prevalent self-centeredness, but have also begun to test the limits of organic social bonds and perhaps even herald their demise.

7.   Feeling Matters

This point calls for further comments on the participation of family and/or friends in the funeral service, as such participation, on the face of it, may be expected to enhance the communal feel of the ceremony. But the capricious nature of, and lack of prior familiarity with, details of any given ceremony, and the sometimes very personal nature of those details, may in fact unsettle and fracture the congregation. Once the funeral service was the prerogative of an appropriately ordained officiating person and, perhaps, a designated eulogist, both acting in predictable ways; by contrast, now the right to pronouncements and evocations of appropriate sentiment is more widely distributed, producing a broad range of performances. (And in a secular funeral, even invocations can be made in lay voices, and to various powers, sometimes within the same service.)

These performances can sometimes be puzzling in an emotional sense and call forth responses that are not necessarily intelligible in terms of the meagre contemporary social stock of knowledge about death and funerals. The meeting ground of mourners at a funeral thus rests on the assumption that everyone present is undergoing an affective (perhaps even affecting) experience of *some* kind. Such an assumption underwrites a social situation which is very different from a ceremony where there is a shared tacit understanding of the significance and meaning of its customary ritual ingredients.

As in other ritual forms of contemporary social and public life (for example, according to Sennett and Mestrovic, politics[28]), overt outpouring of emotion is now a common feature of funeral rites: friends and kin of the deceased frequently relate, as part of the service, minutia of experience and feeling. Though made public, the affect thus revealed is not necessarily shared (although a range of emotions can be, and generally is, provoked by them). One consequence of this is that no service is necessarily like any other, and the degree and manner of expressed grief and pain are quite varied; consequently many mourners may be dissatisfied, lone and even alienated in funeral gatherings. (In exceptional circumstances, things can be different: disasters causing sudden deaths bring people together in very real ways, whatever the form of the funeral service. And wars – acts of terrorism included – often unite mourners into a community as these events provide opportunities for chauvinism to represent common grief as a cause in common. Notably, the services that have followed up such events recently have tended to be extensively choreographed in form and intensively hyperbolic in content, thus representing "celebration of life" ceremonies writ large, as it were.)

Richard Sennett explains that during the 19th. Century (and before), if emotion was to be made public it was expressed in standard, often symbolic, yet always recognisable forms. Such immediate expressivity inspired social effervescence - the only basis, according to Sennett, for a genuinely cathartic experience (on this argument, possible in the traditional funeral form, but increasingly unlikely in the diversified and customised contemporary variants). But as the public domain grows more obscure under its overlay of late capitalism's complex cultural fabric, emotional expressivity necessarily moves from standard modes of presentation to personal re-presentation, in congruence with the modern belief that "social meanings are generated by the feelings of individual human beings".[29]

8.   Community?
The management of death and the disposal of corpses are imperatives in any civilised society; these processes are, in fact, timeless markers of culture. As such, they will be framed by whatever a society holds sacred and important at any given time. But an unified belief system does not any longer characterise modern society, and contemporary individuals are very aware of the variety of convictions and orientations that prevails in their social environments. Another factor in the trend towards a personally oriented funeral service may then be our intuitive understanding that (the importance of) the personal is the only remaining common cultural currency. And, in a sense, that is clearly the case when it comes to funerals, because even those persons who decide on a traditional funeral service (in a multicultural society such as Australia, this may be one of many) are effectively still making a personal choice.

We know that from Palaeolithic times to the present, human beings have responded to death with solemnity and ceremony, thus attempting to render it meaningful in terms of one or another belief- and value-system. As Kessler[30] has pointed out, the manner in which a culture manages death reveals the loci of its reverence for life. In the Western tradition of mortuary rituals, funeral services of the past emphasised and re-validated the established sacred beliefs that underwrote it, and the eulogy implicitly belaboured the moral question of the good and virtuous life through the scrutiny of a particular person's dealings with matters both sacred and profane. Once this question was considered in terms of ethical criteria taken to be universal by a particular community. The fact that the eulogy often fudged actual circumstances of a past life did not invalidate these criteria; on the contrary, it demonstrated their powers not only to be, but also to create, the truth.

Those powers are now dissipating in a social world where human connections are dependent much more on commonality of specific interests and concerns than on a communal mode of existence. Accordingly, the social positions of contemporary persons are distributed over many points of intersection of all their various associations, rather than held in particular communities of place that are recognised as such. In the context of our contemporary mode of sociability, "Our" morality appears to be more a matter of allegiances and beliefs "We" choose to adopt, rather than of the social constraints within which "We" have to conduct our lives. With any particular death, therefore, it may be difficult to imagine a form of funeral service and words spoken in it that will be meaningful to all the assembled individuals in a way that enables them to connect the ceremony with the overall context of their social existence.

Paul Woodruff provides an interesting (American) example: a student has died. Family and fellow students attend the funeral; for some of these young people, this is their first, and therefore a shock. They do not think that their friend was religious – yet the ceremony is. They hear hymns, prayers, and "a sermon about faith and salvation, applied to the case at hand...(yet for them) the one personal thing anyone said about their friend was about her faith, and it is not true".[31] We take his point; but, a few decades ago, this would not have mattered. Personal faith might not have been essential, but observance of social mores was; as obligation rendered funeral practices ubiquitous, their social significance was sustained.

9.   *Caritas*?

But now a variety of approaches obtains – must obtain, in fact – both among and within funeral services; and, if Sennett's argument (as above) holds, individual emotional statements *necessarily* make up much of what takes place during the service. These still have moral implications, however: in the post-modern world virtues are privately owned, as it were, and rest on "emotivism"[32] – the view that morality is the expression of preferences, attitudes or feelings of individuals. At the same time, as Mestrovic points out,[33] presently we confront a panorama of "mediatised" emotional scenarios of both exultation and suffering of others. Exposure to such affective spectacles makes us feel all kinds of things, but luxuriating in second-hand feelings that ensue from these representations ultimately leads, on the one hand, to a shallow emotional life, and, on the other, to compassion fatigue – the separation of emotion and action. "Today, everyone knows that emotions carry no burden, no responsibility to act";[34] if this is the case, mere display of personal feeling in a public context is a breach of good faith and therefore also, Sennett might have said, of civility.

As social roles begin to crumble, except in a functional sense, collective morality seeps out of the public domain. In turn, *caritas* as *routine practice* is severely undermined, since, in normal circumstances at least, very little can rightfully be expected from any particular person. (It is true that many do rise to the occasion, but they do this as compassionate individuals – authentically, as some of us might approvingly say – rather than as a matter of fact, in observance of their social membership.) Perhaps this is why we often feel obliged to claim to be "passionate" about various matters of interest to us. Perhaps also, by way of compensation for the loss of palpable engagement, "caring" has become a conversational idiom of our age - whereby, for example, we talk (sometimes at funerals) about "caring persons"; or, when terminating a routine telephone call, we say (just like in the movies) "I love you", instead of simply "goodbye".

10.   Epilogue

And so it is with funerals, when we do need to say "goodbye", and do so for good. However, this is not what we do. Instead, we play evocative music, we talk about what we remember and how we feel, we celebrate a life that is no more and we rejoice in the life that still surrounds us, and we think that this is a good way of saying goodbye. But it is only a feel-good way which merely papers over the fragmentation of our existence, our terror and ignorance of death, and our inability to accept and deal with the actuality – among much virtuality - of suffering and pain.

This discussion has presented a rather grim view of contemporary responses to the Grim Reaper's task. It is possible that the case has been overstated. The point of the emphasis, though, has been to highlight those aspects of the current mode of our social existence which are reflected in the trend towards individuation and sentimentality – not to say mawkishness - in present-day funeral ceremonies. There is also an implicit message in this critique: however hard we try to avoid it, mortality does confront us when death occurs. In the face of the inevitable nothingness at the end of being, now as before, for us humans there is a need for something – and, in our society, for something beyond the self - to remain sacred. If only we knew how to go about it, a basis for this could well be provided "for the believer as well as the unbeliever...(by) the last moments...the solemn farewells, the funeral, the tomb".[35] Far more trenchantly than any "celebration of life", death, by its very nature, is telling of life's value. It behoves us, then, to pay full respect to the appalling fact that nothing remains of the person who has died. We are truly impoverished if we do not give this voice, do not behold the hiatus created by death, do not honour this great leveller and do not heed its power.

This chapter is dedicated to those who, in their loss, have

Not words, but grief, not messages,
but sorrow,
hard as the earth, sheer, present as
the sea
(Les Murray, from An Absolutely Ordinary Rainbow, 1969)

Notes

[1.] Bertram Puckle. Funeral Customs: Their Origin and Development (London: T. Werner Laurie Ltd, 1926).
[2] Robert Blauner, "Death and Social Structure", in Passing: Visions of Death in America, ed. Charles O. Jackson (Westport: Greenwood Press, 1977), 174-209.
[3] Blauner, 189.

[4] Puckle, 125.

[5] Jessica Mitford, The American Way of Death (London: Quartet Books, 1980).

[6] Duncan Waterson and Sandra Tweedie, "The Funeral Industry in New South Wales", in Essays on Mortality, eds Mira Crouch and Bernt Huppauf (KSHSS, University of New South Wales, 1985), 123-135; Graeme M. Griffin and Des Tobin, In the Midst of Life…The Australian Response to Death (Revised Edition) (Melbourne, Melbourne University Press, 1997).

[7] A double service has a separate committal ritual.

[8] The procession and the committal may feature in vestigial or symbolic forms; for example, the solemn moment, often accompanied by some "meaningful" music, when the curtain closes on the coffin before the body is transported – presumably – to the cremation oven.

[9] Griffin and Tobin, 253.

[10] Robert Nicol, Final Pageant; the Past, Present and Future of Death (South Australia: Uniting Church Historical Society, 1998).

[11] Jane Littlewood, Aspects of Grief: Bereavement in Adult Life (London: Tavistock/Routledge, 1992), 69.

[12] Griffin and Tobin, 148.

[13] Nicol, 17.

[14] Various forms of eulogy most probably have their origins in superstitions regarding the supernatural powers of the dead (of whom one must not ill speak); but they may also be crafted on the basis of another consideration: i.e. that memories of the deceased continue to exercise influence beyond death.

[15] Jessica Mitford, The American Way of Death Revisited (New York: Knopf, 1997).

[16] The discussion here rests largely on observations of circumstances in Australia. Conditions may be different elsewhere in affluent societies, especially in the United States where attitudes to the management of death are said to be unique in many respects (Blauner, 1977; Mittford, 1980; 1997). However, the individualising trend appears to have made inroads into funeral practices everywhere. For example, www.uk-funerals.co.uk lists different types of funerals available (traditional, secular, woodland, DIY – for those who wish to be "personally involved at every stage of saying farewell'); and an American site's (www.ftc.gov/bcp/conline/pubs/services/funerals/htm) leading theme is 'Every family is different, and not everyone wants the same type of funeral". The Sydney Telephone Directory has a sizeable section on "Celebrants – Naming and/or Funeral", with several entries advertising "personalised funerals".

[17] Richard Huntington and Peter Metcalf, Celebrations of Death: The Anthropology of Mortuary Ritual (Cambridge: Cambridge University Press, 1979).

[18] Margaret Visser, The Rituals of Dinner (New York: Grove Weidenfeld, 1991), 21.

[19] Emile Durkheim, The Elementary Forms of the Religious Life, trans. Joseph W. Swain (New York: Free Press, 1965[1915]).

[20] Charles O. Jackson, "Death in American Life", in Passing: Visions of Death in America (ed. Charles O. Jackson, Westport: Greenwood Press, 1970, 229-253.

[21] Griffin and Tobin, 57.

[22] Huntington and Metcalf, 39.

[23] Blauner, 183.

[24] Philippe Ariès, Western Attitudes toward Death, trans. P. M. Ranum, (Baltimore, John Hopkins University Press, 1974).

[25] Zygmund Bauman, "Sociological Responses to Post-modernity", Thesis 11, 23(1989), 35-63.

[26] Anthony Giddens, Modernity and Self-Identity: Self and Society in the Late Modern Age. (Cambridge: Polity Press, 1991).

[27] Thomas A. Kselman, Death and the Afterlife in Modern France (Princeton: Princeton University Press, 1993), 301.

[28] Richard Sennett, The Fall of Public Man (New York: Alfred A. Knopf, 1977); Stjepan G. Mestrovic, Post-emotional Society (London: Sage, 1993).

[29] Sennett, 229.

[30] Clive S. Kessler, "The Cultural Management of Death', (in M. Crouch and B. Huppauf, eds Essays on Mortality, KSHSS, University of NSW, 1985), 135-153.

[31] Paul Woodruff, Reverence: Renewing a Forgotten Virtue (Oxford: Oxford University Press, 2001), 51.

[32] Alistair McIntyre, After Virtue: A Study in Moral Theory (2nd edition) (London: Duckworth, 1985).

[33] Mestrovic, 3.

[34] Mestrovic, 56.

[35] Kselman, 301.

Bibliography

Ariès, Philippe. Western Attitudes toward Death (trans. P.
M.Ranum). Baltimore: John Hopkins University Press, 1974.
Bauman, Zygmund.. Sociological responses to post-modernity. *Thesis 11*,
23(1989): 35-63.
Blauner, Robert. "Death and social structure". In *Passing: Visions of*
Death in America, edited by Charles O.Jackson , 174-209.
Westport: Greenwood Press, 1977.
Durkheim, Emile. (1964 [1915]). The Elementary Forms of the Religious
Life, trans. Joseph W. Swain, New York: Free Press.
Giddens, A. Modernity and Self-Identity: Self and Society in the Late
Modern Age. Cambridge: Polity Press, 1991.
Griffin, Graeme M. and Tobin, Des. In the Midst of Life…The Australian
Response to Death (Revised Edition). Melbourne: Melbourne University
Press, 1997.
Huntington, Richard and Metcalf, Peter. *Celebrations of Death: The*
Anthropology of Mortuary Ritual. Cambridge: Cambridge
University Press, 1979.
Jackson, Charles O. Death in American life. In *Passing: Visions of Death*
        in America, edited by Charles O. Jackson, 229-253. Westport:
Greenwood Press, 1977.
Kessler, C. 'The Cultural Management of Death'. In *Essays on Mortality*,
edited by Mira Crouch and Bernd Huppauf, 135-153. KSHSS, University
of NSW, 1985.
Kselman, Thomas. Death and the Afterlife in Modern France. Princeton:
Princeton University Press, 1993.
Littlewood, Jane. Aspects of Grief: Bereavement in Adult Life. London:
Tavistock/Routledge, 1992.
McIntyre, Alisdair. After Virtue: A Study in Moral Theory, 2nd edition.
London: Duckworth, 1985.
Mestrovic, Stjepan G. *Post-emotional Society*. London: Sage, 1997.
Mitford, Jessica. *The American Way of Death*. London: Quartet Books,
1980.
Mitford, Jessica. *The American Way of Death Revisited*. New York:
Knopf,
1997.
Nicol, Robert (1998). Final Pageant; the Past, Present and Future of
Death, South Australia: Uniting Church Historical Society, 1998.
Puckle, Bertram S. Funeral Customs: Their Origin and Development,
London: T. Werner Laurie Ltd, 1926.

Sennett, Richard. *The Fall of Public Man*. New York: Alfred A. Knopf. 1977.

Visser, Margaret. *The Rituals of Dinner*, New York: Grove Weidenfeld, 1991.

Waterson, Duncan and Tweedie, Sandra. "The Funeral Industry in New South Wales". In *Essays on Mortality,* edited by Mira Crouch and Bernd Huppauf, 123-134. KSHSS, University of New South Wales, 1985.

Woodruff, Paul. Reverence: Renewing a Forgotten Virtue. Oxford: Oxford University Press, 2001.

Mira Crouch is Senior Lecturer in the School of Sociology at The University of New South Wales, Sydney, Australia. Her research concerns, in the main, psycho-social aspects of transitional phases and key events of the life-course in the context of social change.

Neither Dead-Nor-Alive
Organ Donation and the Paradox of 'Living Corpses'

Vera Kalitzkus

1. Introduction

In many European countries and North America organ donation is portrayed as the "gift of life" that renders meaning to an otherwise meaningless death. The bereaved family is said to find consolation and help in the thought that the death of their loved one was not in vain. Yet, "brain death" and organ donation raise fundamental legal, ethical and socio-cultural questions: "What exactly is death – physical, personal, and social", asks medical anthropologist Margaret Lock in her latest study on "brain death".[1] To shed some light on these questions, I want to cover the following aspects:

> ➤ The boundary between life and death is disputable, always culturally defined and embedded in a specific historical context. This is also valid for the assumed objective and universal biomedical definition of death, from which we can learn about social interests and cultural values that informed it.

> ➤ In most, if not all, Western countries, the state of "brain death" officially defines the death of a person; this generates the paradox of a (biologically) 'living corpse'. Thus, humans, who before the raise of the concept of "brain death" were considered dying, yet living persons, are now excluded from the community of the living. This means a shift of the boundary between the living and the dead. How do donor relatives experience the confrontation with "brain death" and cope with the "neither-dead-nor-alive" status of their loved one?

> ➤ As the bodies of "brain-dead" patients can be used for the survival of the living, a new relationship between the living and the dead is created via the transplantation of human organs. How does organ donation affect the relationship between the living and the dead? What can we learn about the social and cultural meaning given to death?

The questions above will be examined in the light of my empirical research (narrative interviews and participant observation) on organ transplantation medicine in Germany.[2] The empirical data consist mainly of narrative interviews (lasting one to four hours) with donor relatives and organ recipients, supplemented by participant observation at meetings of self-help-groups, national and international transplant sporting events (comparable to the Paralympics) and in a transplant unit and ICU of a university clinic in Germany. The heterogeneity of the empirical material enables insights into the complexity and diversity of the experience of patients and relatives. My aim was to identify common features in the wide range of experience, enabling conclusions to be drawn about general culturally conditioned problems of organ transplantation. Although there is a great deal that can be said about coping with the threat and constant fear of death from an organ recipients' point of view – especially as their survival is directly linked to the death of another person – I shall concentrate in this chapter on the donating side of transplantation medicine: the new face of death and the wider implications of organ transplantation for society.[3]

Let me begin with looking at concepts about death and dying in various cultures, in order to shed a new light on the struggles we have with making sense of death and dying – in its old or in its new form.

2.   Culture, Death and Dying

Although every human being is mortal, there is no such thing as a *natural* way of dying, death or grief. Death and dying are always culturally defined and embedded in a system of cultural beliefs and values. This in sum is the main message derived from ethnological studies on death and dying.

Human beings – today and through history – are aware of their mortality and therefore have to react to that fact one way or another. Our mortality makes obvious the tension of our lives between the 'natural' and the 'cultural'. Although the mortality of humans is universal, cultural comparative studies show that there are no universal reactions towards death and dying – neither in respect to the treatment of the dead body, nor concerning the culturally appropriate feelings and display of emotions nor about appropriate conduct during funerals or the expected grieving period.[4] Ethnological and historical studies show that death and dying can only be understood and dealt with via cultural mediation.

Death threatens the existence and self-comprehension of human societies. The living and their communities have to react to this existential threat and the very concrete problems caused to them by death. Each culture has a specific way of answering the following questions:

> What is the definition of death and what is the definition of life?
> How did death enter the world? (causes of death, cosmology)
> How to deal with grief and bereaved people? (code of conduct)
> What happens after death? (meaning of death, transcendence)
> What is a corpse and how should it be treated? (code of conduct)

The cultural answers to these questions constitute one of the main features of a culture's orientation system in the world. They are perceived as 'natural' and therefore 'taken for granted' and unquestionable. This explains why changes in this area and confrontations with alternative answers to these questions can and often do lead to severe conflicts and confrontations – the recent example being the debate about "brain death".

Cultural conceptions of death are always connected with norms, values and goals of human existence. Three aspects are central to all cultural conceptions of death:

> The relation between self/person and body
> The relation between the individual and her/his community
> The relation of humans and their community in the cosmos

Death is embedded in a cultural belief system via death rituals, one of the main rites of passage, through which the social norms and values are expressed.[5] Through the death ritual, the deceased person undergoes a change of status and is excluded from the community of the living. Depending on the beliefs of the community, she becomes a member of the community of the dead, the ancestors, and the spiritual world or simply seizes to exist. It is revealing to look at how this transition from the realm of the living to the realm of the dead is perceived and defined.

3.   The Cultural Definition of Death
        From a Western enlightened and scientific viewpoint death is perceived as a biological fact. Ethnological studies reveal the astounding fact, that the definition of a person as dead – that means her or his exclusion from the community of the living – does not have to be congruent with the biological death of the physical body. As the ethnologists Maurice Bloch and Jonathan Parry state:

This endeavour to control the contingency of death is
highlighted by the commonly encountered discrepancy
between the event of physical death and the social
recognition of it.[6]

The definition of a person as dead is closely connected with
conceptions of the body and the self. Within Hinduism, for example, death
is defined as the moment, when *prana* or the odem of life leaves the body.
Yet, *atman* or the soul is released from the body only during cremation,
and not as part of a natural process, but through human intervention. The
main mourner, most of the time the eldest son, has to smash the skull of
the dead to free the *atman*. Only then, the dead person is given the status
of an ancestral spirit (*preta*). And only with this violent death, the last
glimpse of life is released from the body. With the postponement of the
final point of death to the smashing of the scull, death falls under the
control of the social: it is transferred from the realm of the natural to that
of the cultural.[7] In addition, this example shows the conception of death as
a process and not a single event – an important feature of conceptions of
death in many non-Western cultures.

The transfer of the non-living person from the realm of the living
to the realm of the dead can take a considerable amount of time, during
which she is still considered a member of the community of the living. Let
me provide another ethnographical example. The Toraja from Sulawesi,
Indonesia, are known for their elaborate funeral rituals, both highly time-
and money consuming in preparation. To gather the resources and
assemble the wide spread kinship group for the funeral can take a
considerable amount of time – especially with high-status individuals,
ethnologists Douglas Hallam and Jane Wellenkamp describe. It can take
weeks, months, in exceptional cases even years, from the physiological
death of a person and the performance of the respective funeral. During
this time span the corpse is kept in the house, treated with formalin or
wrapped in layers of cloth and put into reed mats or coffins. Although the
family and the village where the death occurred are affected by it in terms
of ritual impurity caused by death, it is not until the performance of the
funeral rites that the deceased person is referred to as dead:

Aluktu adherents [followers of the traditional religion;
remark by VK] do not formally acknowledge the death
and refer to the deceased as *to macula*, 'person with a
fever', or *to mamma*, 'sleeping person'. The deceased is
offered food and drink, informed of the departure and
arrival of household members, and in general treated as

Vera Kalitzkus 145

if he or she were still alive. (...) Not until the funeral begins is the deceased referred to as *to mate*, literally 'dead person'.[8]

This is a very good example for the possibility of being biologically dead but socially still alive. But also the contrary can be found: being biologically alive but socially dead. Among the Dogon in Mali for example, it is possible that a missing person for whom the death rituals already have been carried out, is not even recognized by his closest relatives, if he returns unexpectedly, and thus has to lead a socially marginalized existence.[9] Venturing into Euro/American homes for elderly people or people with dementia brings parallels to the combination of being biologically alive but socially dead to mind.[10] The cultural construction of death is not confined to the non-Western world; it is also true for Western conceptions – although they haven't been studied that extensively under this perspective.

4.   **"Brain Death" and Organ Transplantation**
      Cultural definitions of death in Euro/American societies are informed by biomedical concepts. Death is defined as the extinction of the last functions of life. But the progress of medical science revealed, that not all parts of the body are dying at the same time. Instead, death is taking place in various body parts at different times – until the last cells eventually die. This shows that physiological death is a process, which also the biomedical view attests to. Foucault pointed out, that the increase of medical knowledge led to an increasing fragmentation of death.[11] In the 18th century medical discussions about the uncertainty of signs of death resulted in a growing fear in the public of suspended animation.[12] Insecurities about this existential pillar, this example shows, can lead to massive fears.
      Insecurities about the definition of death arose again with another hallmark of medical progress: reanimation and artificial respiration during the 1950s. Sebastian Schellong showed convincingly, how former signs of the onset of the dying process (arrest of breathing and heart functioning) became obsolete, as they now could be reversed. As 'natural breathing' – until that time a definite sign of life – could be artificially substituted, it was not clear anymore on which side of the border between life and death these patients were situated.[13]
      With the assistance of artificial ventilators and the support of heart-lung-machines it became possible to keep the bodies of patients with irreversible brain damage in a functional equilibrium. This state was called

coma depassé or irreversible coma and actually constituted a prolongation of the dying process. Doctors now were forced to determine criteria that indicated whether patients were in the state of irreversible coma or whether they still could recover and return back to life. The clinical determination of irreversible coma was above all a criterion to withdraw medical treatment, as the return to life of the patient was impossible. In that phase of the past, these patients were still considered in the last stage of dying, but still alive.[14]

Only with the rise of organ transplantation and the need for organs removed from a biologically functioning body did it become of utmost importance to pinpoint the exact moment of death, as otherwise the removal of organs would constitute a violation of a still living person. The definition of "brain death" as the death of a person was not easily accepted in the medical community and subject to severe debates.[15] Even today, although there is a consensus about the irreversibility of "brain death" and how to determine it (with minor methodological discrepancies in the guidelines in Europe, North America, and Japan), Margaret Lock states "…differences clearly exist about the *significance* of a brain-death diagnosis."[16]

The condition of "brain death" can only be diagnosed in an Intensive Care Unit. Without the support of life sustaining machines, these patients would die a conventional death (arrest of the circulatory system), although, with medical progress, this period of time can expand into weeks, even months (for example in the case of pregnant women in the state of "brain-death").[17] The bodies of these patients display all signs of life: they are warm, the chest is heaving, they can sweat, the heart is beating, spontaneous uncontrollable movements of the extremities can take place (the so called 'Lazarus-signs').

The definition of "brain death" not only as the end of "meaningful life" but as the death of a person signifies a shift of the boundaries of the social, sociologist Gesa Lindemann points out: now a person with a beating heart and biologically functioning body is excluded from the community of the living and declared dead.[18] The actual moment of death signed in the death certificate is – in Germany – the time of the *second* "brain death" protocol.[19] This shows: the moment pinpointed down as the moment of death records a status that already existed and *not* the actual moment of when it happened. The medical diagnosis is therefore defining and influencing the actual point of death of the organ donor. Comparison of countries practicing biomedicine and their regulations for the process of defining "brain death" show differences in the legally accepted point of death. The point of death therefore is socio-culturally defined, or, in the words of anthropologist Veena Das, "…the moment of death does not simply occur any more – it has to be chosen."[20]

In Germany as in many other countries, too, "brain dead" patients are declared medically and legally as dead. Only Japan that also had severe ethical debates about organ transplantation took into consideration that this redefinition of death cannot be imposed on all people regardless of their belief and creed, as Margaret Lock explains:

> … brain death is equated with death only when patients have specified in writing that they wish to become organ donors and their families do not overrule these wishes. Brain-dead individuals who have not indicated that they want to become donors are not considered legally dead.[21]

The definition of "brain death" as the death of a person clearly constitutes a shift of the border between life and death, stripping this 'new' death of the characteristic formerly connected with it: a cold and lifeless corpse. How do relatives of patients in the state of irreversible coma perceive this 'new form' of death? How do they cope with the shift of the boundary between the living and the dead?

5.   Dying and the Hour of Parting under the Premises of Organ Donation

In-depth studies on the experience of the donation process from the donor relatives' side are rare. Donor families in Germany seldom speak about their experience in public (although this has undergone some changes in recent years) and are not – with one exception – organized in self-help-groups. It was difficult to get into contact with them for my research. Most transplant centres I asked where not willing to cooperate. I therefore turned to the option of announcing my project in newspapers, from which resulted the majority of the 21 interviews with 23 immediate next of kin of 19 medically suitable potential organ donors.[22] My sample is very heterogenic concerning the age and kinship relation of donor and relative. The interviews were conducted as soon as three months after the donor's death to as many as twenty years afterwards. The relationship between kin and donor cover all next of kin relations (father, mother, child, spouse).

Germany is operating with the informed consent regulation: either a person decides during her life to be a potential organ donor and documents her will in a so called donor card or relatives are requested on her behalf. In the majority of the cases, relatives have to decide whether or not to consent to the "harvesting" of organs. In Germany, between 1997 till 1999 only about four percent of the organ donors had documented their will in a donor card.[23]

This decision whether to grant or withhold consent to the removal of organs has to be made under emotionally extreme conditions: at the Intensive Care Unit, when the relatives are confronted with the message of a mostly sudden death. At that time they are in a state of mental shock. To remove organs suitable for transplantation, the donor has to be in the state of "brain death". The condition of "brain death" can only be diagnosed at the Intensive Care Unit. Without the support of life sustaining machines, these patients would die a form of conventional death (arrest of the cardiac and pulmonary system). This fragile condition can only be sustained for a limited period of time. Therefore, the decision has to be made under pressure of time. The period of time for the decision the relatives loose from the farewell of their loved one that is of utmost importance in the grieving process.

In addition to that, the sensual experience confronts the relatives with all signs associated with life, but not with death. From their outer appearance, patients in the state of irreversible coma cannot be distinguished from other comatose patients: their bodies are warm to touch, the chests are heaving, and the heartbeats can be felt – although only due to the life-support machines. This creates a difficult situation for the relatives to cope with:

> Then, I sat there and thought, 'How long do you want to stay here?' It was very difficult to have on the one hand the impression, that she's alive, and then to leave her. On the other hand, there was the knowledge that I have to leave her in that state, because they will carry her away like that for the organ removal at sometime. Being dead one associates with the fact that someone's not breathing any more. But that was not the case, she was breathing, well, the machine was breathing for her. And then to decide: 'Well yes, now you are dead. Now, only your body lives on and you don't need me anymore. Now I can let you go.' That was hard. … Because I didn't see my wife in a state, that she was cold and not breathing. (translated by VK)

As my interview material clearly showed, the dominant problem with "brain death" is not an intellectual one, but a problem of the sensual experience and perception involved. The majority of the relatives, who were for various reasons not confronted with their loved one in the state of "brain death", judge their donation experience in retrospect as positive. But for little more than half of the relatives, who were confronted with "brain death" at the Intensive Care Unit, the organ donation meant an additional burden and quite often a very painful experience. As the relatives are confronted with the signs of life, but not of death, they are insecure and full of doubts.[24] A young mother of a two-year-old child that died in a car accident put her experience in the following words:

> It might sound funny, but death is not a sensual experience any more. One cannot grasp it. [...] It deprives us of death, the experience of dying. ... Of course a brain-dead person is not breathing any more, otherwise one couldn't do it. And this is the fact that I cling to. If the respirator had been turned off, then he really would have died. But the last image I have of my child is that of a breathing child. And that makes it very hard to cope with and go on living. (translated by VK)

The time between the "brain death" diagnosis and the end of the organ removal is an additional burden for the bereaved. This time span can extend up to 24 hours, in exceptional cases even longer. The bereaved have to wait for the message or a phone call from the clinic, that the removal operation is over and the corpse is ready for the mortuary. Now the body of the brain-dead person has turned into a corpse in the traditional sense and also can be experienced as a corpse on the sensual level. "My son has died two deaths", a donor father expressed his experience. The first death refers to the "brain death", the second death to the one after organ removal.

Donor relatives are confronted with a 'new face' of death that is not congruent any more with former cultural interpretation schemes. In their experience three distinctive phases of death can be distinguished:

> ➤ The "brain death", which can only be understood intellectually, but not to be experienced with the bodily senses in confrontation with a brain-dead person. For the relatives, therefore, the brain-dead patient is still considered a dying person.
> ➤ The actual death after organ removal, when they can see the corpse and thus realize, that there is no life left in their relatives' body.

> ➤ The *final death*, when the transplanted organs also died in or with the body of the organ recipient. As there is strict anonymity between the donor and recipient side, they never know, when that actually happens.

This third point is connected to the often stated belief of donor relatives, that part of the organ donor still lives on in the body of the recipient. Therefore, the transplanted organ is perceived, even after death, as still saturated with aspects of the donor's self: in a sense they constitute his prolongation. For some bereaved this is a consoling thought – some aspect of their loved one still exists. For others – especially if they had traumatic experiences in the clinic and/or with the donation process – this perception can be very painful.

6.   Conclusion

My analysis shows that the main problem for the bereaved is in coping with death in its new form as "brain death" and the underlying concept of the person with the brain as its essence. Because of the close connection between the body and the self not all people are able and willing to alienate the corpse after death. Organ donation also means to sacrifice the hour of parting, the last moments they share with their dying/dead relative and surrender this intimate and private moment of life to the necessities and the regime of the transplantation process. The experience of the donor families clearly support the assumption of Margaret Lock in her study on "brain death", that it is necessary to take into consideration the social and cultural aspect of death:

> It is quite possible to conceive of social death as of primary significance and biological demise as secondary to it, as has been the case until relatively recently in most societies. A decaying body will never return to a living condition, and many of us readily agree that a brain-dead body will never revert to consciousness or breathe again, but death and dying are nevertheless social constructs.[25]

In the public discourse organ donation is portrayed as the ultimate altruistic deed, the "gift of life", that gives meaning to an otherwise meaningless death. Yet, there is a kind of cultural amnesia about where the organs for transplantation come from and what the donation process entails for the bereaved family. For them it is an additional burden: a decision quite often derived at under duress as they know the living of other people depending on their willingness to approve the donation. It also entails severe disturbance during the hour of parting form their beloved. To minimize the burden for the bereaved open acknowledgement of the circumstances and open information about the stressful and problematic aspects of organ donation are needed. In the last instance this implies, on an individual as well as on a societal level, the acknowledgement of and appeasement with death. Only then could one speak of a free choice of giving in its true sense of the word – the gift of life given in death.

Notes

[1] Margaret Lock, *Twice Dead. Organ Transplants and the Reinvention of Death* (Berkeley: University of California Press, 2002), 37.
[2] The study was part of a larger research project sponsored by the German Research Foundation (Deutsche Forschungsgemeinschaft) and conducted at the Institute of Ethnology at the University of Göttingen, Germany, under the chair of Prof. Brigitta Hauser-Schäublin. In this project we also looked at reproductive technologies. The results are published in Brigitta Hauser-Schäublin et al., *Der geteilte Leib. Die kulturelle Dimension von Organtransplantation und Reproduktionsmedizin in Deutschland* (Frankfurt a. Main / New York: Campus, 2001). The results of this research on organ transplantation constitute my dissertation and are published under Vera Kalitzkus, *Leben durch den Tod. Die zwei Seiten der Organtransplantation. Eine medizinethnologische Studie* (Frankfurt / New York: Campus, 2003).
[3] I addressed the situation of organ recipients in my paper for the first conference on "Making Sense of Health and Illness", in Oxford, July 2002 (publication in progress).
[4] Ample examples of cultural ways of dealing with death can be found in Nigel Barley, *Dancing on the Grave: Encounters with Death* (London: Abacus, 1997); Maurice Bloch and Jonathan Parry, *Death and the Regeneration of Life* (Cambridge: Cambridge University Press, 1982); Robert Hertz, *Death and the Right Hand*, transl. Needham, R. and C. Needham (Aberdeen: Cohen & West, 1960 [1907]); Richard Huntington and Peter Metcalf, *Celebrations of Death. The Anthropology of Mortuary Ritual* (Cambridge: Cambridge University Press, 1979).
[5] For the concept of the rites of passage see Arnold van Gennep, *The Rites of Passage*, 17th print (Chicago: Chicago University Press, 2001 [1909]).
[6] Bloch and Parry, 12-13.

[7] See Jonathan Parry, "The End of the Body," in *Fragments for a History of the Human Body*, ed. Michael Feher, Vol. 2 (New York: Zone, 1989).

[8] Douglas W. Hallam and Jane C. Wellenkamp, *The Thread of Life. Toraja Reflections on the Live Cycle* (Honolulu: Hawai'i Press., 1996), 174.

[9] Bloch and Parry, 13.

[10] Elisabeth Hallam et al., *Beyond the Body: Death and Social Identity* (London: Routledge, 1999), 3.

[11] Michel Foucault, *Die Geburt der Klinik. Die Archäologie des ärztlichen Blickes*. 5. ed. of the German Issue (Frankfurt am Main: Fischer, 1999 [1963]), 156.

[12] Martina Kessel, "Die Angst vor dem Scheintod im 18. Jahrhundert. Körper und Seele zwischen Religion, Magie und Wissenschaft," in *Hirntod. Zur Kulturgeschichte der Todesfeststellung,* ed. Thomas Schlich and Claudia Wiesemann (Frankfurt am Main: Suhrkamp, 2001).

[13] Sebastian Schellong, "Die künstliche Beatmung und die Entstehung des Hirntodkonzepts," in *Hirntod. Zur Kulturgeschichte der Todesfeststellung,* ed. Thomas Schlich and Claudia Wiesemann (Frankfurt am Main: Suhrkamp, 2001), 205.

[14] Sociologist Gesa Lindemann analysed that process in detail, see Gesa Lindemann, *Die Grenzen des Sozialen. Zur sozio-technischen Konstruktion von Leben und Tod in der Intensivmedizin* (München: Fink, 2002), 105 – 138.

[15] Analysis of these debates in historical perspective are given by Lindemann 2002; Claudia Wiesemann, "Instrumentalisierte Instrumente: EEG, zerebrale Angiographie und die Etablierung des Hirntodkonzepts," in *Instrument – Experiment – Historische Studien*, ed. Christoph Meinel, (Berlin, Diepholz: Verlag für Geschichte der Naturwissenschaft und der Technik, 2000), 225-234.

[16] Lock, 2002, 37.

[17] Margaret Lock, "On Dying Twice: Culture, Technology and the Determination of Death," in *Living and Working with the New Medical Technologies. Intersections of Inquiry*, ed. Margaret Lock et al. (Cambridge: Cambridge University Press, 2000), 233.

[18] Lindeman, 2002.

[19] In order to "harvest" organs the German Transplant Law prescribes that "brain death" has to be diagnosed twice by two independently and experienced doctors, who are not further involved with the transplantation process.

[20] Veena Das, "The Practice of Organ Transplants," in *Living and Working with the New Medical Technologies. Intersections of Inquiry*, ed. Margaret Lock et al. (Cambridge: Cambridge University Press, 2000), 269.
[21] Lock, 2002, 3.
[22] Two contacts were facilitated by a transplant coordinator, another one by a pastor working in a clinical setting.
[23] Deutsche Stiftung Organtransplantation, *Organspende und Transplantation in Deutschland 1999* (Neu-Isenburg: Deutsche Stiftung Organtransplantation, 2000), 14.
[24] As other studies showed, even medical professionals and nurses, who directly work with brain-dead patients experience this uncertainty in perception concerning the status of a brain-dead patient. See Hauser-Schäublin et al. 2001, Linda F Hogle, *Recovering the Nation's Body. Cultural Memory, Medicine, and the Politics of Redemption* (New Brunswick / New Jersey: Rutgers University Press, 1999); Lindemann 2002; Lock 2000.
[25] Lock, 2002, 374.

Bibliography

Barley, Nigel. *Dancing on the Grave: Encounters with Death*. London: Abacus, 1997.
Bloch, Maurice and Jonathan Parry. *Death and the Regeneration of Life*. Cambridge: Cambridge University Press, 1982.
Das, Veena. "The Practice of Organ Transplants and the Determination of Death." In *Living and Working with the New Medical Technologies. Intersections of Inquiry*, edited by Lock, Margaret, Allan Young and Alberto Cambrosio, 233-262. Cambridge: Cambridge University Press, 2000.
Deutsche Stiftung Organtransplantation. *Organspende und Transplantation in Deutschland 1999*. Neu-Isenburg: Deutsche Stiftung Organtransplantation, 2000.
Douglas W. Hallam and Jane C. Wellenkamp. *The Thread of Life. Toraja Reflections on the Live Cycle*. Honolulu: Hawai'i Press, 1996.
Foucault, Michel. *Die Geburt der Klinik. Die Archäologie des ärztlichen Blickes*. 5. ed. of the German Issue. Frankfurt am Main: Fischer, 1999 [1963].
Gennep, Arnold van. *The Rites of Passage*. 17th print. Chicago: Chicago University Press, 2001 [1909].

Hallam, Elisabeth, Jenny Hockey and Glennys Howarth. *Beyond the Body: Death and Social Identity*. London: Routledge, 1999.

Hauser-Schäublin, Brigitta, Vera Kalitzkus, Imme Petersen and Iris Schröder. *Der geteilte Leib. Die kulturelle Dimension von Organtransplantation und Reproduktionsmedizin in Deutschland*. Frankfurt a. M. / New York: Campus, 2001.

Hertz, Robert. *Death and the Right Hand*. Translated by R. Needham, and C. Needham. Aberdeen: Cohen & West, 1960 [1907].

Hogle, Linda F. *Recovering the Nation's Body. Cultural Memory, Medicine, and the Politics of Redemption*. New Brunswick / New Jersey: Rutgers University Press, 1999.

Huntington, Richard and Peter Metcalf. *Celebrations of Death. The Anthropology of Mortuary Ritual*. Cambridge: Cambridge University Press, 1979.

Kalitzkus, Vera. *Leben durch den Tod. Die zwei Seiten der Organtransplantation. Eine medizinethnologische Studie*. Frankfurt / New York: Campus, 2003.

Kessel, Martina. "Die Angst vor dem Scheintod im 18. Jahrhundert. Körper und Seele zwischen Religion, Magie und Wissenschaft." In *Hirntod. Zur Kulturgeschichte der Todesfeststellung*, edited by Thomas Schlich and Claudia Wiesemann, 133-166. Frankfurt am Main: Suhrkamp, 2001.

Lindemann, Gesa. *Die Grenzen des Sozialen. Zur sozio-technischen Konstruktion von Leben und Tod in der Intensivmedizin*. München: Fink, 2002.

Lock, Margaret. "On Dying Twice: Culture, Technology and the Determination of Death." In *Living and Working with the New Medical Technologies. Intersections of Inquiry*, edited by Lock, Margaret, Allan Young and Alberto Cambrosio, 233-262. Cambridge: Cambridge University Press, 2000.

Lock, Margaret. *Twice Dead. Organ Transplants and the Reinvention of Death*. Berkeley et al.: University of California Press, 2002.

Parry, Jonathan. "The End of the Body." In *Fragments for a History of the Human Body*, edited by Michael Feher, 490-517, Vol. 2. New York: Zone, 1989.

Schellong, Sebastian. "Die künstliche Beatmung und die Entstehung des Hirntodkonzepts." In *Hirntod. Zur Kulturgeschichte der Todesfeststellung*, edited by Thomas Schlich and Claudia Wiesemann, 187-208. Frankfurt am Main: Suhrkamp, 2001.

Seale, Clive. *Constructing Death. The Sociology of Dying and Bereavement.* Cambridge: Cambridge University Press, 1998.

Wiesemann, Claudia. "Instrumentalisierte Instrumente: EEG, zerebrale Angiographie und die Etablierung des Hirntodkonzepts." In *Instrument – Experiment – Historische Studien,* edited by Christoph Meinel, 225-234. Berlin, Diepholz: Verlag für Geschichte der Naturwissenschaft und der Technik, 2000.

Avoidable Death
Multiculturalism and Respecting Patient Autonomy

Andrew Fagan

1.   Introduction

This chapter presents a philosophical analysis of the phenomenon of patients' refusal to consent to life-saving medical treatment on the grounds that the specific method of treatment necessarily involves a fundamental violation of patients' deep and inviolable cultural or religious beliefs. Clinical practice is no longer singularly determined by the pursuit of the most optimal medical outcome, irrespective of patients' wishes. In theory at least, satisfactorily respecting the principle of patient autonomy will entail patients' dying from curable or at least medically remediable conditions. The principle of patient autonomy, if it is to be taken seriously by clinicians, places a non-clinical, moral constraint upon the principles of beneficence and nonmaleficence and may appear to strike at the very heart of the purpose of medical treatment: alleviating physical and mental illness and restoring health. This chapter does not attempt to reassess the validity of the application of personal autonomy to clinical practice in general. Nor does it attempt to fully consider the extent to which, in practice, the various conditions for respecting patient autonomy can be fully satisfied in the cut and thrust of medical treatment. I recognise just how problematic the principle of respecting patient autonomy is, in both theoretical and practical terms. Indeed, it is precisely one aspect of this difficulty that provides the starting point and motivation for my analysis.

The autonomy principle does not provide the patient with an absolute and unconditional veto on medical treatment. Autonomy is not to be confused with mere licence and nor is autonomy to be identified with anything an individual desires. Clearly, clinicians' legal duty to respect patient autonomy entails an identification of the necessary and sufficient conditions for the exercise of autonomy. In practice, this typically entails a determination of patients' mental or cognitive capacities. Within culturally pluralist societies the dominant social and political convention for determining individual autonomy typically restricts the criteria to the formal manner in which individuals' arrive at and exercise their decision. The actual substance of the decision itself and the specific beliefs underlying it are typically not considered to be determinative in this respect. In general, individuals' rights to freedom of expression and religious and cultural association are not conditional upon the presumed veracity of the beliefs to which they subscribe and public servants cannot thereby withhold the all-important attribution of autonomy from those individuals whose beliefs do not coincide with established opinion and belief. This general situation is, of course, somewhat more problematic in clinical treatment. After all, diagnosing mental illness, for example, necessarily includes an evaluation of the content of individuals' beliefs and of the manner in which those beliefs are held. Unlike many other public servants, medical clinicians' determination of personal autonomy does necessarily extend to include some stipulative concern for the rational character of patients' beliefs. The specific focus of this chapter is to examine the extent to which respecting the principle of patient autonomy is consistent with extending respect to patients' cultural and religious beliefs, where these beliefs provide the ultimate grounds for a refusal to consent to life-saving treatment.

At present medical clinicians do not have a legal duty to respect patients' cultural or religious beliefs per se. However, many patients' refusal to consent to life-saving treatment is precisely motivated by their concern for their deepest religious and cultural beliefs: consent is withheld where the sole course of medical treatment will entail some gross violation of the specific social or ethical code in accordance with which patients seek to live and die. In judging the merits or validity of such claims, medical professionals are typically concerned to evaluate patients' mental and cognitive competence. Attempts to determine patients' capacity for exercising rational judgement do not, typically, extend to include any detailed consideration of the philosophical merits of the cultural or religious beliefs in question. In theory at least, whether patients' wishes are to be respected or not is determined by whether they can be deemed to be acting autonomously. Outside of medical ethics and clinical practice there is a wealth of literature on the phenomenon of multiculturalism and the political and moral consequences of religious and cultural diversity for legitimising public authority. In much of this literature there is a tendency to defend multiculturalism on the grounds of equality and autonomy. Public authority is deemed legitimate to the extent that it actively protects and promotes cultural and religious diversity. I will refrain from engaging with the detail of this literature but aim instead to critically analyse the assumption that respecting personal autonomy is generally consistent with respecting the fundamental beliefs and practices of any given culture or religion. I aim to caution clinicians against the assumption that conforming to cultural and religious beliefs is necessarily consistent with autonomy.

2.   Multicultural Medicine?

Many societies have increasingly come to recognise themselves as being 'multicultural' in character. Within the urban conurbations of many countries in Europe and North America one can find a veritable Babel of immigrant native languages being spoken, designating the existence of a similarly diverse array of cultural communities that have survived and even thrived despite geographical dislocation. The implications and effects of cultural and religious diversity for the formulation of democratically legitimate political constitutions have been widely discussed and analysed.[1] However, relatively little attention has been paid to the extent to which such conditions impact upon the provision of medical treatment and the fundamental ethical principles which attempt to guide medical practice. This lack of attention to the possible effects of cultural and religious diversity upon the principles and working practices of medical clinicians appears to offer some support to those who have consistently criticised biomedicine for ignoring the importance of culture generally in the successful provision of medical treatment, at all levels. Biomedicine does not exist in a social or political vacuum.[2] While not necessarily strictly determined by underlying material structures, clear relationships have been demonstrated to exist between medical systems and the social, political, and moral values of the societies in which they are found. However, this relationship is a complicated and even, in places, contradictory one. On the one hand, the inclusion of the principle of respect for patient autonomy within medical practice is typically restricted to those societies where the ideal of personal autonomy commands a high degree of political and moral authority. On the other hand, a number of critics have argued that biomedicine, though itself a cultural and social entity, unduly ignores the importance of culture generally in the successful provision of medical treatment. Thus, critics such as Helman present biomedicine's epistemological commitment to a physiologically reductivist model of disease as largely excluding the possibility of fully appreciating the extent to which patients' subjective understanding of the nature and causes of an ailment can be influenced by the beliefs and values of the particular cultures to which they belong.[3] This is important for biomedical treatment to the extent to which such beliefs directly inform patients' decisions concerning their own treatment. Within increasingly diverse societies, medical clinicians can expect to be confronted by situations in which patients' wish to comply with their fundamental religious and cultural beliefs and practices will conflict with the methods and aims of medical treatment. Patients have refused to sanction medically essential treatment on the grounds that such treatment entails an unacceptable violation of the beliefs to which they adhere. In so doing, patients appear to be, in effect, prioritising their cultural and religious interests over their interests in health and well-being. In so doing, they appear to be rejecting the fundamental ethos of biomedicine and its guiding presumption that the prolongation of life and the restoration of health are of ultimate, incontrovertible value, to which are minimally rational individuals would assent. Examples of such a conflict between the cultural and religious values and the values of biomedicine abound.

The most frequently cited example is that of the Jehovah Witnesses' general prohibition of blood transfusion on the grounds that such a practice constitutes an intolerable violation of that faith's fundamental religious beliefs and practices. However, a relatively recent reformist trend amongst some Jehovah Witnesses' has complicated the picture somewhat. Though still very much in a minority, some followers have begun to allow for the exercise of individual discretion in respect of consenting to blood transfusions. One cannot rest one's case, so to speak, solely upon an appeal to Jehovah witnesses therefore. Fortunately, there exist other religious communities whose values prohibit their members receiving various forms of potentially life-saving treatment. Thus, the Christian Scientist church has long prohibited the use of vaccinations and inoculations amongst its members on the general grounds that any such medical intervention constitutes an unacceptable violation of that faith's central tenets. Similarly, though more speculatively, one may question the potential effects of the growth of an interest in various Eastern religions amongst some sectors of European and North American societies. One may ponder how members of both the Jain and Buddhist religious communities are likely to respond to the emergence and progressively extensive deployment of xenotransplantation, given both religions' prohibitions against the use of animals in this fashion. Similarly, the transplantation of animal organs into human bodies constitutes a clear violation of the human/non-human animal distinction which is so sacred within the Judaeo-Christian tradition generally.

Looking slightly further afield, it is interesting to note that Japanese culture has generally long rejected the absence of brain activity as the sufficient criterion for determining death. This has been contrasted with western biomedicine's emphasis upon brain activity as the key criterion of the persistence of life.[4]   Ohnuki-Tierney, a medical anthropologist, argues that western culture generally differs form its Japanese counterpart on the central issue of the location of personhood, of which organ is thought to be constitutive of personhood. She argues that the principal importance which western biomedicine accords to the brain in this respect is entirely consistent with a western philosophical perspective that views the exercise of reason as the key distinguishing characteristic of personhood. In contrast, Japanese conceptions of personhood are described as more pluralist in character, identifying not one, but several bodily organs, such as the liver and the stomach, as essential sites of personhood. Japanese conceptions of personhood exert a profound influence upon Japanese perceptions of the ethical legitimacy of organ transplantation. Japan has some of the lowest rates of organ donation in the developed world. Amongst the more secularly minded inhabitants of Japan this may be accounted for, in part, by a more rigorous measure of determining when the death of the would-be donor has actually occurred, combined with a cultural reluctance to accept such symbolically significant organs such as the stomach and the liver. In addition, Confucian religion generally insists that the successful rebirth of the soul is dependent upon retaining an intact body, in life and after death. Thus, amongst the Japanese generally there exist powerful forces which serve to limit the medical use of organ transplantation as a means of preserving and prolonging life.

The above examples are illustrative of the phenomenon in question and are not intended to be exhaustive, by any means. A fully comprehensive empirical survey of the diverse cultural and religious communities found within industrialised societies will reveal the full extent to which prospective patients' cultural and religious beliefs may conflict with the methods and aim of medical treatment. In some instances it will be possible to proceed with alternative forms of treatment, acceptable to both clinician and patient alike. Thus, while the medical prospects of Jains and Buddhists (and other strict vegetarians) requiring organ transplantation may be affected by a growing utilisation of xenotransplantation, the technique itself is not intended to wholly replace the use of human organs. While a refusal to accept an animal's kidney on cultural or religious grounds may extend the time spent on dialysis, thereby reducing the patient's chances of survival, this need not, by itself, result in that patient's medically avoidable death so long as the, albeit inadequate, supply of human organs persists. In a situation such as this clinicians are not faced with an immediate life-and-death scenario. However, such scenarios do arise. Patients have refused to consent to medically essential treatment on the grounds that such treatment entails an unacceptable violation of the fundamental cultural and religious beliefs to which they adhere. Medical clinicians are confronted by the question of how they may best ethically respond to those patients' who refuse to consent to medical treatment even where such a refusal, if respected, will result in a medically avoidable death?

3.   **Autonomy, Multiculturalism and Respect for the Other**

The phenomenon confronting clinicians necessarily concerns the imposition of a constraining non-clinical, moral principle upon the pursuit of optimal medical outcomes. A sole dependence upon the twin bioethical principles of beneficence and nonmaleficence would, on the face of it, invalidate acquiescing in the occurrence of medically avoidable deaths on the grounds that such action was entailed by a respect for patients' cultural and religious beliefs. Clearly, such an outcome is entirely inconsistent with the underlying ethos and rationale of biomedicine. Yet, it occurs. Clinicians are confronted by a prima facie claim to respect patients' cultural and religious beliefs in so far as these beliefs provide the basis for patients' exercising their autonomy. The principle of respect for patient autonomy provides the means by which clinicians are expected to give due consideration to such apparently non-biomedical factors as religion and culture. The philosophical principle of personal autonomy is deceptively easy to state and notoriously difficult to explicate.[5] Personal autonomy is typically conceived of as referring to an individual's capacity and opportunity to exercise rational self-determination over the content and general course of her life. To be autonomous is to possess the cognitive ability to reason combined with the existence of sufficiently diverse social conditions as the object of one's choice and the means by which one's autonomy is expressed. Thus, for example, John Stuart Mill's defence of individual liberty attempts to erect an inviolable boundary around the rational individual who is deemed to be free to act as she wills without any external interference or coercion by others. The only substantive condition Mill attaches to this account of individual liberty is that the only legitimate constraints that may be placed on individual freedom concern those actions identifiable as harmful to others, so-called other-regarding actions. All forms of self-regarding actions, by contrast, are to remain free from the imposition of external constraints.[6] During much of the previous three centuries, philosophers have tended to conceive of autonomy in relatively formal, or negative terms. On this view, individuals' enjoyment of freedom was presented as sufficiently attainable by the removal of any and all external interference with the exercise of the will. However, this approach tended to obscure the extent to which the exercise of personal autonomy presupposed and required the existence of a sufficiently diverse external environment. Advocates of 'negative liberty' tended to measure individual freedom by the extent to which individuals were free from all but the most minimal and formal social requirements. In contrast, advocates of personal autonomy as 'positive liberty' argued that the exercise of autonomy required the positive promotion and protection of social institutions and forms, as an instrumental means for securing the conditions for autonomy.[7] Over the previous two decades or so, philosophical accounts of autonomy have increasingly emphasised the importance of the necessity of particular social environments as a prerequisite for the exercise of autonomy.[8] A principal effect of this account of understanding the conditions for autonomy is the emergence of a view that personal autonomy and culture are, potentially, complimentary, rather than mutually exclusive. Increasingly, political philosophers have come to recognise the promotion and protection of specific cultures as an indispensable means for promoting and protecting individuals' opportunities for exercising their autonomy through the promotion of cultural diversity. The social and philosophical background to this relatively new development rests with the recognition that many complex societies are multicultural in character. The normative doctrine of multiculturalism primarily consists of a combination of this empirical observation with a normative claim that individual well-being is inherently dependent upon the existence of suitably supportive social and cultural conditions.

The existence of a diverse collection of cultural and religious communities within a single society presents the provision of publicly funded and regulated services with a relatively new problem; namely, how to respond to the expressed wishes of those communities whose values and beliefs are found to be, in certain important respects, fundamentally incompatible with the principles upon which the provision of such services is based? Given the potential life-and-death consequences of medical treatment, medical clinicians may be reasonably thought of as peculiarly exposed to this particular problem. Hence, the question many clinicians require an answer to is why patients' culturally-determined wishes should be respected at all, where respecting these wishes will result in medically avoidable deaths? The answer to this question is complicated and multifaceted but begins with a consideration of the importance of culture to the development of our identity as individual human beings.

In recent years many philosophers and social theorists have begun to recognise the role which cultural membership plays in the development and lives of human beings generally. In contrast to a well-established, earlier liberal philosophical tradition that presents individuals as mostly self-constituting, ultimately self-reliant beings, philosophers such as, for example, Charles Taylor and Joseph Raz (to name but two) have consistently stressed the cultural basis of human identity and individual agency.[9] As representatives of a wider constituency, both philosophers argue that human identity is constituted through culturally embedded relationships and practices. Our identities are acquired through our membership of, initially at least, one cultural community. Similarly, the acquisition of our personal identities is itself constituted through our identification with the varying culturally determined and constituted values, beliefs, and practices. For philosophers such as Taylor and Raz, each individual's identity is shaped by, and is thereby ultimately dependent upon, the culture they have grown up within: we come to be the kinds of people we are as a consequence of the cultures we inhabit. As Taylor states, *'we become full human agents, capable of understanding ourselves, and hence of defining our identity, through our acquisition of rich human languages of expression.'* [10]As a veritable corollary to the claim that all human identity has a cultural basis, both philosophers argue that, as culture-inhabiting beings, our exercise of choice always occurs within a general cultural setting and that, further, the very objects of even our most significant choices are themselves culturally dependent. Thus, Raz argues, fairly incontrovertibly, that the choice to pursue a medical career is only possible within societies that both recognise the existence of such a specific profession and within which there exists the institutional infrastructure to support such a practice. [11]

Based upon the initial claim that all human identity is culturally constituted and that the objects of individual choice concerning such choices as one's career presuppose specific cultural infrastructures, philosophical advocates of multiculturalism such as Taylor and Raz proceed to argue that individual well-being is significantly dependent upon membership of a respected cultural community, one which is duly recognised within the wider society as a legitimate entity. The reason for this may be simply stated: because our identities as individuals are constituted through our relations with others and are prefigured, to a significant extent, by how others evaluate and perceive one as a member of a recognisable cultural community, the development of one's identity may be adversely affected by being associated with a cultural community that is the object of discrimination and prejudice. The general policy of multiculturalism is intended, in large part, to rectify the systematic discrimination which many members of minority cultures testify to having experienced in their attempts to practise their own cultural beliefs and values within complex, heterogeneous societies. If individual identity is culturally constituted it follows that a given individual's well-being is dependent, to some degree, upon the general well-being of the culture to which she belongs. Advocates of multiculturalism typically go further in arguing that the state has a moral obligation to protect and promote its citizens' essential interests and that these interests include membership of a respected cultural community. Taylor specifically requests of the state and individuals alike that due recognition and respect be extended to each individual's cultural community. He insists that *'due recognition is not just a courtesy we owe people. It is a vital human need.'*[12]

The doctrine of value pluralism is an essential component of the defence of multiculturalism. Multiculturalists address their arguments to culturally and religiously diverse societies. These societies are typically described as normatively diverse in character in that there exist a number of differing, perhaps even incompatible, visions of how life ought to be led and thus differing opinions as to which practices and beliefs are genuinely valuable and worthy of respect. Against those who argue that there can be only one correct way to lead a morally valuable life, multiculturalists argue from the central premise of value pluralism: that valuable human lives can be achieved in a diverse number of indeterminable ways. According to value pluralism there is no singly correct way to lead a morally valuable life. Value pluralism has long provided a normative basis to the argument that, in liberal political societies, the state should refrain from attempting to dictate or determine how its citizens' should seek to lead their lives, beyond a mere respect for the law. Value pluralism is therefore closely related to the ideal of personal autonomy. Many multiculturalists thereby argue that the promotion and protection of cultural and religious diversity is entirely consistent with the ideal of personal autonomy, if not a veritable instrumental means for securing that end. In addition to the argument that recognition of one's culture is a vital human need, multiculturalists also argue that the existence of a genuinely multicultural society testifies to the realisation of the liberal ideals of value pluralism and personal autonomy. Taken together, these two arguments constitute the basis of multiculturalism's claim to philosophical legitimacy. However, what specifically does the implementation of multicultural principles require of the state and what implications might this have for the provision of medical treatment?

Both Taylor and Raz unequivocally insist that the withholding of recognition of the value of cultural communities can constitute a form of social and political oppression, in so far as the well-being and sense of self-worth of the individual members of those communities is likely to be adversely affected as a direct consequence. However, neither philosopher is prepared to advocate extending equal recognition to all groups which designate themselves as 'cultures'. Rather, both insist that enjoying the political status which multiculturalism can confer upon cultures is dependent upon the satisfaction of certain conditions. Thus, Raz argues that, *'multiculturalism requires a political society to recognize the equal standing of all the stable and viable cultural communities existing in that society.'*[13] For Raz the determinative criteria for extending equal respect to any given culture is not based upon the values and beliefs of that culture conforming to those of the majority, or those approved by the state, but depend instead upon the stability and viability of the particular culture in question. One might think of these last as functional, as opposed to normative, criteria. While they remain somewhat vague in character, Raz clearly intends the stability and viability conditions to serve as threshold criteria for determining which cultures ought to enjoy equal respect and recognition by the liberal multiculturalist state. Providing the basis for some institutional 'gate-keeper', such criteria might act to exclude the claims of, for example, newly-established religious cults or political associations from claiming the status of a viable and stable culture. In practice, this is bound to provoke some controversy in determining who may and may not enjoy the protection of a multiculturalist state. However, it seems reasonable to assume that all of the cultural and religious groups I referred to earlier would satisfy any likely test and thus would have a legitimate claim to equal treatment by public authorities. Multiculturalism requires that the state formulate its political and legislative procedures in such a way as to be equally acceptable to all of those cultures that fall under its jurisdiction. Similarly, it also requires that the state and its various public authorities allocate the provision of public services and goods in a manner which accords equal respect and recognition to all of the relevant cultures. What implications does this have for the ethical provision of medical treatment? In particular, how would the realisation of this moral obligation affect the relationship between medical clinicians and those patients who refuse to consent to treatment on grounds of culture and religion? Can this be adequately assimilated by the principle of respect for autonomy?

4.   Respecting the Patient – Autonomy and Multiculturalism
        Within complex, multicultural societies there exist numerous cultural and religious communities whose fundamental beliefs and practices are incompatible with central tenets of biomedicine and the biomedical model of diagnosis and treatment. Patients continue to refuse to consent to essential life-saving medical treatment on the grounds that such treatment is culturally and religiously unacceptable. There can be little doubt that the full implementation of a multiculturalist policy within the health sector will entail numbers of individuals dying from medically treatable and curable conditions. For clinicians, as public servants, to act in accordance with the ethics of multiculturalism entails a suspension of their medical duties to patients. At present, this unpalatable situation is typically assuaged by appeal to the autonomy principle. On this view, clinicians are not so much being asked to respect patients' cultural and

religious beliefs per se, as to respect their patients' exercise of autonomy. This position finds clear support in much of the literature on multiculturalism. Many advocates of multiculturalism, such as Joseph Raz and Charles Taylor, similarly argue for multiculturalism on the grounds of its presumed generally beneficial effects upon the exercise of autonomy. Neither Raz nor Taylor appear prepared to unconditionally endorse a protectionist policy towards cultural integrity at the expense of the autonomy of individual members. Liberal multiculturalists, the only form that enjoys any credible recognition within liberal democratic societies at present, characteristically restrict their arguments to a presumed compatibility between defending multiculturalism and defending personal autonomy. One may question whether such an approach can ultimately be squared with the defence of multiculturalism. Personal autonomy is not an ideal that enjoys universal validity in all cultures and religions. Many of these communities may be, in other respects, both stable and viable, whilst simultaneously restricting their individual members' scope for autonomous action and thought. Put simply, advocates of multiculturalism must be clear as to what they ultimately wish to defend: personal autonomy or cultural autonomy. In many cases one cannot achieve both. The defence of cultural autonomy will entail extending respect to cultures and religions that do not value personal autonomy, while the defence of personal autonomy will necessitate some form of discrimination against those very same cultures. What bearing does this have for medical clinicians and the issue of medically avoidable deaths? How far can the principle of respect for patient autonomy assimilate considerations of patients' cultural and religious beliefs?

It would be naïve to assume that the principle of respect for patient autonomy itself has been unproblematically assimilated within biomedical practice. The principle is not amenable to a simple formulation and so it is not always readily apparent precisely when or how the requirements of the principle have been met. In addition, medical clinicians are increasingly subject to myriad conflicting pressures and demands. On the one hand, patients, patients' representatives and many ethicists are demanding that patient autonomy be fully respected, whilst on the other hand, bureaucrats continue to impose various health 'targets', the possible realisation of which appears to require the imposition of treatment regimes as means for attaining the targets: hitting one's targets may often require compliant, and not autonomous, patients. Perhaps, more than at any other time since the establishment of the principle, respecting patient autonomy has become deeply problematic. Even when one places such concerns to one side, it is clear that many clinicians have considered the principle of patient autonomy as placing a medically invalid constraint upon the pursuit of the most optimal health outcomes. The principle of respect for patient autonomy is grounded, in large part, upon individuals' essential interests in the exercise of autonomy. Biomedical treatment, in contrast, has been grounded upon the promotion and protection of health, as expressed through the principles of beneficence and nonmaleficence. The latter requires that clinicians seek to avoid causing any unnecessary harm to the patient, whereas the former *'asserts an obligation to help others further their important and legitimate interests.'[14]* Not surprisingly, medical clinicians have tended to construe 'harm' and 'interests' in biomedical terms, as referring primarily or even exclusively to the physiological well-being of the patient as determined by the objectively-verifiable diagnostic procedures of biomedicine. One may think of this as the telos, or ultimate purpose, of biomedical treatment. From within this biomedical paradigm, the relationship between clinician and patient is an unavoidably hierarchical one to the extent that the clinician's perspective is necessarily accorded priority over that of the patient. The clinician's authority is grounded in the presumed objectivity of scientific rationality and is thus justified to the extent that the clinician restricts her attention to the identification and appropriate treatment of the underlying physiological causes of a given ailment. It follows, however, that the clinician could undermine this authority by extending her diagnosis to include what might be termed 'medically inappropriate factors', such as the patient's own subjective beliefs about the causes of her ailment or about how treatment should proceed, if at all. As Helman argues, *'because medicine focuses more on the physical dimensions of illness, factors such as personality, religious belief, culture, and socio-economic status of the patient are often considered largely irrelevant in making the diagnosis or prescribing treatment.'[15]* The principle of respect for patient autonomy does, however, entail the medical team according due recognition to patients' subjective, potentially medically ill-informed, beliefs about their own treatment. Respecting patient autonomy will entail a suspension of the very telos of biomedical practice in some cases. The extension of the principle of respect for patient autonomy contains the potential for significantly altering the relationship between clinician and patient to the degree that the principle restricts the clinician from performing any medical procedures to which the patient has not consented. In accordance with the principle of respect for autonomy, medical clinicians are generally expected to operate under a moral and legal obligation to respect patients' wishes concerning the forms of treatment they are to be subjected to.

However, in both practice and in principle, respect for patient autonomy does not require that clinicians' unconditionally accept whatever decision a patient arrives at. Evaluating the legitimacy of patients' actual decisions is subject to certain, well-established conditions and limitations. It is precisely at this point that the whole question of patients' cultural beliefs, values, and practices becomes especially problematic. The principle of patient autonomy must obviously allow for the possibility of patients' challenging and rejecting clinical advice. If the principle is to be adequately respected then this must extend to allow for the possibility of patients' refusal to consent to life-saving treatment. However, the principle itself does not require clinicians' to accept and respect every decision made by each and every patient. On the contrary, the autonomy principle clearly only requires that patients' autonomous decisions be accepted. Determining when a patient is acting autonomously is therefore crucial in clinical practice. Conventionally, the key tests for determining patient autonomy focus upon whether the patient possesses the capacity for autonomous deliberation and whether the patient was free from undue external coercion or manipulation in her deliberations. When combined, these two conditions provide medical clinicians with a criterion or standard against which to judge whether patients' decisions should be respected. In so doing, they also provide a means for deliberating upon patients' appeal to their cultural and religious standards as the principal justificatory ground for the refusal to consent to treatment.

In respect of patients' capacity for the exercise of autonomy, the conventional test applied by medical clinicians is the so-called 'mental competence test' [16] This test might be thought of as concerned with the functional character of the capacity for autonomous decision-making. Typically, the test has been applied in such a manner as to enable clinicians to identify those categories of patients who are deemed to be either permanently or temporarily incapable of exercising autonomous choice, such as, for example, children, the mentally ill, or those suffering from dementia. These categories of patients are deemed incapable of functioning as autonomous agents. Little, if any, concern is paid to the importance of the actual substance of these patients' beliefs or attitudes. Once classified as incompetent in this respect, clinicians may proceed to administer treatment without requiring the consent of patients themselves. Clearly seeking to apply such a test to patients refusing to consent to treatment on the grounds of their cultural and religious beliefs would be wholly illegitimate. Such a move would, if nothing else, severely restrict patients' general rights to freedom of expression and religious affiliation. The mental competence test does not allow for a sufficient scrutiny of the conditions under which patients' take such decisions in this respect.

Before clinicians are capable of determining the extent of patients' ability to exercise autonomy they must still provide an answer to the question of whether the patient was free from external interference or coercion in exercising their decision. Addressing this issue sheds some very interesting light on the clinical application of the autonomy principle. In contrast to the first condition, a satisfactory answer to this question will entail a consideration of the substance of the grounds and substantive reasons cited by patients' in arriving at their decisions. It must be said that there is widespread reluctance to include any such considerations in determining the extent to which a person can be said to be acting in a genuinely autonomous manner. Our liberal culture has been founded upon the concept of the sovereignty of the individual. The legal, political, and economic systems in liberal societies largely proceed on the assumption of individual autonomy, on the belief that individuals' may be generally considered to be autonomous. Thus, proposed legal restrictions on individual liberty must typically demonstrate that such restrictions are primarily required to ensure the equal opportunities of all to possess and exercise personal autonomy. So long as what we wish to do does not pose a potential harm to others, where the harm suffered principally consists of some diminuation of others liberty, then the political and juridical systems of a liberal society must refrain from seeking to impose any constraints upon one's actions. However, such a presumption of autonomy can only legitimately be applied to those agents who were in a position to act autonomously when they reached the decision they did. A general means, or procedure, for determining this must include some consideration of the specific reasons individuals appeal to in accounting for their decision or action. The justification for this should not be difficult to discern. On close inspection, the very nature of some cultural and religious beliefs appear to be thoroughly incompatible with the principle of personal autonomy in so far as they demand not so much the individual's critical deliberation, as her unquestioning obedience. Such cultural beliefs simply exclude the possibility of an individual legitimately acting in any other way than that prescribed by the fundamental tenets of her culture on pain of alienation, or exclusion from the cultural or religious community. Thus, one can identify a category of cultural and religious beliefs which aim to exclude the very possibility of autonomous deliberation. Patients' are heteronomously complying with the demands of their cultural or religious community in refusing to endorse the clinician's advice. This is not an autonomous act. No matter how mentally competent the patient may be, her capacity for exercising autonomy has been severely restricted by her desire to comply with the demands of her cultural or religious community. In cases where such beliefs exclude the legitimacy of reaching any other decision than that which has been culturally prescribed, one must conclude that the patient is acting under duress and is subject to significant externally coercive forces. Under these circumstances, a principal condition for the autonomy principle has not been satisfied. Respecting a patient's decision in such circumstances could not be defended by appeal to the autonomy principle.

I suspect that this line of argument may be troubling to many. If nothing else, it appears to move clinicians from a rock to a hard place. As it stands clinicians are under no legal obligation to unconditionally respect the cultural and religious beliefs and background of their patients. However, clinicians are under a legal obligation to seek and gain patients' (or their legal representatives') informed consent to proposed medical treatment. This legal obligation is morally grounded in the principle of respect for personal autonomy and the satisfactory realisation of this principle must allow for the possibility of clinicians respecting patients' refusal to consent to treatment. However, clinicians are not unconditionally bound to respect patients' decisions. The crucial test is whether these patients' can be said to have been acting autonomously. This necessarily requires some consideration of the substantive reasons determining patients' decisions. Within increasingly culturally and religiously diverse societies, it is inevitable that clinicians will be exposed to a far broader range of such reasons than was previously the case. On the face of it, a recognition of the constitutive importance of culture and religion in forming individual identity requires, at the very least, that clinicians pay due consideration to how such conditions affect patients' understandings of their own ailments. It does not, though, require clinicians to simply accept as autonomous any decision based upon an appeal to the fundamental tenets of patients' religion or culture. The autonomy principle requires clinicians to accept only those decisions based upon reasons which themselves do not exclude the legitimacy of autonomous deliberation. While it will entail clinicians appearing to pass judgement upon others' religious and cultural beliefs in some cases, the autonomy principle cannot be extended to apply to those cases where patients' decisions are determined by conditions that are themselves prohibitive of the exercise of autonomy. The ethics of multiculturalism were clearly not intended to provide justification for a succession of medically preventable deaths. Avoiding this will, however, entail clinicians resorting to an appeal to a paternalist ethic which necessarily places distinct limits upon the extent to which culture and religion may be assimilated within considerations of biomedical treatment.

5.   Conclusion

The principle of respect for patient autonomy extends a liberal ethical principle to the provision of health care and the treatment of sick and vulnerable people. In certain circumstances, medical clinicians are under a duty to respect the wishes of their patients, even where respecting these wishes will result in the occurrence of medically avoidable deaths. In such circumstances, respecting the ethical principle of personal autonomy appears to be entirely incompatible with the purpose, or telos, of medical treatment. This is a difficult area, fraught with many potential ethical dilemmas. The phenomenon of multiculturalism serves to potentially complicate matters still further. Clinicians will be confronted with a vast array of significantly diverse cultural and religious beliefs, some of which may be utterly incompatible with the ethos and practice of biomedicine. Multiculturalism generally calls for public authorities to respect such beliefs and attempts to encourage a climate in which individuals feel free and able to express their cultural and religious affiliations without fear of censure. Patients' expression of their religious and cultural beliefs is bound to come into conflict with clinicians views on optimal treatment outcomes. In such circumstances, what is required is a determination of whether patients' deliberations were genuinely autonomous, or whether the need to comply with the fundamental strictures of culture or religion effectively prohibited the exercise of autonomy. In these circumstances, medical clinicians may be unable to avoid the role of moral guardian, in having to adopt what many may consider an ostensibly illiberal stance towards those religious and cultural communities for whom there are worse things than dying. In their defence, medical clinicians will need to appeal not so much to the teleological principles of biomedicine, but the non-clinical, ethical principle of personal autonomy.

Bibliography

Barry, Brian. *Culture and Equality* New York: Oxford University Press, 2000

Beauchamp, Tom L. & Childress, John F. *Principles of Biomedical Ethics,* (4th. Edition), New York: Oxford University Press, 1994

Berlin, Isaiah. *Four Essays on Liberty,* Oxford: Oxford University Press, 1969

Charlesworth, Max. *Bioethics in a Liberal Society*, Cambridge: Cambridge University Press, 1993

Dworkin, Gerald. 'The concept of autonomy', in John Christman (ed.) *The Inner Citadel: Essays on Individual Autonomy*, New York: Oxford University Press, 1989

Goldberg, David T. (ed.), *Multiculturalism; a Critical Reader,* Oxford: Blackwell, 1994

Helman, C.G. *Culture, Health, and Illness,* 4th. Edition, Oxford: Heinemann-Butterworth, 2000

Lindley, Robert. *Autonomy,* Basingstoke: Macmillan, 1986

Mill, John S.*On Liberty and other Essays,* Oxford: Oxford University Press, 1991

Ohnuki-Tierney, C. 'Brain Death and Organ Transplantation: Cultural Bases of Medical Technology.', Current Anthropology, 35, 3 (June 1994)

Raz, Joseph. *Morality of Freedom,* Oxford: Clarendon, 1986

Raz, Joseph. Ethics in the Public Domain: Essays on the Morality of Law and Politics, Oxford: Oxford University Press, 1994

Taylor, Charles. *Multiculturalism and "The Politics of Recognition": an Essay,* Princeton, N.J.: Princeton University Press, 1992

Taylor, Charles. *Philosophy and the Human Sciences (Philosophical Papers, Vol. 2),* Cambridge: Cambridge University Press, 1985

Notes

[1] See Brian Barry, *Culture and Equality* (New York: Oxford University Press, 2000) & David T.Goldberg (ed.) *Multiculturalism: a Critical Reader* (Oxford: Blackwell, 1994).

[2] See, Max Charlesworth, *Bioethics in a Liberal Society*, (Cambridge: Cambridge University Press, 1993)

[3] C. Helman *Culture, Health and Illness* (4th. Edition) (Oxford: Heinemann-Butterworth, 2000)

[4] See Ohnuki-Tierney 1994

[5] For a philosophical introduction to the concept of personal autonomy see R.Lindley, *Autonomy*, (Basingstoke: Macmillan, 1986). See also Gerald Dworkin's, 'The Concept of Autonomy', in J.Christman (ed.) *The Inner Citadel: Essays on Individual Autonomy* (New York: Oxford University Press, 1989). In bioethical literature the convention is to cite John Stuart Mill's *On Liberty and Other Essays* (Oxford: Oxford University Press, 1991) as the classic statement on personal autonomy as individual liberty.

[6] Mill, *On Liberty*

[7] The terms 'negative liberty' and 'positive liberty' are associated with Isaiah Berlin and his 'Two Concepts of Liberty' in his *Four Essays on Liberty* (Oxford: Oxford University Press, 1969)

[8] Joseph Raz's *Morality of Freedom* (Oxford: Clarendon Press, 1986) is one of the best examples of this literature.

[9] Raz, *Morality of Freedom* and *Ethics in the Public Domain: Essays on the Morality of Law and Politics* (Oxford: Oxford University Press, 1994). Charles Taylor *Multiculturalism and "the Politics of Recognition": an Essay* (Princeton, N.J.: Princeton University Press, 1992)

[10] Taylor, *Philosophy and the Human Sciences (Philosophical Papers, Vol2.)* (Cambridge: Cambridge University Press, 1985) p.79

[11] Raz, *Morality of Freedom*

[12] Taylor *Philosophy and the Human Sciences,* 74

[13] Raz *Ethics in the Public Domain,* 159

[14] Tom Beauchamp & John Childress *Principles of Biomedical Ethics* (4th. Edition) (New York: Oxford University Press, 1994) 260

[15] Helman *Culture, Health and Illness,* 260

[16] See Beauchamp and Childress, *Principles of Biomedical Ethics*

The "Euthanasia Underground" and its Implications for the Harm Minimization Debate: an Australian Perspective

*Roger S Magnusson**

"I thought an overdose of an anti-depressant would be best, so in the notes I wrote that [my patient] was depressed and I gave him a prescription of [amitriptyline] – enough to do the job" (Gary, general practitioner).

Gary is one of many doctors and nurses who are involved in assisted suicide and euthanasia in Australia today. In terms of frequency, Gary's career is fairly unremarkable. He gave me six detailed descriptions of his involvement, although that was years ago and I know that he has been involved since then. Others I spoke to claimed to have been involved 40-60 times.

"I'm not [a] hit-man", he said, as we sat talking during his lunchtime in a small, windowless treatment room in a busy, inner-city surgery. "Once I've got the needle in their arm, they can change their mind at any time, till they're unconscious. I always give them ample opportunity to take it out, but every single one who's got so far as to set a date [has gone through with it]". "The Medical Board would probably not take a great view of the fact that I've killed quite a few patients", says Gary, "but they're all frumps, and they're not operating in the real world".

The "euthanasia underground" is the underbelly of nursing and medicine – a dimension of health care work that professional medical bodies choose to ignore. At the empirical level, its existence is undeniable. There is a substantial body of literature quantifying levels of involvement in the practice of covert, physician-assisted suicide (PAS) and active voluntary euthanasia (AVE) in the United States,[1] Britain,[2] Australia,[3] and other countries. Despite this, remarkably little is known about the social context of these practices.

This chapter draws briefly on my study of covert ("underground") physician-assisted suicide and euthanasia as practiced by health care workers specializing in HIV/AIDS care in Sydney, Melbourne and San Francisco, and published in *Angels of Death: Exploring the Euthanasia Underground* (2002), and other papers.[4] Drawing on detailed, first-person accounts of involvement, I will illustrate how the ideals of "medical professionalism" frequently become corrupted in the euthanasia underground.

The practice of covert euthanasia raises difficult policy challenges. The criminal law neither effectively inhibits the practice of euthanasia, nor adequately protects the vulnerable patients who most desire it. This chapter aims to give a sense of the practices involved, and to illustrate the relevance of "underground" PAS/AVE to the debate about harm minimisation and the legalisation of euthanasia. The debate about legalisation usually polarises advocates and opponents of PAS/AVE, with neither side giving an adequate account of the balancing exercise that is called for. At the same time, political factors make legalisation and statutory regulation of PAS/AVE an unlikely prospect in many jurisdictions. The chapter concludes by arguing that, regardless of whether it is ever legalised, covert PAS/AVE presents a moral challenge to the professional medical bodies to confront this divisive issue and to seek to educate and influence the practices of their constituencies in a way that better protects vulnerable patients.

1.   Survey Evidence of "Underground" Euthanasia

With the exception of Oregon, [5] the Netherlands and Belgium,[6] the overwhelming response of western countries towards assisted death is one of prohibition, backed up by criminal penalties. Despite this, surveys suggest that PAS/AVE occurs to a significant degree, informally and without safeguards. A national survey of 1902 American physicists found that 3.3% had written at least one "lethal prescription", while 4.7% had provided at least one lethal injection.[7] A survey of American oncologists found that 3.7% had performed euthanasia, while 10.8% had assisted suicide.[8] In a random sample of American physicians, 44.5% favoured the legalisation of physician-assisted suicide (PAS), although 33.9% were opposed.[9]

Similar themes are evident in Australia. In one survey of 1268 doctors in New South Wales and the Australian Capital Territory, 46% of respondents reported that they had been asked by a patient to hasten his or her death. Twenty-eight per cent (12.3% of all respondents) had complied with that request. Fifty-nine per cent agreed in principle that AVE is sometimes right, and 58% believed the law should change.[10] In a more recent survey of Australian general surgeons, 5.3% reported administering a bolus lethal injection, while 36.2% reported giving an overdose of drugs with the intention of hastening death; more than half (or 20.4% of respondents), did so without a clear patient request).[11]

There is evidence that levels of involvement in PAS/AVE may be higher within HIV/AIDS medicine. In one Dutch study, the rate of

PAS/AVE in men with AIDS was found to be 12 times the national euthanasia rate of 2.1%.[12] In 1997, Slome et al. reported that 52% of respondents drawn from a network of San Francisco HIV/AIDS specialists had assisted a patient to suicide by prescribing a lethal overdose.[13] Similarly, in a survey of members of the Australasian Society for HIV Medicine, one in five doctors had assisted an HIV patient to die.[14]

2.   Researching Covert, Illicit Euthanasia: My Methodology
The methodology for my study has been reported in more detail elsewhere.[15] I conducted 49 interviews with doctors, nurses, therapists, community workers and one funeral director.   All specialised in HIV/AIDS health care or worked closely with the HIV community in Sydney, Melbourne or San Francisco.   Prior to interview, each person chose a pseudonym and no "master list" of the identity of interviewees was retained. Each interview was taped and transcribed. The study was approved and monitored by the Human Research Ethics Committee of the University of Melbourne.   Details of each respondent's "PAS/AVE credentials" emerged during interview and were confirmed through specific accounts of involvement, through discussion of the various interventions respondents had taken (from a spectrum of practices facilitating the organisation and delivery of PAS/AVE), and through estimates of the number of times each interviewee had been involved.[16] Post-interview, respondents were asked to complete a substantial questionnaire that collected demographic information and facilitated the verification of claims and estimates of PAS/AVE involvement made during interview. *Table 1* gives an overview of the nature and extent of involvement of the "top dozen" interviewees.

Thirty-seven of the 49 interviewees reported participating in specific episodes of PAS/AVE. Their testimony also provided evidence of the collaborative dimensions of euthanasia, drawing on the overlapping friendships and professional connections that have grown up around involvement in the gay community and in HIV medicine. Collaboration was evident at all stages of the euthanasia process. Health care workers cooperate with each other in referring patients to activist doctors for "assessment", in writing lethal prescriptions, charting lethal infusions, in accessing veins and administering lethal injections or infusions at the bedside, in concealing suspicious evidence and disposing of the body, signing death certificates and counter-signing cremation forms, and in de-briefing and counselling after the event. Collaborative euthanasia was evident both in community settings (among general practitioners and community nurses), and in institutional settings (hospital wards and hospices).

3.   **What is the "Euthanasia Underground" Really Like?**
On many – perhaps most – occasions, death comes peacefully.
Joseph, an eminent physician, was asked by his hairdresser to prescribe a
lethal dose of drugs to assist the death of the hairdresser's lover, who was
dying from AIDS.   Joseph had heard about the man's deterioration
second-hand, during haircuts, but Joseph had never met him.   Joseph
admits, "there was no assessment involved whatsoever". He recalls:

I wrote a prescription to a patient who I had never seen and I sent it to him
in the mail. I heard that next time I went in to get my hair cut that it was
the most beautiful experience that my stylist had ever had.   It was [St]
Valentine's Day and they had a lovely meal with champagne…and they
held each other and then his partner took his pills and was released.

Not all deaths end as sweetly as this. My interview with Gordon,
an experienced doctor, provides one illustration. Gordon was called in to
"remedy" a botched suicide attempt. Gordon had been treating Stephen –
a young man of 26, who had some AIDS-defining conditions – for a
period of six weeks. Stephen was estranged from his family, who had
rejected him because he was gay.   Gordon tried to assist in a
rapprochement, and to monitor Stephen's pain. At one point Gordon
arranged for Stephen to go into a hospice, which gave Stephen's 22-year
old partner a break. "He just decided that he wanted to die", said Gordon.
"He'd had enough…he was *over it*".
        "He had dreadful self-esteem and…was a very anxious, obsessive
person", said Gordon. "I actually felt that he had an immense amount of
guilt". He'd grown up being called "fag" and "poof", and his family was
from a non-English speaking background. "Stephen was…an absolute
misery guts. I think he'd never had a joyful experience in his life. He
might have occasionally [smiled] at 2 o'clock in the morning under
amphetamines on the dance floor, but he was terribly, terribly miserable".
        Gordon pointed out to me that Stephen's friends were supportive
of his decision to suicide. They said, "yes, you've got this right". Gordon
felt as if the friends were "conspiring" in the decision – "everyone in that
social circle agreed yes, this was the right thing to do, and he followed that
decision". "His self-esteem was so poor", said Gordon, "I think he wanted
to make other people happy".
        Stephen's 22-year old partner did a bit of doctor shopping and
managed to obtain three prescriptions of Tryptanol, an anti-depressant.
He told the doctors "I just need a repeat of this; I'm depressed and my
partner's dying of AIDS". Gordon had also stockpiled morphine tablets
obtained from the hospice.

On the night in question, Stephen invited his friends to dinner. (A final meal, a pre-death wake was a recurrent phenomenon in interviews. Interviewees described final meals of oysters and champagne, and even Kentucky Fried. The bedside role of one interviewee, a former priest, regularly extended to creating pre-death rituals).[17] Stephen took a combination of Tryptanol, MS-Contin (a slow release morphine), a barbiturate called Soneryl (once used for epilepsy), together with an anti-emetic.

"I got this phone call about one or two in the morning", recalls Gordon. "I remember having this shocking flu at the time…[and when I arrived] here were [Stephen's] nursing friends all expecting him to die. Stephen was in a deep coma, his pupils were very dilated, and he was Cheyn-Stokes breathing.

Between 2am and 6am, Gordon injected Stephen with all the morphine he had brought with him in his doctor's bag, together with an anti-emetic, Seranace. "I gave him everything from my doctor's bag, *and he still breathed*", Gordon recalls.

"When I got there I realised 'well, he's not going to survive this; he's going to be dead anyway – I might as well speed it along'…I think also *because it was 4 o'clock in the morning, I had a cold and I felt dreadful and I just wanted to get out of there*…and I knew that if I didn't do something that they would find some other way to do it and I was really concerned that…he didn't suffer".

Around 6 o'clock in the morning, while Gordon was in the lounge room, one of Stephen's friends went into the bedroom. Gordon says, "I'm not sure to this day but I'm almost certain that the nurse did a 'pillow job'…I think it was asphyxiation with a pillow". Gordon certified Stephen's death. A funeral director who had been "booked" in advance of the death arrived, and Stephen was cremated.

During this interview, Gordon complained of feeling "cajoled", "assaulted" and "abused" by Stephen's friends to assist in the death. At the same time, Gordon felt that Stephen had also been "cajoled into it", as a result of his poor self-esteem, and years of homophobic abuse. He went on to say that "so many gay men are just utterly miserable and this is one of the reasons I believe that there's such a high suicide attempt".

How do we make sense of this story? Called out in the middle of a winter's night, suffering from flu and anxious to get home, a doctor pumps a comatose patient full of drugs in order to fulfil friends' expectations, all the while conceding that the patient had serious, unresolved emotional problems.

4.   "Anti-Professionalism" and Underground Euthanasia
Gordon's account is *not* an especially shocking one, when compared to the many other accounts given by interviewees. But it does illustrate an important theme: that the euthanasia underground is characterised by the very opposite of those features we usually associate with the concept of "medical professionalism".

A "profession" is a self-regulating organisation, characterised by specialised training leading to unique skills, accountability, and a tradition of disinterested service:

In the euthanasia underground, however, there is no specialised training, and hence no unique skills. Participants remain ignorant about what is needed to achieve a gentle death. "Botched attempts" are common.

Accountability is also absent. The medical profession for the most part turns a blind eye to the practice of illicit euthanasia by its members. Participation is shrouded in secrecy and deception.

In the absence of a professional framework, there are few established norms or principles to guide involvement in PAS/AVE. Participation is triggered by highly idiosyncratic factors, with evidence of casual and precipitative involvements.

In place of a tradition of disinterested service to patients, there is evidence of a complete lack of professional distance, conflicts of interest, and examples of euthanasia without consent.

Below, I give some typical examples drawn from the interviews to substantiate my claims about the "anti-professionalism" of underground euthanasia.[18]

Firstly, because euthanasia is unlawful, it must be practiced in secret. Each participant must re-invent the wheel. "Botched attempts" are common. Desperate doctors end up suffocating and strangling their patients in a desperate attempt to "finish the job". Of the 88 first-hand accounts that interviewees gave as illustrations of their involvement, 17 (19%) involved "botches". The real percentage is probably much higher, since many of my interviewees were experienced participants who had perfected their drug strategies and success ratios. "It was horrible", said one doctor. "It took four or five hours. It was like Rasputin, we just couldn't finish him off". "I tried insulin, I tried just about everything else that I [had] around and it just took forever…[It was] very hard for his lover. So I um sort of shooed the lover out of the room at one stage and put a pillow over his head, that seemed to work in the end [laughs, nervously]…That was one of the worst [clearing throat] one of the most horrible things I've ever done".[19] Suffocations following failed PAS/AVE attempts were referred to euphemistically as "pillow jobs" by several interviewees.

The degradation involved is disturbing. Stanley, a therapist, told of a case where a patient self-administered 15 Seconal tablets (Seconal is a barbiturate). But he failed to take an anti-emetic and threw up the whole mixture. Desperate, the patient succeeded on the second attempt, after he ate his own vomit.

Secondly, accountability – another characteristic of medical professionalism – is also absent in the euthanasia underground. The euthanasia underground reflects an all-permeating culture of deception that eliminates any possibility of accountability. Deceit begins with the methods used to procure drugs; it permeates the planning and orchestration of the death itself, and extends to the disposal of the body and associated paperwork. It permeates and distorts discussions between medical colleagues.

In many cases, the euthanatic strategy involves massive overdoses of analgesics, sedatives, and anti-depressants – drugs that have a therapeutic purpose, and which the patient is already taking. Building a plausible (if fabricated) basis for prescribing or administering massive doses is an important means of self-protection. As Gary says, "I thought an overdose of an anti-depressant would be best, so in the notes I wrote that he was depressed and I gave him a prescription of [amitryptyline] – enough to do the job". My interview with Merril, a physician, provides another example:

RM   [But] what if, for example, the patient isn't in chronic pain and so Demoral [a barbiturate] is not really medically indicated?

Merril ...probably in that instance *I would develop some chronic pain* [very quiet]

RM   ...[so] you're hoping to fudge the system to some extent?

Merril To protect me and the patients.

Several interviewees admitted to the outright theft of drugs. Others – particularly in hospital – hoarded the excess morphine left in the vials after the charted dose had been given.

Where the "euthaniser" holds a senior position, lethal doses may simply be charted and administered by nurses upon doctors' orders. In one case, a patient who had bungled a suicide attempt was admitted directly into the care of "experienced" palliative care nurses, who helped to complete the attempt.

At the level of language – the intention to kill frequently masquerades as routine palliation. Language is often deliberately ambiguous, reflecting the apprehension and mixed feelings of participants. Erin, a nurse, gave a nice illustration of this. Erin was approached by a physician who was aware of his involvement in a previous case. The physician told Erin: "Use as much morphine as you need. I'll sign for it".

Erin was surprised. "Do you know what I mean?" said the physician.

"I'm not sure", said Erin. "Do you want me to make [the patient] comfortable, or do you want me to make him *ultimately* comfortable".

"Yes", replied the physician, ambiguously.

The patient died that night.

In another hospital ward, Liz, a nurse, detailed a more explicit culture of euthanasia. The focus of Liz's interview – which took place in the quiet corner of a department store coffee shop – was a detailed and confessional allegation of involuntary euthanasia. During our conversation, however, Liz explained how the unit where she worked would "book in" patients to receive a lethal infusion of drugs. Nurses would be told that "the cocktail is going up" and no attempt was made to hide its significance.

On one occasion, Liz told of an old man with no family who was quickly going downhill. "He wouldn't have his infusion for about three days", said Liz. "He watched telly, and ate and went outside and smoked, and sat in the garden and did all those sort of things, and then one morning he just said 'today is the day'". Liz herself was involved in administering this particular infusion.

While euthanasia is sometimes explicit, in many cases, those involved prefer to hide their involvement by absenting themselves before the point of death. Paula, a GP, told of how she drew up a lethal quantity of potassium chloride obtained from a doctor colleague, and gave it to the patient and his partner. She then walked around the suburb for an hour, waiting for the call on her mobile phone. After the death, she returned to the patient's home to fill out the death certificate.

Lying on the death certificate and cremation forms is a regular part of post-euthanasia practice. As one GP said:

RM   You signed the death certificate?
Josh   Yes
RM   What did you put…as the cause of death?
Josh   Well I certainly didn't put "Lethabarb" [a veterinary drug] as the cause of death [laughter]. I am forced to lie. I said that [the patient] died of AIDS and disseminated Kaposi's

Sarcoma...The cremation certificate also [asks] questions like 'Do you know [if] there could have been any foul play? Could this death have resulted from poisoning?' and I have to lie there...I mean, you've got to protect yourself.

I conducted one, very detailed interview with a funeral director, John, who stood at the centre of a series of activist doctors and nurses in one city. He was the undertaker of choice for AIDS-related death. The transcript of our conversation reveals:

RM   [Are there many community nurses that you know of who are open to assisted suicide?]
John   Three or four, which is enough to help [the client] along.
RM   And how many doctors?
John   I [can] probably think of ten.
RM   So you would say that there's an informal network?
John   Yeah, I would certainly say that; in fact, at one stage the group was given the nickname "Angels of Death"
RM   Angels of Death?
John   Yes [laughs]...[An] informal network of people who...co-operate and help, facilitate [euthanasia] under the right circumstances.

John went on to detail how sometimes he would bump into doctors socially who would remark, casually, "I probably need you on Friday night; hope you're not doing anything". "You just know", he added, "nothing more needs to be said". John estimated that assisted death accounts for no more than 10% of his client base, or about 15 to 20 deaths a year.

Cremation is the favoured way of disposing of the body. Peter, a nurse, describes the "window period" between death and cremation in the following terms:

After death, prior to cremation, anyone can ask the question and the Coroner can intervene [to] test the body...for drugs, and then find out that they were killed, and then there's questions asked, and then you can be charged...*You sit in sweat waiting for cremation to occur*...All of the people you speak to, if they're being honest, will say the same thing, *we're all waiting for the smoke to go up in the crematorium.*

In some jurisdictions, when a body is to be cremated, a second doctor must counter-sign the certificate to confirm that there are no suspicious circumstances. John noted that trusted doctors from the "network" would frequently counter-sign the cremation certificate, without viewing the body, and with no questions asked.

As these examples illustrate, deception is central to illicit euthanasia. Deceptive practices contribute to the *invisibility* of euthanasia, and help to perpetuate the myth that because euthanasia is prohibited, it never occurs.

A third feature of medical professionalism is that there are established norms, principles and procedures to guide clinical interventions. In the euthanasia underground, however, there are no requirements for second opinions from psychiatrists or palliative care specialists. Participation in assisted death is triggered by gut instinct. There is also evidence of casual and precipitative involvements.

Gary, a general practitioner, detailed how he gave a lethal injection to a patient he had only met the same day. He had a chat to a hospital physician who had been involved in the patient's care who "seemed to think that death would be a nice thing". It later emerged from a community nurse I interviewed, who was involved in the same incident, that the patient had only told his parents a week before that he was HIV positive. Even those closest to the patient were concerned about depression. Another GP gave me a detailed account of a case in which the patient had brought his death forward a week, so as to fit in with the GP's scheduled holidays.

There were several examples of euthanasia upon patients with HIV, but not AIDS – surely a disturbing finding, given the success of protease inhibitors and other therapies. One interviewee justified her actions by telling me her patient was "emotionally, spiritually and psychologically terminal – he was in a state from which no recovery was possible".

Some interviewees had thought about how euthanasia *should* be regulated, and several suggested the safeguards they thought should be followed:

> I think that the death certificate should say euthanasia or assisted suicide. I think it should be reported to the Coroner. I think that there needs to be further consultation with at least two doctors. (Gordon, GP)

> I see that the Dutch system probably works – I don't know a lot about it – but I think there [should] be two medical opinions, I would

actually go so far as saying that...it's worth getting a psychiatric review...[to] eliminate depression as a major influence. (Josh, GP)

Perhaps unsurprisingly, these doctors failed to follow their own advice. Gordon, as described previously, had tried to "finish off" a patient without consulting any other doctor, in circumstances where he felt pressured by the patient's friends. Josh had performed euthanasia without obtaining a psychiatric opinion, using drugs sourced from a vet who was "on side".

A fourth indication of "anti-professionalism" within the euthanasia underground is the fact that, in place of a tradition of disinterested service to patients, there is evidence of a complete lack of professional distance, conflicts of interest, and even non-consensual and involuntary euthanasia. In nearly a third of the 88 detailed accounts of involvement that interviewees described, they were involved in a personal capacity, with friends, as distinct from in a professional capacity, with patients. Involvement brings its stresses and risks of burnout. Peter, a community nurse, described the stress and sadness of strangulation and suffocation. He says:

Peter   You've got to resort to some other form of, you know, bringing death on, and...it's very very hard to do.
RM   Such as?
Peter   Strangulation, or suffocation.
RM   which must be extremely stressful to you?
Peter   ...I don't think you ever get rid of it. There may be people you've spoken to who will comfortably say [that they are] all-together about it. I know them in a different light, and I know that they all carry lots of sadness and lots of stuff inside them about what's happened.

In one, troubling case, Liz, a hospital nurse, described a case where the doctor in her hospital unit sent the mother of a patient (who apparently had AIDS dementia) home to have a shower. "Once mum had left the ward", said Liz, the physician charted an infusion of midazolam, morphine and Tegratol "designed to kill" the patient. According to Liz, the doctor's words were "get it up, and get him out of here by sundown".

Feeding the patient breakfast earlier that morning, Liz recalled that he had said "Hey, do they know what's wrong? When am I going home?"

"It was obvious to me that [the patient] wanted to go home", said Liz. "He wanted us to make him better, he didn't want to die..."

Liz made it clear that euthanasia had occurred in her unit on other occasions, but always with the patient's consent. On this occasion, the lethal infusion was drawn up by Liz and another nurse. The patient had "two or three" infusions running already, so [the family] didn't really notice that another bag was there. The patient died nine hours later, and his bed was vacant the next day.

5.   Responding to the Harms of Underground Euthanasia

The "anti-professionalism" of underground euthanasia raises difficult policy challenges. The criminal law's blunt prohibition of all intentional killing makes it unable to effectively regulate PAS/AVE when it nevertheless occurs within a medical context. On the other hand, if evidence of HIV/AIDS-related assisted death in Sydney, Melbourne and San Francisco is any guide, these practices cannot safely be left to the discretion of health care workers themselves. How, then, should the law respond, if it aims to protect patients from the harms of "anti-professionalism"? In terms of policy choices, there would seem to be three major alternatives to the status quo:

To protect patients by trying to eliminate underground euthanasia.

To legalise, and thereby seek to "re-regulate" euthanasia.

To educate and influence those involved in covert, illicit euthanasia.

A. First Option: "Prosecute the Offenders"

The first option is to "prosecute the offenders" in the hopes of wiping out underground practices. To moral conservatives, evidence of the "anti-professionalism" associated with covert euthanasia confirms the importance of keeping euthanasia illegal, because it illustrates the true horror of delivering the power of life and death into the hands of doctors. On the other hand, opposing legalisation, rather than attempting to stamp out illicit PAS/AVE, is likely to remain the priority for moral conservatives.

It seems clear that any genuine attempt to suppress the covert practice of PAS/AVE would require a massive commitment to *policing clinical functions*. Increasing levels of surveillance over drug prescribing and administration practices, however, would almost certainly have an adverse impact on those in pain and those who were dying. The most common "euthanasia recipes" consist of overdoses of relatively accessible, therapeutic drugs. A more aggressive policing of analgesics, sedatives and anti-depressants would have a disastrous impact on pain relief and symptom management. The resulting climate of "defensive medicine" could seriously undermine palliative care efforts.

Doctors are also likely to be hostile towards any policy that involved closer scrutiny of their clinical functions. There is a powerful argument that the medical profession is wary of legalising euthanasia precisely because "legislation to provide legal legitimacy for forms of euthanasia that are already occurring shifts the locus of control from the private to the public realm, or from health professionals to the State".[20] If seriously advocated by moral conservatives, a policy of surveillance and prosecution would also weaken the alliance between the conservative churches and representative medical organisations that remains, at least in countries like Australia, a significant impediment to euthanasia law reform. For their part, professional medical organisations are likely to ignore or play down evidence of underground euthanasia out of self-interest, or because PAS/AVE is a divisive issue that can bring few political rewards. The conservative churches and moral conservatives are likely to ignore or dismiss evidence of covert euthanasia because it undermines a key assumption of "slippery slope" theorising: that *if* euthanasia is legalised, the killing will start and this will lead to the *creation* of a vulnerable class of patients.

In real terms, a policy of prosecuting the offenders would almost certainly fail. Interview evidence suggests that covert euthanasia is well hidden, and that (show trials aside) there is no realistic chance of purging the health professions of those who participate in assisted death. Australia, like other countries, has a healthy tradition of dissident doctors admitting in the media to having performed euthanasia, with few legal consequences.[21] While participation in PAS/AVE is not without its risks, one has only to remember the lengths that Jack Kevorkian went to in order to become a martyr for the cause![22]

The fact that a punitive response to underground euthanasia is likely to fail does not mean that a policy of prohibiting PAS/AVE is not the best available option. What must be recognised, however, is that a policy of doing nothing, or relying on the criminal law's ineffective prohibition of PAS/AVE to combat covert practices, carries very real costs for patients. This point is rarely acknowledged by euthanasia critics, who emphasise the symbolic, protecting functions of prohibiting PAS/AVE and confidently assert that "the potential for abuse is increased even more when euthanasia is legal".[23] In reality, both advocates and opponents may over-emphasise the capacity for law to regulate a space that is inevitably personal, discretionary, and infused with emotion and personal values. If we are to debate policy from a perspective of wanting to protect vulnerable patients, however, we must balance the detriments, as well as the benefits, of the status quo – including the clandestine practice of PAS/AVE – against the benefits and detriments of the most obvious alternative: legalisation.

B. Second Option: Legalising and "Re-regulating" Euthanasia

Advocates for the legalisation of euthanasia argue that a statutory PAS/AVE regime creates an opportunity for law to re-regulate euthanasia and to protect vulnerable patients by incorporating safeguards into the law. Opponents of legalisation assert that statutory safeguards would fail to adequately "screen out" vulnerable patients, that doctors would in any event ignore the statutory process and its safeguards, and that a legal precedent for euthanasia would result in a "slippery slope" towards involuntary euthanasia and other forms of killing. These criticisms can be summarised in the following claims: that legalisation will fail to reduce underground PAS/AVE, that it will fail to ensure that "above ground" assessments are safe, and that it will generate more unsafe killing, both above and below ground.

These assertions call for evidence. My aim in this chapter, however, is not to review whether the available empirical evidence (such as it is) from places like Oregon or the Netherlands supports a policy of legalisation. Rather, I want to briefly explore what evidence of underground euthanasia contributes to the debate about harm minimisation, and to ask: what should a policy of legalisation be aiming for, in terms of what counts as policy "success"? Two points need to be emphasised.

Part of the confusion surrounding the legalisation debate arises from disagreement about what criteria should be used to judge the success of any statutory PAS/AVE regime. This disagreement, in turn, reflects the difference between arguments based on assessments of likely consequences, and arguments grounded in beliefs about the inherent rightness or wrongness of euthanasia. If a statutory euthanasia regime worked effectively, according to the safeguards embodied within it, people would use it and would die. Conceivably, a significant number of people would access PAS/AVE, depending on factors including their clinical condition, personal values, the effectiveness of the available palliative care, and the willingness of treating physicians to provide assistance in accordance with legislated procedures. On the one hand, any sudden rise in lawful euthanasia deaths, both initially and over time, might be seen as evidence that previously covert practices were gradually being "re-regulated" and driven above-ground (policy success). Advocates would argue that the policy was compassionate because those dying were dying better deaths. On the other hand, for those who see euthanasia as inherently wrong, any lawful killing would be grounds for concern, and for suspicion about the failure of safeguards (policy failure). For these opponents, the only good euthanasia law is one whose safeguards are so complex and bureaucratic that no patient could ever qualify for assistance. When euthanasia deaths become, for the first time, *visible*, the temptation for moral conservatives – particularly those who are unaware of (or who wish to ignore) the reality and the extent of covert practices – is to interpret anything other than minimal use of PAS/AVE statutes as evidence of a slippery slope.

The debate about what are appropriate safeguards for inclusion in any PAS/AVE statute is a legitimate and important one. This issue cannot ever be divorced from beliefs about when (if ever) killing is justified. Once those safeguards have been articulated, however, it is helpful to the debate about harm minimisation to keep separate any broader moral critique of the law from any narrower evaluation of whether the law is working successfully *as policy*, in achieving its own aims. The former will rarely be an empirical issue; the success of legalisation as a policy, however, is definitely an empirical issue, even if conclusive evidence is hard to obtain and harder to interpret.

The second point relates to the design of any euthanasia law, and its safeguards. One important aim of a policy of legalisation is to seek to make PAS/AVE safer by channelling previously unregulated and invisible practices into a statutory context. The "safer" the safeguards inserted into any statute (to protect the vulnerable, or to minimise the number killed), the harder it will be for a patient to access assistance under the statute, regardless of their circumstances. Furthermore, since the policy of prohibition has failed to prevent covert practices, any statutory euthanasia protocol must – if it is to improve on the current situation – attract the support and voluntary compliance of doctors. The risk is that a law that is too bureaucratic, too intrusive, and that gives insufficient protection to doctors acting in good faith will be ignored in practice and will thus have minimal impact on underground euthanasia. Making the law too "safe" may not be the best way to minimise the harm caused by the "anti-professionalism" of covert euthanasia. The challenge is to identify the middle ground, a dilemma made all the more controversial because of the feared consequences of "unsafe" law. For some, the difficulty of this challenge will be seen as a reason to give up, to embrace the familiar failure of prohibitionism. For those concerned about minimising harm, however, the debate must go on.

Opponents of legalisation point to the gap between the "ideal" safeguards embodied in any PAS/AVE law, and the reality of how they will be implemented within clinical practice. The New York State Task Force on Life and the Law warned, for example, that while "one can posit 'ideal' cases in which all the recommended safeguards would be satisfied....the reality of existing medical practice in doctors' offices and hospitals across the state generally cannot match these expectations, *however* any guidelines or safeguards might be framed".[24]

Contrary to the assumptions of some, no PAS/AVE law is ever likely to be perfectly safe. This is because the process of assessing patients and "operationalising" safeguards will always require *judgments* that are value-laden, difficult and uncertain. As Caplan and colleagues point out, the fact that concepts like "unbearable suffering", terminal illness, depression or competency have fuzzy edges does not mean that they provide no constraints on behaviour.[25] Judgments are called for, and the point of any statutory protocol is to ensure that these judgments are made carefully. Here, as elsewhere, hard cases do not necessarily make bad law. Furthermore, even partial compliance with statutory safeguards may represent an improvement on the kinds of clinical decisions that are occurring in a covert context. The more influence a statutory protocol has upon underground practices, the safer patients will be.

C. A Final Option: Influencing the Underground

One important contribution of medical sociology to the debate over euthanasia policy is to remind us that for all the debate about ethics and the illicit practice of PAS/AVE, euthanasia (like abortion) remains a political issue that will be resolved in political terms.[26]

In May 1995, in a brief but controversial experiment with euthanasia, the Northern Territory Parliament passed the *Rights of the Terminally Ill Act*. Between 1 July 1996 (when the Act took effect) and 25 March 1997 (when Australia's federal Parliament overrode the Territory legislation, drawing on its constitutional power to make laws for the territories), four patients died in accordance with the statutory protocol, assisted by euthanasia advocate Philip Nitschke.[27] All other attempts to introduce euthanasia statutes in Australian State and Territory Parliaments have so far failed.

It is not possible in this chapter to provide an adequate review of the politics of euthanasia law reform in Australia or anywhere else. Suffice it to say that there are serious obstacles to the enactment of

PAS/AVE statutes in Australia and probably other countries, at least in the medium term. Putting to one side those cases where politicians have deeply-felt moral objections to euthanasia, politicians stand to lose far more, in political terms, from defying the wishes of the minority of social and moral conservatives who vehemently oppose PAS/AVE, than from the majority whose support for legalisation is, in comparative terms, much weaker. The "moral minority" was a potent lobbying force during debate over the federal *Euthanasia Laws Act*, which overturned the Northern Territory legislation.[28]

The fact that legalisation currently remains politically unrealistic may be a comfort to some. But it is false comfort, if one is concerned about vulnerable patients or the harm caused by ill-considered, covert practices.

Regardless of whether PAS/AVE is ever legalised, there remains the policy option of actively seeking to influence underground practices in the hopes of improving the quality of the decisions that lead to illicit assisted death. A recurrent theme in my interviews was that interviewees felt compelled to try to assist their patients, but felt isolated, and lacked information. Regardless of whether PAS/AVE is ever legalised, an important opportunity remains for professional medical bodies (in Australia, the Australian Medical Association, and the royal colleges that preside over various medical specialties) to educate and to influence their members in an effort to reduce the harm caused by idiosyncratic and haphazard practices. Even if doctors will continue to ignore the criminal law's prohibition on assisted death, they might nevertheless *do less harm* if they had the opportunity to calibrate their actions against some sort of benchmark, some minimum set of criteria. Such guidelines could, if necessary, be deliberately vague, and need not advocate assisted death. But they should be specific enough to address the issues, risks and pitfalls that are present when health carers do choose to assist.

The argument that professional medical bodies – long the guardians of medical ethics – should produce guidelines for use by those who are committing the crimes of assisted suicide or murder may be seen by some as offensive, or as a last-gasp effort to promote and to legitimise euthanasia. These critics may need to separate their private views about the inherent wrongness of euthanasia, from harm minimisation efforts. Euthanasia policy shares a tension between moralistic and consequentialist approaches also seen in the context of drugs policy, and in Australia, in the debate about clean needle distribution and exchange programs.

It may be naïve to hope for any consensus on assisted death either among or within professional medical bodies. Nevertheless, precedents do exist for the development of guidelines for the practice of assisted suicide by stakeholders with differing views. Hillyard and Dombrink have described how, in January 1995, the Center for Ethics in Health Care at Oregon Health Sciences University convened a Task Force to develop professional standards and regulations for the implementation of Oregon's Death With Dignity Act. The Task Force produced a detailed guidebook to assist health carers in considering their roles beneath the legislation, implementing assessment procedures, and clarifying their own ethical beliefs (there is no legal requirement on health providers to participate).[29] There are also examples in the literature of multi-disciplinary collaborations between both advocates and opponents of assisted death to consider what safeguards should be included in a PAS law, assuming such a law *will be enacted*.[30] The common feature of these processes is not a shared belief about the morality of PAS/AVE, but a commitment to the common goal of reducing harm, and making law as safe as possible.

Conclusion

Illicit, covertly practiced PAS/AVE calls on us to script a new debate. The choice is not between having euthanasia or not having it, but between letting it stay underground, and trying to make it visible. The new debate is a troublesome one for moral conservatives, whose bottom line is that intentional killing is always wrong, regardless of the consequences. It is equally difficult for the medical profession, which is keen to avoid criticism, and the prospect of more intrusive forms of scrutiny and regulation. For professional medical bodies, in particular, euthanasia is a divisive issue, and there are few incentives to confronting its covert practice.

I have argued, however, that patients need protection from the inexperience, enthusiasm and occasional recklessness of their carers. Ultimately, euthanasia policy requires us to weigh the potential for the abuse of vulnerable patients, in an environment where – in an effort to regulate it – PAS/AVE was legalised, against the "anti-professionalism" that results from the criminal law's prohibition of PAS/AVE, despite its inability to control it. This is a debate which has barely begun, but one which promises opportunities for constructive dialogue between advocates and opponents of assisted death, in so far as they are ultimately motivated by their concern to protect vulnerable patients. Even if political factors retard the introduction of PAS/AVE legislation, important opportunities remain for professional bodies to try to foster *safer*, albeit covert and illicit practices.

Notes

[1] Meier, D.E., Emmons, C.A., Wallenstein, S. et al., "A National Survey of Physician-Assisted Suicide and Euthanasia in the United States," *New England Journal of Medicine*, vol. 338 (1998): 1193-1201.
[2] Ward, B.J. & Tate, P.A.., "Attitudes Among NHS Doctors to Requests for Euthanasia", *British Medical Journal*, vol. 308 (1994): 1332-1334.
[3] Kuhse, H, Singer, P., Baume, P. *et al.*, "End-of-Life Decisions in Australian Medical Practice", *Medical Journal of Australia*, vol. 166 (1997): 191-196.
[4] Roger S. Magnusson, *Angels of Death: Exploring the Euthanasia Underground*, (New Haven, Connecticut & London, England: Yale University Press, 2002). See also R.S. Magnusson, "Challenges and Dilemmas in the 'Aging and Euthanasia' Policy Cocktail", in D.N. Weisstub, D.C. Thomasma, S. Gauthier & G.F. Tomossy (eds), *Aging: Decisions at the End of Life*, Dordrecht: Kluwer Academic Publishers, 2001), pp 107-137.
[5] Hillyard, D & Dombrink, J., *Dying Right: The Death with Dignity Movement*, (New York: Routledge, 2001).
[6] For English versions of the Dutch and Belgian legislation, see *Monash Bioethics Review*, vol 20, (2001), pp 11-19 (recent Dutch legislation, confirming requirements previously established in caselaw); *Bulletin of Medical Ethics*, January (2002), pp 9-11 (recent Belgian legislation).
[7] Meier et al, above n 1.
[8] Emanuel, E.J., Fairclough, D., Clarridge, J. et al., "Attitudes and Practices of U.S. Oncologists Regarding Euthanasia and Physician-Assisted Suicide," *Annals of Internal Medicine*, vol. 133 (2000): 527-532.
[9] Kohlwes, R.J., Koepsell, T.D., Rhodes, L.A., Pearlman R.A., "Physicians' Responses to Patients' Requests for Physician-Assisted Suicide," *Archives of Internal Medicine*, vol. 161 (2001): 657-663.
[10] Baume, P and O'Malley, E., "Euthanasia: Attitudes and Practices of Medical Practitioners," *Medical Journal of Australia*, vol. 161 (1994): 137-144.
[11] Douglas C.D., Kerridge I.H., Rainbird K.J. et al., "The Intention to Hasten Death: A Survey of Attitudes and Practices of Surgeons in Australia," *Medical Journal of Australia*, vol. 175, (2001), pp 511-515.
[12] "Euthanasia and Physician-Assisted Suicide in Homosexual Men with AIDS," *The Lancet*, vol. 347, (1996), pp 499-505.

[13] Slome L.R., Mitchell T.F., Charlebois E. et al., "Physician-Assisted Suicide and Patients with Human Immunodeficiency Virus Disease", *New England Journal of Medicine*, vol. 336 (1997): 417-421.

[14] "Doctors Help in HIV Patients' Suicides", *The Australian*, 17 November (1995), p 3.

[15] Magnusson, above n 4, pp 128-130, 282-284.

[16] Magnusson, above n 4, pp 130-138.

[17] Magnusson, above n 4, pp 141-143.

[18] These themes are discussed in more detail in Chapters 10-11 of *Angels of Death*, above n 4, pp 200-247.

[19] Magnusson, above n 4, pp 202.

[20] Lewins F., "The Development of bioethics and the Issue of Euthanasia: Regulating, De-regulating or Re-regulating?" *Journal of Sociology*, vol. 34 (1998): 123-134, at 132.

[21] Magnusson, above n 4, pp 23-34. In the absence of direct evidence that an accused administered the drug that has independently been shown, through toxicology reports, to have caused the patient's death, then prosecutions, let alone convictions, are unlikely. Even then, there is the prospect of a perverse jury verdict, based on public sympathy for the motivations of the accused doctor.

[22] Magnusson, above n 4, pp 28-32.

[23] Somerville M., *Death Talk: The Case Against Euthanasia and Physician-Assisted Suicide*, (Montreal & Kingston: McGill-Queen's University Press, 2001), p 55.

[24] New York State Task Force on Life & the Law, *When Death is Sought: Assisted Suicide and Euthanasia in the Medical Context*, (1994), New York: The New York State Task Force on Life & the Law, p 120 (emphasis supplied).

[25] Caplan A.L., Snyder L., Faber-Langendoen K., for the University of Pennsylvania Center for Bioethics Assisted Suicide Consensus Panel, "The Role of Guidelines in the Practice of Physician-Assisted Suicide," *Annals of Internal Medicine*, vol. 132 (2000): 476-481, at 478-9.

[26] Lewins, F. *Bioethics for Health Professionals*, (Melbourne: MacMillan Education Australia Pty Ltd, 1996), pp 105-112.

[27] See Magnusson, above n 4, pp 61-63; D.W. Kissane, A. Street and P. Nitschke, "Seven Deaths in Darwin: Cases Studies Under the Rights of the Terminally Ill Act, Northern Territory, Australia", *The Lancet*, vol., 352, (1998), pp 1097-1102.

[28] Magnusson, above n 4, pp 62-63.

[29] Hillyard and Dombrink, above n 5, pp 167-174.

[30] See J.A. Tulsky, R. Ciampa, E.J. Rosen, for the University of Pennsylvania Center for Bioethics Assisted Suicide Consensus Panel, "Responding to Legal Requests for Physician-Assisted Suicide", *Annals of Internal Medicine*, vol. 132, (2000), pp 494-499; L. Snyder and A.L. Caplan, "Assisted Suicide: Finding Common Ground", *Annals of Internal Medicine*, vol. 132, (2000), pp 468-469.

* Roger S. Magnusson, BA/LLB(Hons), PhD; Faculty of Law, The University of Sydney, 173-175 Phillip St, Sydney, NSW, Australia; <rogerm@law.usyd.edu.au>

"Suicides Have a Special Language": Practicing Literary Suicide with Sylvia Plath, Anne Sexton, and John Berryman

Clare Emily Clifford

> *Dying*
> *is an art, like everything else.*
> *I do it exceptionally well.*
> Sylvia Plath, "Lady Lazarus"

> *...and I see now that we store him up*
> *year after year, old suicides*
> *and I know at the news of your death,*
> *a terrible taste for it, like salt.*
> Anne Sexton, "Sylvia's Death"

Confessional Poetry was the term given to the works of a group of American poets—including Robert Lowell, Anne Sexton, John Berryman, Sylvia Plath, W. D. Snodgrass, and less often Theodore Roethke and Allen Ginsberg—who were writing verse in the late nineteen-fifties and sixties. This label, "confessional," was so named—misnamed—by critic M. L. Rosenthal in a 1959 review of Robert Lowell's *Life Studies*, because of the personal voice and colloquial style the volume presented which was unlike the formality of Lowell's previous collections. For their subject matter these poets used parts of life not ordinarily presented in the public domain, such as frank revelations about marital infidelities, experiences with drug and alcohol addictions, mental breakdowns, and suicide attempts. Yet Rosenthal's term, "confessional," radically simplified the work that it labelled. Accordingly, a great deal of criticism charts the fallout of this label's assumptions, implications, and inadequacies, but this line of inquiry is not where my investigation is concerned. What interests me is the way in which three of these poets—Sylvia Plath, Anne Sexton, and John Berryman—use their poems as a public forum for engaging in literal and philosophical conversations about suicide.

It is true that the poetry of the Confessionals is a radical departure from what had came before it, primarily in regard to the perceived intimacy of the poetry's subject matter. With the frequent use of "I"-driven narratives, colloquial diction, and frank revelations of personal failure, the writing of Plath, Sexton, and Berryman *appeared* to be wholly unveiled and autobiographical. Indeed, their work is similar to much post-WWII poetry that challenged strict formal conventions and T. S. Eliot's high-modernist insistence on the impersonality of the poet as *modus operandi*. Specifically though, the work of these three poets constitutes a distinct attempt to blur the boundaries between author and a poem's speaking persona—a technique which affected their critical reception in a number of ways.

Critical reception to the work of Plath, Sexton, and Berryman reveals commonly-held cultural attitudes about the subject matter of their work, defining what poetry could and should not talk about. I believe that bulk of critical attention these three poets have received—particularly the claims of manic-depression, unabashed self-indulgence, and shocking exhibitionism—has been about the poets themselves, and not about their poems. This creates an extremely limiting rubric for considering these poets' work, and subsequently the criticism of them takes predominantly two modes, neither of which opens new conversation addressing how to understand this poetry within a philosophical or aesthetic context. The first mode is comprised of dismissing critics shocked by the transgressive subject matter of this verse, who are obsessed with the mythic stories about the lives that created it. Often these critics only look at the poetry of these writers inasmuch as it can be tied to the author's controversial and fascinating biography. The second mode of critical dismissal occurs because many critics simply disdain poems that consider taboo subjects like mental institutions and repeated suicide attempts as fit subject matter for poetry.

The hurdle that this presents for the *poetry* of Sexton, Plath, and Berryman continues even today. In the classroom students are mesmerized and buzzing with their knowledge of Sylvia Plath's own controversial suicide, but extremely uncomfortable and reluctant to discuss in detail any poems written in the voice of suicidal speakers. Could this be because we still don't understand suicide—the philosophical quandary, the literal act—despite our repeated cries to understand it? Suicide, as a subject, has been pathologized; subsequently, poetry that engages the subject of suicide has suffered a similar pathologizing rather than receiving critical attention usually credited to poems that pose and answer similarly important philosophical questions about language, subjectivity, and existence.

With these three issues in mind, in this study I intend to examine modern cultural attitudes about suicide and illustrate how the work of Sylvia Plath, Anne Sexton, and John Berryman engages in the very lively process of defining (and redefining) the act and subject of suicide, both broadly and specifically. I am also interested in the way that these writers responded to and facilitated changing social attitudes about suicide. I do not believe it was at all coincidental that at the same time these three poets were writing about suicide in their poetry, the field of suicidology was beginning to take flight. Edwin Shneidman, the century's foremost suicidologist, began his first foray into the field of suicide studies in 1949 upon finding a series of suicide notes collected in the Los Angeles Hall of Records, in the Coroner's vault[1]. I also find it extremely telling, as Richard Sanderson notes, that with Schneidman's discovery "modern suicidology began not with a study of suicidal acts but with a study of *writing*" (author's emphasis)[2]. In this account, the written act and the suicidal act are married, and this is an example of what I define as *textual suicide*, wherein suicide becomes the occasion for and subject of a text. In the poetry of Plath, Sexton, and Berryman, the poem is the written locus of suicidal ideation and functions as a literary example of textual suicide rather than a physical suicidal act; the language we use to describe suicide—whether in essay, story, or poetry—defines our understanding of the act itself.

The work of these poets is long overdue for critical reconsideration; in particular, the poetry of Plath, Sexton, and Berryman practices a sophisticated and philosophical investigation of American attitudes toward death and suicide by stirring up the placid surface of what Robert Lowell called the "tranquillized *Fifties*"[3]. These poets have left us a literary legacy charting a dialogue of grief, as suffered by individuals and communities alike. As critic Stephen Hoffman explains, "confessional autobiography becomes the cutting edge for a detailed examination of life in the post-war period, its characteristic anxieties, its multitudinous threats to psychic stability, and finally its ominous tendency to erode the very concept of viable human identity"[4]. What these poets especially mourn is the impersonality of death in a century punctuated by mass death and atrocity.

More specifically, the poetry of the Confessionals—at its zenith in the late fifties and sixties—anticipates the need to create awareness about suicidal individuals, and thereby individualize death and dying. This need becomes more publicized and culturally validated with the American publication of Emile Durkheim's *Suicide* in 1951, Edwin Shneidman and Norman Farberow's edited volume *The Cry for Help* in 1961, Jessica Mitford's controversial and award winning *The American Way of Death* in 1963, Elizabeth Kübler-Ross' *On Death and Dying* in 1969, and A. Alvarez's *The Savage God: A Study of Suicide* in 1971. Even more astonishing, is the way that these three poets express a common cultural desire for a more personalized approach to death—and understanding of suicide in particular—evidenced in the way that these poets repeatedly, in the poems, figure their deaths at their own hands. This poetic trend is part of a larger collective project occurring in the middle half of the twentieth century, wherein social and scientific disciplines like thanatology and suicidology emphasize the importance of contemplating the function of death in contemporary society so as to elicit a greater cultural openness about loss, mortality, and the mystery of self-destruction. In this context, then, suicide can be regarded as one of the most personal, self-defining, and individual, of acts anyone can execute.

In this project, I would like to look at the way that current thinking in thanatology examines the trajectory of cultural attitudes toward death in the twentieth century. Some of the discipline's major thinkers have argued, as Geoffrey Gorer does in his groundbreaking 1965 article, "The Pornography of Death," that to contemporary society death has become as obscene and pornographic as sex was a taboo subject to the Victorians. With the "public denial of mourning," Gorer argues, has come increasing "public callousness...excessive squeamishness about references to death, pain or mourning, [and] treating these human experiences as though they were obscene, so that any mention or depiction of them is considered unpleasant for the mature and corrupting for the immature"[5]. In the same way that embalming is an "art of complete denial"—not coincidentally, embalming is a funerary practice that gained popularity in the early part of the twentieth century—it is no surprise to the student of thanatology that the cultural anthropologist Phillipe Ariès' groundbreaking text *The Hour of Our Death* has entitled its section devoted to twentieth century attitudes toward death "The Invisible Death"[6].

Ariès charts changing attitudes toward death, and has given considerable attention to studying the notion of "forbidden death" as, what he calls, a deadly "characteristic of modernity"[7]. Through his work, he traces the way that death has undergone a sublimation in the early part of the twentieth century, and he questions the way our culture desires that it be a "given that life is always happy or should always seem to be so"[8]. He describes how with the beginning of the twentieth century "people had already begun to empty [rituals of death] of their dramatic impact; the procedure of hushing up had begun"[9]. This quietude of death reinforces the notion that, as an event, it is a cultural and topical taboo, and empties the drama of traditional death rituals. This encourages individuals and communities alike to silence their grief, and with their newly banished dead, bury their heads in the sand.

In 1959—the year Lowell's *Life Studies* was published—Kenneth Rexroth explained that   "The society in which we live is destroying the person and the communion of persons"[10]. Not only does the notion of community become eradicated with urban—and suburban—ization, but the acknowledgement of the individual and the notion of personal experience becomes even further dismissed. Shortly before her death in 1963, Sylvia Plath was interviewed by the BBC, and questioned about the importance of contemporary poetry's movement toward restoring the value of individual experience as a poetic reality. She explained:

> Perhaps this is an American thing: I've been very excited by what I feel is the new breakthrough that came with, say, Robert Lowell's *Life Studies*, this intense breakthrough into very serious, very personal, emotional experience which I feel has been partly taboo. Robert Lowell's poems about his experience in a mental hospital, for example, interested me very much. These peculiar private and taboo subjects, I feel, have been explored in recent American poetry. I think particularly the poetess Anne Sexton, who writes about her experiences as a mother, as a mother who has had a nervous breakdown, as an extremely emotional and feeling young woman, and her poems are wonderfully craftsman-like poems and yet they have a kind of emotional and psychological depth which I think is something perhaps quite new, quite exciting. [11]

While Plath does not explicitly mention death here, I would argue that death is indeed one of the "intense breakthrough[s]" that Plath so values here about the work of her contemporaries. Subtly, one effect of the Confessionals' poetry acts to refute what Phillipe Ariès calls "forbidden death," and what Geoffrey Gorer calls the "modern pornography of death"[12]. These poets aim "to give back to death... its parade and publicity, readmit grief and mourning" back into the life of their numbly silenced society[13]. Their work is a testament to making death more than merely mentionable in polite society, to awakening a dialogue about the pain of struggling with the literal and philosophical fact of human mortality.

The broader philosophical implications to the Confessionals' poetic endeavours is similarly clear from Camus' famous opening lines of *The Myth of Sisyphus*: "There is but one truly serious philosophical problem, and that is suicide. Judging whether life is or is not worth living amounts to answering the fundamental question of philosophy"[14]. Suicide is simultaneously a private and public act, much like the writing of a poem. Suicide is frequently accused of being a selfish act, and yet in actuality it is an act committed by an individual who has consciously chosen to relinquish the most selfish desire we can imagine—the desire to live. For the existentialist, and certainly the suicidal poetics of the Confessionals are exemplary in their recording of existential crisis, contemplating what suicide is—in a poem—is precisely the occasion for examining the options available for an individual to achieve meaning from life. In the poetry of Sexton, Plath, and Berryman this meaning is derived through a rigorously focused query into death and suicide.

In the decades following the Second World War, it should not at all surprise us to find literature preoccupied with identity, death, and suicide. As Frederick Hoffman elucidates,

> The erosive influence of a depersonalized world of "others," in wars, in concentration camps, in organizational maneuvers of one kind and another, is a major threat to the chances of preserving self-identity... to kill the self that was and to make it another self. Modern literature abounds in illustrations of this kind of depersonalizing strategy. A crucial feature of the existentialist view of death (for Sartre, as for Heidegger and Jaspers) is that in each case it is a unique event: I will die, and it is the act that *only* I can perform.[15]

Hoffman's argument—in the existentialist vein—is that the self's awareness of its freedom, in defining itself as a conscious and choosing individual at every moment of life, is complicated by the "depersonalization in modern life," which serves to limit "the self's balance of choice within life and in terms of death"[16]. Therefore one mode of repersonalizing the self, reconstructing a thinking choosing self, is accomplished by the suicidal writer's choices at portraying the suicidal minds of suicidal characters. My interest is in examining the choices that these poets make in *textualizing* suicide.

Alicia Ostriker claims that the poetry of this time is the "truth of a national predicament," that "the suicides of our poets—Berryman, Sexton, Plath—exemplifies our culture of American narcissism and American self-destructiveness"[17]. Indeed, America's national value for "individual liberty...[also] includes the liberty to suffer" just as fervently as it proclaims to value the pursuit of happiness[18]. Yet in opening up a reconsideration of this "national predicament," Susanne Kimball speculates that "perhaps the poet is the only member of society who deals with [suicide] in such a way as to stimulate the rethinking of conventional views on the subject"[19]. The common view of suicide is that the act occurs at the behest of an irrational mind, serving to further alienate suicidal individuals and survivors of suicide. This perpetuates the notion that suicide is a reality to be shocked by, ashamed of, and whispered about in hopeless defeated tones. Yet to treat suicide in this manner—unable to even say the word, let alone admit the suffering and truth of its reality—is to do a disservice to our own capabilities for human compassion. The poetry of Sylvia Plath, Anne Sexton, and John Berryman actively rewrites our conventional understanding of the entanglements of the suicidal mind. Their poetry shows us that there is a way out of what A. Alvarez calls "the closed world of suicide"[20]. Instead of taking sword in hand, these poets take pen in hand and write suicide, thus opening our opportunities to find a language that speaks about suicide.

While the field of thanatology has immense value for any study considering literary meditations on cultural attitudes toward death, the application of suicidology to post-war American poetry can offer extremely surprising discoveries. Advancements in suicide studies in the last fifty years have worked to promote a greater understanding of the suicidal mind and foster cultural awareness about suicide. Simultaneous to this field's development, the poetry of Anne Sexton, Sylvia Plath, and John Berryman was also gaining enormous public attention for treating suicide as one of its predominant poetic subjects. Even Kay Redfield Jamison's most recent book, *Night Falls Fast: Understanding Suicide* (1999) is a pointedly literary study. Jamison's dissection of the complexity of suicidal ideation has valuable use beyond the clinical forum when applied, surprisingly, to poetic practice.

The poetry of these writers offers a poetic casting of suicidal ideation as an alternative to the act itself, and in doing so the Confessionals present "a public face to what had been very private thoughts"[21]. In contemplating her own feelings and reasons for suicide, Sylvia Plath weighs how to emerge, and learn, from her own death wish: "How is it done? Talking and becoming aware of what is what and studying it is a help"[22]. In fact, Plath's most successful poems are spoken by personas who address their survival of attempted suicide. It is her speakers that wish to die and so defiantly fail at completing their own suicides that interest me most. The speaker of the poem "Lady Lazarus" infamously claims that "Dying / is an art," and it is Plath's artistry of suicide which makes her poetry so successful[23]. Her speakers are perfected in their inability to die—thus, Plath's success of the failed suicide.

As a poet Anne Sexton is an example of the working suicide, the worked suicide, the drafted and industrious world of suicide. In a letter she proclaimed, "Suicide is, after all, the opposite of the poem" and in writing a poem about suicide, she says: "as I work on it I create it (instead of doing it)... a fine substitute!"[24]. It is this fine line between writing suicide and committing it that Sexton toes as a poet. One speaker explains that "the business of words keeps me awake," and in the poem "Wanting to Die" we are taught that "suicides have a special language. / Like carpenters they want to know *which tools*. / They never ask *why build*"[25]. Sexton carefully builds a career of capitalizing on the publicity of her poetry's obsession with death—in fact she won the Pulitzer for her 1966 volume of poetry entitled *Live or Die*. Yet she is clear about the distinction between attempting suicide and writing about it. She tells of the rigorous drafting process of her poem "Suicide Note," the first draft of which she had written on a paper napkin in crayon: "I never heard of anyone committing suicide with a crayon in their hand, but then I wasn't committing suicide, was I, I was only writing about it"[26]. She continues saying that the poem went through about ten drafts, and that "If it were a real suicide note, there would have been one draft, I imagine. One does not perfect at gunpoint"[27].

In the poetry of John Berryman we find his speakers struggling with, what "The Ball Poem" defines as, the "epistemology of loss"[28]. The desire to understand this loss is the driving force for nearly all of Berryman's poetry, including his epic poem *The Dream Songs*. Writing is the driving force for the main character of this 384 poem volume; as Henry struggles to reconcile the loss of his father to suicide he proclaims himself "Bluffed to the ends of me pain / & I took up a pencil"[29]. Henry feels he has "a living to fail," because his living as an elegiac poet has been built on the deaths of others[30]. Out of terror and seeking comfort, Henry writes continually of his father's suicide as an unhealed wound singing to him like a siren. Henry fears that his father's fate is his own as well, serenading him into the grave. Berryman's work is focused on what Jeffrey Berman calls "the legacy—or illegacy—of suicide," how those who live on after a loved one's suicide struggle with the aftermath[31]. Berryman's poetry is haunted by the elegiac task of commemorating the dead he has lost, while still wrestling with his own desire to surrender to that very death himself. As Edwin Shneidman aptly explained, "A suicide puts their skeleton in the psychological closet of all who survive them," and this is the territory that Berryman's Henry sends his dispatches from[32]. Ironically Henry's creative process *is* his written lifeblood—his suicidal urge and his parasuicidal behaviour are driven by the same urge that fuels his composition process. His art is the making and unmaking of his own death, as when Berryman explains, "Henry stabbed his arm and wrote"[33]. There is much more contemporary poetry from 1945 to the present which treats suicide for its subject. Further examination continues to expose the evolution of this topic, the term, and the act it describes as attitudes toward suicide continue to modulate even as we move into a new century. I see the depiction and treatment of suicide in our poetry as a contribution to our cultural definitions and understanding of suicide as a chapter in the larger history of death studies. The written life is the place of life's continual revision, even the revising and revisioning of suicide. It is important to remember that a suicidal communication—verbal or written—by implication carries with it the desire to maintain a "connection to life and individuals"[34].

As Kay Redfield Jamison explains, the suicidal mind in crisis settles on suicide *only* when other "options appear spare or nonexistent, their mood is despairing, and hopelessness permeates their entire mental domain. The future cannot be separated from the present, and the present is painfully beyond solace"[35]. Yet for the artist—the poet—writing is an option one step removed from the hopelessness precipitating the suicidal act itself. Therefore, we can see the role that *poetic* suicidal ideation plays in the conception and reformulation of life in the context of ruminating on dying. Exploring suicide, textually, does not carry the same consequences of actually taking one's own life. For a poet, writing about suicide is *still* an option preferable to actually committing it, and it seems that as long as writing is an available option for exploring creative—and thus hopeful—opportunities in life, the suicidal act itself is kept at bay.

Sadly we can see evidence of language's failure as a life-sustaining force in the works of these poets. While poetry is a viable place to work out one's suicidal ideations, life is not lived in a poem. One of Sexton's later poems announces of words that "often they fail me. / I have so much I want to say... But the words aren't good enough"[36]. Berryman's Henry, while underground but alive in his coffin cries aloud, "My wood or word seems to be rotting. / I daresay I'm collapsing"[37]. And the final poem in Plath's *Collected Poems* says, "we have come so far. It is over"[38]. Indeed, while Sexton, Berryman, and Plath did eventually die by their own hands, they did *come so far*. By all accounts, it was their pointed task of writing—it was the poetry—which kept them alive for as long as they lived.

In an elegy for John Berryman, Robert Lowell writes, "We asked to be obsessed with writing, and we were"[39]. The Confessional poets used language as if they made it, and they did; or rather, it made them—language made their lives until they could invent it no longer. Inventing literature from moments of desperation can be a salvation, and in a footnote Camus wrote "To talk of despair is to conquer it. Despairing literature is a contradiction in terms"[40]. It is certain that the suicidal despair of these writers was astonishing for their contemporaries to be confronted with. It is the willingness of these writers to assert over and over again that, indeed, the triumph of literature is its ability to continually surprise us with an "accident of hope"[41].

Contributor Note:

Clare Emily Clifford is finishing her PhD at The University of Alabama where she currently teaches in the Department of English. Her dissertation is a multidisciplinary examination of Post-WWII American culture and poetry as it intersects with the field of suicidology.

Notes

[1] Shneidman's account of this occurs in two of his works. The first is: Edwin Schneidman, *The Suicidal Mind* (New York: Oxford UP, 1996). The second account of this incident is in his superb article which traces the evolution of the fourteen entries on "suicide" in the *Encyclopedia Britannica* over its 220 year history: Edwin Shneidman, "Suicide on my Mind, *Britannica* on My Table," *American Scholar* 67:4 (Autumn 1998): 93-104.
[2] See Richard K. Sanderson, "Relational Death's Narratives of Suicide Survivorship. *True Relations: Essays on Autobiography and the Postmodern*, ed. Thomas Couser and Joseph Fichtelberg (Westport, CT: Greenwood Press, 1998): 44n1.
[3] This phrase is found in the poem entitled "Memories of West Street and Lepke," in Robert Lowell, *Selected Poems* (New York: Noonday Press, 1998).
[4] See Steven K. Hoffman, "Lowell, Berryman, Roethke, and Ginsberg: The Communal Function of Confessional Poetry," *The Literary Review: An International Journal of Contemporary Writing* 22 (Spring 1979): 332.
[5] See Geoffrey Gorer. *Death, Grief, and Mourning* (NY: Doubleday, 1967): 131-2.
[6] See Phillipe Ariès. *The Hour of Our Death.* (NY: Oxford UP, 1981) 196.

7 See Phillipe Ariès, "Forbidden Death." *Passing: The Vision of Death in America*, ed. Charles O. Jackson (Westport, CT: Greenwood Press, 1977): 149.

8 Phillipe Ariès, "Forbidden Death," 149.

9 Phillipe Ariès, "Forbidden Death," 149.

10 See Kenneth Rexroth, *Bird in the Bush* (NY: Ayer Publishers, 1959) 84.

11 See Peter Orr, *The Poet Speaks: Interviews with Contemporary Poets.* (New York: Barnes & Noble, 1966): 167-8.

12 Ariès, "Forbidden Death," 1; and Gorer, 199.

13 Gorer, 199.

14 See Albert Camus, *The Myth of Sisyphus and other Essays*, trans. Justin O'Brien (New York: Vintage, 1991): 3.

15 Hoffman, 448.

16 Hoffman, 449.

17 See Alicia Ostriker, "The Americanization of Sylvia," *Critical Essays on Sylvia Plath.* ed. Linda W. Wagner (G.K. Hall & Co: Boston, MA, 1984): 108.

18 Ostriker, 108.

19 See Susanne B Kimball, "Literary Death and Suicide" *Germanic Notes and Reviews.* 31:1 (Spring 2000): 27.

20 See A. Alvarez, *The Savage God: A Study of Suicide* (Norton: New York, 1990): 96.

21 Kay Redfield Jamison, *Night Falls Fast: Understanding Suicide* (New York: Knopf, 1999): 35.

22 See Sylvia Plath, *The Unabridged Journals of Sylvia Plath: 1950-1962*, ed. Karen V Kukil (New York: Anchor Books, 2000): 447.

23 From the poem "Lady Lazarus," in Sylvia Plath, *Collected Poems*, ed. Ted Hughes (NY: HarperPerennial, 1992).

24 See Anne Sexton, *A Self-Portrait in Letters*, eds. Linda Gray Sexton and Louis Ames (Boston: Houghton Mifflin, 1991): 273, 232.

25 From the poems "The Ambition Bird" and "Wanting to Die," respectively, in Anne Sexton, *The Complete Poems* (Boston: Houghton Mifflin, 1982): 299, 142.

26 See Diana Hume Geroge, "Anne Sexton's Suicide Poems," *Journal of Popular Culture* 18:12 (Fall 1984): 30.

27 See Diane Wood Middlebrook, *Anne Sexton: A Biography* (NY: Vintage, 1992): 240.

28 From the poem "The Ball Poem," in John Berryman, *Collected Poems: 1937-1971*, ed. Charles Thornbury (New York: Noonday Press, 1989): 11.

29 From "Dream Song 30" in John Berryman, *The Dream Songs* (NY: Noonday Press, 1994).

[30] From "Dream Song 67," Berryman, *The Dream Songs*.
[31] See Jeffrey Berman, "'The Grief that Does Not Speak": Suicide, Mourning, and Psychoanalytic Teaching," *Self-Analysis in Literary Study: Exploring Hidden Agendas*, ed. Daniel Rancour-Laferriere (NY: NYU Press, 1994): 41.
[32] Quoted in Sanderson, 33.
[33] From "Dream Song 74," in Berryman, *The Dream Songs*.
[34] See Ronald W. Maris, Alan L. Berman, and Morton M. Silverman *Comprehensive Textbook of Suicidology* (London: Guilford Press, 2000): 282.
[35] Jamison, 93.
[36] From the poem "Words," in Sexton, *The Complete Poems*, 464.
[37] From "Dream Song 85," in Berryman, *The Dream Songs*.
[38] From the poem "Edge," in Plath, *Collected Poems*, 272.
[39] From the poem "For John Berryman," in Robert Lowell, *Day by Day* (Boston: Faber and Faber, 1978).
[40]See Albert Camus, *The Rebel: An Essay on Man in Revolt*, trans. Anthony Bower (New York: Vintage, 1991): 263.
[41] From the poem "For John Who Begs Me Not to Enquire Further," in Sexton, *The Complete Poems*, 34.

Time To Die: The Temporality of Death and the Philosophy of Singularity

Gary Peters

1. The Death of Socrates

The first philosopher (in the "modern" sense)---Socrates---is the also the first, and perhaps only philosopher to die a philosopher's death. Famously declaring that philosophy was itself primarily concerned with providing the means by which we learn to die, his own death has come to represent an ideal---the "good death", a death that is "good" because it secretly speaks of (and to) life, of happiness and contentment rather than anxiety or fear.

> For I deem that the true votary of philosophy is likely to be misunderstood by other men; they do not perceive that of his own accord he is always engaged in the pursuit of dying and death; and if this be so, and he has had the desire of death all his life long, why when his time comes should he repine at that which he has always been pursuing and desiring? (1)

The "death of Socrates", as any student of philosophy or the humanities will know is a long death! The time of this death is not one of suffering or pain, it is not a time of dying. There is no deterioration, decline or decay involved in this death. It is without emotion (on Socrates' part) and without the tragedy of the Greek dramas that pre-exist it. Indeed, for Nietzsche, it is the "birth" of Socrates that signals the death of tragedy, and the death of tragedy that, in turn, signals the birth of philosophy as an academic subject devoid of tragic pathos.

The death of Socrates is instantaneous like all death, but its significance as a philosophical death has a duration that, like a reversed comet's tail, streams out before it as a light---an enlightenment---illuminating a dialogical philosophical arena. Such illumination is, however, not something visible, not something seen, but rather an enlightenment that is spoken---Socrates is literally talked to death, he talks himself to death. As such, death here loses its sting in the to and fro of a continuous stream of dialogues terminating in Socrates' final ironization of death...."I owe Asclepius a cock". Having transported Socrates and his interlocutors the furthest imaginable distance from tragedy, dialogue and irony here arrive at the greatest tragedy of all---the tragic absence of tragedy. This chapter will be concerned with, amongst other things, rethinking the relationship between irony and death.

To say again, the secret of a "good death" is that it is, in reality, a death for the sake of the living, offering, to use Wittgenstein's phrase, a "form of life" rather than the formless vanishing point of death. As is often said, one cannot die an other's death, but one can die *in the place of* an other---a form of self-sacrifice much-vaunted in the mythologization of war. Hegel gives it an infamous formulation in the *Phenomenology*:

> War is the spirit and the form in which the essential moment of ethical substance, the absolute freedom of ethical self-consciousness from all and every kind of existence, is manifestly confirmed and realized. While, on the one hand, war makes the particular spheres of property and personal independence, as well as the personality of the of the individual himself, feel the force of negation and destruction, on the other hand this engine of negation and destruction stands out as that which preserves the whole in security. (2)

To die for a perceived truth or Idea is to die for those who will live on in the company of this truth. It is, thus, a singular death for the sake of a continuing collective *life*. In these terms the death of Socrates is the ultimate maieutics, the final and absolute act of midwifery, that delivers from the body of the collective the philosophical reason it will need to continue its evasion of death.

Socrates "dies well" because he ensures, through his dialectical method, that the collective agility of dialogue occupies those around him, filling up their time with discourse while protecting them from the silent void they all fear. Death by philosophy is, thus, the evasion of death, the loquacious postponement of time's end.

2.   Hegelian Dialectics and the Sublation of Fear

The philosophy of singularity in its different guises proposes a philosophy that faces death, not as a topic of conversation or the object of dialectical sublation---thus raising the thought and the thinker above the horrific nullity of its visage---but as the limit of philosophy itself and the failure of its absolute ambition. In fear, trembling, and anxiety, the philosophy of singularity confronts the temporal continuity of philosophical systems---reaching its apotheosis in the absolute idealism of

Hegel---with the radical discontinuity of a lived-time that ends. And, what is more, a lived-time that ends alone, in absolute solitude, outside of reassuring philosophical discourses. But, if the philosophy of singularity itself is to rise above the triviality of everyday life---"everydayness" in Heidegger's terminology---it must first acknowledge the formidable philosophical power of Hegelian dialectics and find a way of re-instating death as that which refuses to be sublated into the "system". As said, this means introducing either fear or anxiety into philosophy or pitting a certain existential defiance against the virility of Hegel's confrontation with death, a virility that, as Franz Rosenzweig puts it…"plugs up its ears before the cry of terrorised humanity…".

To begin from here; Hegel's most famous account of death can be found in the "Lordship and Bondsman" section of the *Phenomenology of Spirit* where it is seen as necessary to "stake one's life" and face death in order to achieve the necessary "recognition" of the self. However, as a philosophy utterly dependent on the self-recognition of the individual as one moment of the absolute self-recognition of "Spirit", Hegel's phenomenology, while facing death, must be a death-less philosophy if it is to transcend the annihilation of one individual by an other, thus prematurely terminating the phenomenology of recognition that requires life. To "stake one's life", is, thus, not the same as to lose one's life or to end the life of an other. On the contrary, it is a risk that does in fact reinforce a form of life by introducing a specific structure into it--- the reciprocal structure of mastery and servitude. The movement of Hegel's phenomenology, then, requires a fearless virility on the part of the recognition-seeking combatants, one fought out, be it noted, in the public sphere, in the company of the other, for the sake of a certain reciprocity which, though contradictory, nevertheless keeps death at bay.

Yes, there is death in Hegel's philosophy, the crucifixion of Christ of course, as well as the aforementioned mass death of war, necessitated by the self-realisation of Absolute Spirit; but there is no *fear* of death, no "terrorised humanity". What is more, from the most insignificant death (if such exists) to the most appalling catastrophe, the instant of death here evaporates into the teleology of universal history, the continuous temporality of Spirit's self-realisation irreducible to all death events. In this respect, no-one dies alone, everyone dies together, a collective sacrifice strewn across all time as the very movement of a shared history and a shared time.

> The death of the Divine Man, *qua* death, is abstract negativity, the immediate result of the process which terminates only in the universality belonging to nature. In spiritual self-consciousness

death loses this natural significance; it passes into its true conception...Death then ceases to signify what it means directly--- the non-existence of *this* individual---and becomes transfigured into the universality of the spirit, which lives in its own communion, does, dies there daily, and daily rises again. (3)

In Hegel there is an infinite time to die, but as he demonstrates in the *Logic*, his conception of the infinite is "true" (rather than "spurious") in that it returns back into itself in an absolute self-presence that holds death within its unbreachable horizon as a rational moment of the life of Spirit (4)

As a rational form of life death enters into the seamless continuity of a philosophical discourse that renders everything communicable. From one (apparently) solitary existence to another, death can be shared within the common objective time of the Absolute either through identification or contradiction, both of which *over time* are reducible to the same. Death gains a language---albeit a language of evasion---and thus, as Nietzsche shrewdly recognized, is brought back to life as "grammar", the very grammar that keeps God alive after his own (Nietzschean) "death.

The great Jewish thinker of singularity, Franz Rosenzweig, in his *The Star of Redemption* is compelled at the outset to confront Hegel and "the philosophy of the All" as he describes the Absolute idealism of the latter. He opens his account with a stunning passage.

Concerning Death

All cognition of the All originates in death, in the fear of death. Philosophy takes it upon itself to throw off the fear of things earthly, to rob death of its poisonous sting, and Hades of its pestilential breath. All that is mortal lives in this fear of death; every new birth augments the fear by one new reason, for it augments what is mortal. Without ceasing, the womb of the indefatigable earth gives birth to what is new, each bound to die, each awaiting the day of its journey into darkness with fear and trembling. But philosophy denies these fears of the earth. It bears us over the grave which yawns at our feet with every step. It lets the body be a prey to abyss, but the free soul flutters away over it. (5)

Having thus re-established the primordial fear of death as the necessary presupposition of all thought, and the thought of the All, Rosenzweig challenges the claim made by Hegel in the Introduction to the *Phenomenology of Spirit* that his philosophy is able to commence without presuppositions, a necessary purity for the "system" to be able to claim absolute validity. Such a claim constitutes, for Rosenzweig, a refusal to acknowledge the substantiality of fear as the prior and primordial existential category of mortality. In other words, the time of death, both as the instant which interrupts the continuity of temporality and the lived duration of that instant experienced singularly as life-long fear is a time prior to the instant of philosophical speculation and the "birth" of objective time figured as history.

> By denying the sombre presupposition of all life, that is by not allowing death to count as Aught but turning it into Nought, philosophy creates for itself an apparent freedom from presuppositions. For now the premise of all cognition of the All is---nothing. Before the one and universal cognition of the All the only thing that still counts is the one and universal Nought. Philosophy plugs up its ears before the cry of terrorised humanity. Were it otherwise, it would have to start from the premise, the conscious premise, that the nought of death is an aught, that the nought of every new death is an aught, ever newly fearsome, which neither talk nor silence can dispose of. (6)

3.   Kierkegaard's Deathly Irony

Following Rosenzweig's trajectory of thought, I would like to turn briefly to Kierkegaard's engagement with the objective idealism of Hegel. Kierkegaard always speaks from the position of "the single-one" thus announcing a singularity that is defined by solitude rather than mere particularity. This radicalisation of individuality in the face of philosophical objectivity leads, in turn, to a problematisation of communication that echoes in the final remarks of Rosenzweig above---the conjuncture of speech and silence. Kierkegaard wants to speak of subjectivity, and he wants to speak subjectively. He wants to speak of his own fears and anxiety, he wants to relate the guilt, sin and suffering of SK not of objective spirit or, indeed, of "man". When he speaks of death he wants to speak of actual death and not the dialectical sublation of death into life.

This, then, is the problem; how does one "single-one" speak to another "single-one" without betraying this singularity in the grammar of the "All", the collective, the "They" (as Heidegger expresses it)? Kierkegaard speaks instead of the "universal" and "universality" saying..."as soon as I speak, I express the universal, and if I do not do so, no one can understand me". (7) His answer is to propose a form of what he calls "indirect communication" whereby the single one remains absent from what is said without, thus descending into the evasiveness of silence. The most obvious example of this is Kierkegaard's use of pseudonyms in many of his early texts, a strategy that enables him to mark out a negative space of singularity by speaking from the place, and with the voice of the Other---something like a negative egology. Another example of "indirect communication", one which takes place *within* the pseudonymous texts, thus further problematizing the status of what is said, is irony, something of a hallmark of Kierkegaard's writing and one which sits very uncomfortably alongside Hegelian dialectics as is witnessed by the latter's vehement critiques of the romantic ironists throughout his work.(8) Significantly, and in spite of the fact that Kierkegaard's first published text is entitled *The Concept of Irony*, it is in his later work that he arrives at a more sophisticated (and less ironic) understanding of the nature of irony and its peculiar suspension between speech and silence. In particular it is his extended discussion in *Fear and Trembling* of the intended sacrifice of Isaac by Abraham that the limit-case of irony is considered, the case of a father knowingly bringing his own son to the moment of death. What is important here is not the instant of death---Isaac's "demise"---which, of course, never arrives, but the time of dying that commences with God's commandment to sacrifice the boy. Crucially, the time of dying is Abraham's time and not Isaac's, and it is not an abstract temporality but the lived-time of a single-one in fear and trembling struggling with the foreknowledge of, and the responsibility for an other's death. On more than one occasion Kierkegaard reminds us of the exact time it takes to reach the moment of death...

We forget that Abraham only rode an ass, which trudges along the road, that he had a journey of three days, that he needed some time to chop the firewood, to bind Isaac, and to sharpen the knife. (9)

Even more precisely...

If I were to speak about him, I would first of all describe the pain of the ordeal. To that end, I would, like a leech, suck all the anxiety and distress and torment out of a father's suffering in order to describe what Abraham suffered...I would point out that the journey lasted three days and a good part of the fourth: indeed, these three and a half days could be infinitely longer than the few thousand years that separate me from Abraham. (10)

So, Kierkegaard, in his separated, singular being cannot directly speak about, let alone to Abraham, and yet that does not change the fact that, for him, the climax of the story concerns precisely the particular manner in which speaking nevertheless takes place, albeit in a "strange tongue"---"God himself will provide the lamb for the burnt offering, my son!". (11) This speech is ironic. It is irony that allows something to be said that amounts to nothing, a spoken silence "too silent for silence" (Nietzsche) that, contra Hegel and prefiguring Rosenzweig, neither talks of death or disposes of it in silence.

But a final word by Abraham has been preserved, and insofar as I can understand the paradox, I can also understand Abraham's total presence in that word. First and foremost, he does not say anything, and in that form he says what he has to say. His response to Isaac is in the form of irony, for it is always irony when I say something and still do not say anything. (12)

Kierkegaard speaks of Abraham's anxiety which, following a line from his thought to Heidegger's, emerges out of a recognition of death's dual nature---its *certainty* coupled with its *indefiniteness* described here by the latter...

...the "they" covers up what is peculiar in death's certainty---that it is possible at any moment. Along with the certainty of death goes the indefiniteness of its "when". Everyday Being-towards-death evades this indefiniteness by conferring definiteness upon it. But such a procedure cannot signify calculating when the demise is due to arrive. In the face of definiteness such as this, Dasein would sooner flee. Everyday concern makes definite for itself the indefiniteness of certain death by interposing before it those urgencies and possibilities which can be taken at a glance, and which belong to the everyday matters that are closest to us.

But when this indefiniteness has been covered up, the certainty has been covered up too. (13)

On the strength of this, is Kierkegaard right to describe Abraham's emotions as anxiety, given that from God's commandment onwards Isaac's death is both certain *and* definite? That is to say, Isaac's dying begins at a specific time and its duration is terminated at the precise moment preordained for Abraham to act. Surely, it is within this, his own deathly time---given Isaac's ignorance---that Abraham feels *fear* not anxiety? And indeed, this would be in harmony with Rosenzweig's view that fear of death is always felt for the Other, it being impossible to conceive of one's own death. He writes:

...only Others can die; man dies only as an Other, as a He. The I cannot conceive of itself as dead. Its fear of death is the horror of becoming the only thing which its eyes can see in the deceased Others: a deceased He, a deceased It. Man does not fear his own death. (14)

Whether or not Kierkegaard considers Abraham to be fearful however, remains in doubt, a doubt strengthened by Heidegger's characterisation of the fearful "they" who turn and flee when confronted by a death as definite as Isaac's, preferring instead to make definite precisely the indefiniteness of death in inauthentic forms of life.

But Abraham *does* face the certain and definite death of his son, and one would assume he is afraid, otherwise this trial of faith would lack existential substance. If so, then this is a different fear, one that locks the sufferer into the time of death rather than propelling it away from this unbearable teleology into the ritualistic distractions that, in the name of death and the dying, sustain an inauthentic life. Such a fear, if such exists, is not, then, expressed in the terrorized cry of humanity heard by Rosenzweig echoing through all time (rather than the time of the All), but in the measured blankness of irony, delivered with an apparent indifference to the plight of the Other on the threshold of death. Such an irony, in all its profound seriousness, speaks in the knowledge of an irresolvable paradox that the great romantic ironist, Friedrich Schlegel, expressed as follows "...irony emerges out of the impossibility and yet the necessity of complete communication". (15)

Isaac speaks from anxiety, Abraham speaks from fear, one speaks of the indefinite, the other of the definite, normally one would associate irony with the indefinite rather than the definite but here we encounter an irony that inhabits or (better) is created within the inconceivable space between the two. There is absolutely nothing ironic in Abraham's words, as words, it is, rather, their transition from the definite to the indefinite that renders them ironic---impossible, yet necessary.

The case in question is an unusual one in that the certainty and definiteness of an Other's death is not normally given to us in the way described here, but it does, nevertheless, highlight, through a consideration of a collective experience of a singular death, the problematic of speaking out of one experience of time into another; in this instance, the time of death and the temporality of an anxious life respectively.

4.   Phenomenology and the Internal Time-Consciousness of Dying

There is insufficient space here to introduce and discuss phenomenology so I will have to go straight to what is normally perceived as one of the key "problems" of this philosophical perspective and then radicalise this problem further by reflecting briefly on the phenomenology of internal time consciousness: the problem in question is solipsism.

The clarion call of phenomenology is the "return to the things themselves", a philosophical project that requires the suspension of the "natural attitude" naively situated and secure within the given world and its social organisation. The famous "epoche" or "bracketing" amounts to a phenomenological reduction of the world to the intentional activity of the pure ego, with all alien otherness under erasure. It is precisely here that the problem of solipsism arises. Having suspended the world and the other, how can phenomenology re-constitute intersubjectivity, sociality and totality from the monadic solitude of the "reduced" ego?

The root of the problem can be seen clearly in one of Husserl's earlier works, *Ideas 1*, where he accepts that, in spite of the mirroring of one organic body by an other, what he calls "pairing" in the *Cartesian Meditations*, (16) the "consciousness stream" of one ego can never be reduplicated by another ego. (17) More graphically we could say that the physical signs of suffering, decline and damage of an Other's body in the process of, or at the instant of death are phenomenologically accessible but the intentional situatedness of the Other stream of consciousness within the suffering body is not.

In one view this might be considered via an ontology of space, as do Heidegger, Levinas and Blanchot in their much-used notion of "proximity", referring to a simultaneous closeness and remoteness of the Other, but there is also a temporal dimension to solipsism rendering each instant of time irreducible to another and thus closed to the experience of an Other. This is evident in Husserl's analysis of the phenomenology of internal time consciousness where the very identity of the ego as a continuous being is something that can only be constituted through memory and expectation, retention and protention, to use his terminology. (18) Forever located in the present instant, self-identity nevertheless avoids discontinuity, fragmentation and non-identity by carrying over into "subjective time" the memory of past instants and the foreknowledge of events to come, each confirming the temporal substance of the self-same ego within the eternal flux of difference and differentiation. However, while this explains, to Husserl's satisfaction, the temporality of the transcendental ego, his distinction between objective and subjective time compounds the problem of solipsism in that his constitution of the ego depends upon retentions and protentions that are, as past and future instants of a particular life, untranslatable into the life-time of an Other. Strictly speaking, then, the transcendental ego of phenomenology not only dies alone, thus echoing Kierkegaard and Rosenzweig, but also *lives* alone within a stream of time that, no doubt, flows into, and is itself flowed into by other streams of subjective time, but which never dissolves into the absolute flow of objective time.

To my knowledge Husserl rarely if ever discusses death, which is a pity because a fully worked-out phenomenology of death and dying would surely offer some real insights into the nature of this experience both for the dying as well as those who are proximal to the death of an Other. I will attempt to briefly sketch out some initial thoughts here.

To begin with, Husserl's treatment of retention and protention is neutral, that is to say, devoid of the existential weight one might associate with actual memories and expectations. His metaphorical illustration of internal time consciousness is almost exclusively musical---melodic coherence and continuity—which, speaking as a musician, is illuminating but, nevertheless, existentially abstract. Following Nietzsche, it might be more fruitful to consider the past and the future, as they constitute the present "now", as having a specific gravity that is, not merely given but which changes radically depending upon the place of the "now" on the time-line of an individual life and the manner in which a particular, singular self occupies the moment. This is especially the case in the face of death where the existential balance of past and future is seriously disrupted and, one assumes, the constitutional phenomenological acts of retention and protention take on a very different significance.

In Nietzsche's case the deplorable weight of the past is a "disadvantage" for life if it is not counterbalanced by the lightness of a future protained (if there is such a word) as pure creativity---the creation of a life.(19) In the face of imminent death, however, the Nietzschean challenge will be more difficult to take-up, the suspension of the self between past and future will now be more engaged with the deplorable lightness of the future rather than the weight of the past. Indeed, in the face of death it is, perhaps, precisely the weight of the past that offers some substance to the self as it approaches the point of its own vanishing. It is, of course, a cliché to think of ageing and old age as dominated by memories and nostalgia, but a phenomenological investigation might help us understand better the particular existential structure of feelings such as regret, hope and, indeed, hopelessness as part of the singular temporality of dying.

As death approaches, as a certain and definite event the experience of time must change. That is to say, where continuity itself becomes an issue for the self, there might be observed an intensification of the experience of time that radically transforms temporal experience in a manner that problematizes intersubjectivity and communication. In other words, this intensification of internal time consciousness draws our attention to the way in which the "now" is not merely the instant where the immediate past and the immediate future are mediated but, more importantly, where the retention of retentions and the retention of protentions come to weigh upon the present in a complex (and singular) knot of loss and gain, regret and hope.

To explain; starting from Husserl's musical example, listening to a piece of music requires the subject, through retention and protention, to remember the notes of the melody as they pass into the past, and anticipate future notes through a flowing extrapolation from what has already occurred. However, although this offers us considerable insight into the production/reception of melody as a coherent and continuous structure rather than a mere conglomeration of unrelated sounds, it tells us nothing about the *significance* of the piece within the existential being of one singular life. That is to say, it contributes a great deal to the understanding of subjectivity and its persistence through time, but more or less nothing to the aesthetic experience of music and its considerable emotional power--- its intensity. A phenomenological account of aesthetic experience, then, requires more than mere retention and protention to explain, for example, aesthetic pleasure. Indeed, it is only through an analysis of retained retentions and retained protentions that the *meaning* of time consciousness can be adequately considered. It is precisely here that it is necessary to go beyond Husserl's account of the phenomenology of internal time consciousness which, as he confirms himself, is restricted to immediate intuition rather than the non-intuitive engagement with the past and future typical of death experience.

...all our explanations are restricted to the immediate intuition of temporal objects, and the question of mediate or non-intuitive expectations and memories is left alone. (20)

Looked at in turn; the internal time consciousness of a retained retention differs from pure or primary retention in that it does not simply mediate a prior moment within the flux of ongoing experience but, rather, introduces into this flux an intentional knot that interrupts the abstract flow with existentially significant memory. In this way the horizontality and flowing linearity of an "experience stream" is intercepted by a vertical ecstasis that has gathered up within itself a series of prior intentional acts that now take on the emotional force typical of life in all its intensity. Thus understood, the past is not a singular stream (a misunderstanding of the phenomenology of singularity), but, rather, a unique concatenation of unrepeatable transitory points and recurring retained retentions that, in being retained again, bring to bear on the present a plurality of intentional pasts that, in their shifting patterns, configure the singular temporality of one solitary transcendental ego.

Two questions to note that will be returned to at the end of this chapter. Firstly: if it is the case that the approach of death leads to an intensification of time-consciousness, what impact does this have on the fine balance between past, present and future necessary for the maintenance of self-identity? Secondly; to "die alone" is something normally reserved for the moment of death which cannot be shared by an other. But is the approach of death, the time of dying, something that can be shared? Was Phaedo correct to say that Socrates did not die alone?

Turning now to the retention of protentions, once again an analysis of melodic continuity confirms that it is the anticipation of future events as congruent with those that have fallen into the past that allows the ego to experience novelty not as absolute novum but as the ongoing arrival of the past's expected continuation. Unlike Walter Benjamin's "angel" who can only look backwards at the ruination of (and in) time, protention allows the ego to look both forwards and backwards simultaneously, given that one can only expect what has already been. Protentions confirmed in the now make manifest a deeply harmonious temporality that, within the dominant aesthetic of the West, is experienced as pleasure. Following Levinas however, it might be concluded that it is precisely the rootedness of protention in the past that compromises the experience of the future by stripping it of its futurity. Such a radicalisation of futurity is epitomised in the attempted anticipation of one's own death, a task that will be returned to below.

As with retention, the protention of a particular structure of musical events only speaks of the manner in which separate moments are experienced phenomenologically as a coherent and cohesive work of art persisting in time beyond the instant of reception. Questions concerning meaning or emotional content however, will need to be addressed through a more sophisticated notion of protention, one which recognises that particular patterns of past protentions, retained by the ego as existentially significant complexes of anticipations, interrupt the largely unconscious protentional flow of time experience with the upsurge of intense feelings of anticipation, registered variously as expectation, hope and desire, often coupled with anxiety or fear.

Again, some questions: what impact does the foreknowledge of imminent death have on the existential function of retained protentions such as hope or longing which rely upon a future which is now waning? Given that protentions are rooted in the past and not the future, are unfulfilled hopes, now unfulfillable in the face of death, cast back into the past, as regret, thus creating a painful disequilibrium in the experience of internal time consciousness? Is the precise nature of this pain communicable to the other situated not only within another stream of time but, more importantly, a different structure of time?

There is a familiar mystification that at the moment of death one's whole life passes before one's eyes, such a claim, in spite of its recognition of the crucial importance of memory, nevertheless misunderstands both life and the complex temporal structure of passage. To begin with, life and death are not so easily separated, as Heidegger famously recognised in his phenomenological analysis of "being-towards-death". (21) Life is always already death, and death is only "authentic" to the extent that it is lived. Having said that, Heidegger does not consider being-towards-death at the point where death is imminent, when it is both certain *and* definite and thus the source of fear rather than anxiety; not the fear of the "they", but what might called, with reference to the earlier discussion of Abraham and Isaac, an authentic fear for the other rather than for the self. Such is not the fear of the other's death but, I would like to suggest, the fear of the other's life in the face of one's own death, a death which now comes to dwell within that other life as an irrevocable absence. It is, perhaps, the fear of this absence that compels the dying to consolidate their lives through an intense engagement with the process of retention for the sake of the other. So, given this, before considering the dying, those whose death is certain and definite, Heidegger's analysis of anxiety in the face of certain but indefinite death compels further consideration here. In particular it is the existential knot of anxiety, being-towards-death and "care" that implicitly (although not directly considered by Heidegger) raises the question of death and the post-mortem life of the other.

To *care* for the other amounts to more than merely accounting for the fragility of their own lives---although this is, of course, a fundamental demand and duty---unavoidable anyway. Care exceeds the parameters of an other life, in all its necessary carelessness, and turns back upon itself in an effort to satisfy the, perhaps as yet unformulated and all-too-often unfelt, needs of the other as they relate to, or ultimately *will* relate to the one who cares at the time of their death. Anxiety, then, as Heidegger rightly affirms, is the authentic way in which death enters life as care, but it is not (to use Foucault's terms) the care of the self that is the crucial issue here but, rather, the care of, and for, the *other*, in the face of an eventual death that will leave them floundering in the appalling absence of a loved one, that creates anxiety and not the speculation on the indefiniteness of certain death. Whether anxious or fearful, a distinction unnecessarily polarised by Heidegger, it is this, the re-alignment of the experience of death from the perspective of the other, that raises the possibility of an authentic fear (as well as anxiety) in the face of death, one that works to enrich life rather than flee death, for the sake of the afterlife---of the other, of course. The question, to return to phenomenology, is what impact does this have on the fine balance between past, present and future constitutive of internal time consciousness and temporal identity? This is, in turn, a question of the form or structure of consolidation, something that can only be sketched out here.

5.   Two Times of Dying
        Two temporal models of dying might be considered briefly: firstly, one where the known diminution of the future results in an intensification of the phenomenological process of retention and the consequent displacement of the present instant by the substantiality of a recollected past. Here, prior to the rituals of collective memorial after the moment of death, the dying self remembers itself as it might have been, as it should have been, as it was (or wasn't). Both Kierkegaard and Nietzsche understand this imbalance of past, present and future as disadvantageous to life---but for whose life? (22)
        While it might be true that turning one's back on death through the inauthentic distractions of memory and nostalgia can enervate life, intersubjectively, the retention of retentions offers the dying self a stock of significant temporal moments or time periods from which it can draw, and thus flesh out a life (now almost lived) for those who would remember. In

this sense, what might be disadvantageous to one life can be advantageous to an other.

There is an undeniable poignancy here; if, as suggested, the fear of death is, in large part, the fear for the life of the other after that death, then the substantiation of identity through the intensification of temporal retention works against the slipping of the dying self into an abstract oblivion incapable of substantial retention by the other---an insignificant demise. However, by offering-up a self capable and, indeed, worthy of remembrance, the dying man or woman (and, perhaps, not the child who cannot offer the other enough to grasp...a terrible predicament...which raises many issues which cannot be tackled here) compress a "life" into a discourse of memory that significantly heightens the sense of loss experienced by the other after the death of the one who dies. To "die well" within the context of this model, is to take responsibility for providing the other with a life that is capable of being lost, it is to provide the other with the material necessary for their own suffering and a form for their own sadness and regret.

The second model shifts attention away from the past to the future, indeed the futurity of the future. It is a model that returns us to the question of protention within an internal time consciousness which, in the face of imminent death, must confront the sudden diminution of the future but which refuses nonetheless to cast unfulfillable hopes back into the past as regret. Instead, the anticipation of a future, now denied, results not in the drawing of the past into a "now" increasingly emptied of its "now-ness" as a consequence, but rather the opposite, a reaching forth into the future in an urgent effort to bring forward into an intensified "now" anticipated moments that would otherwise remain unrealised at death.

As with the previous model, it might be suggested that this peculiar distortion of internal time consciousness is not motivated by a fear of death but rather a concern that the Other would otherwise be denied the possibility of sharing a life in the future that, instead, must now be lived in advance, albeit with an intensity that is only practicable in the short term. As such intensity indicates, it is here that the retention of protentions takes on real force by providing the means by which the futurity of the future can be compressed into a discourse of anticipation that substantiates in the present a future that can no longer be lived in the future. Here, again, imminent death appears to drive life back (or backwards?) into the present, thus providing the Other with what is, in fact, an impossible idealisation of an existential engagement with the lifeworld; one essential to the experience of loss, not only of the one who dies but also of an existential ideal that can, perhaps, only be lived through the death of an other.

In both of the above models the other has been identified as the beneficiary (whether intended or not) of the different but comparable distortions of internal time consciousness in the face of death. But to come back to the earlier question, does this mean that, while death is an event that can only be experienced or endured alone, dying is a temporal process that is fundamentally intersubjective? Can death and dying speak to life and living? Or is the time of dying ontologically different to the (non)-time of death?

6.   Irony and Death

This chapter will not attempt any answers at this juncture but, instead, would advise caution, and remind those sensitive to the fundamentally temporal nature of human life and living, that death and dying highlight in a particularly radical way, the profound differentiation of internal time structures during a terminal duration that is poignant precisely because it problematises in a phenomenologically explicable but nonetheless irresolvable manner the "common" or "objective time" necessary for communication to take place. Neither death nor dying are unspeakable, on the contrary they speak volumes---but they speak of and from within a time that is not of the living. They speak in a "strange tongue", an ironic tongue that neither speaks or evades death but which resonates with a fear that philosophy---the most anti-ironic of discourses---has proved largely incapable of hearing.

Something of an exception, Derrida, after years of mourning his own friends (23), has in his more recent work increasingly found himself in the proximity of that deathly irony that accompanies (and at times informs) the present text. More than most, he senses the silence, the absolute secret, at the heart of the "strange tongue" of irony. In *The Gift of Death* he writes:

> Speaking in order not to say anything or to say something other than what one thinks, speaking in such a way as to intrigue, disconcert, question, or have someone or something else speak...means speaking ironically. Irony, in particular Socratic irony, consists of not saying anything, declaring that one doesn't have any knowledge of something, but doing that in order to interrogate...(24)

This is Abraham's irony in most respects, but his is also something radically different, radically *un*-Socratic---it interrogates nothing or no one. In his incomprehensibly comprehensible words nothing is communicated, there is no opening onto knowledge and no intersubjective sharing of the appalling secret silently voiding this peculiarly solitary language---one "too silent for mere silence", to note the "double stillness" in Nietzsche's *Thus Spake Zarathustra.* (25). The irony of such a spoken ignorance is absolutely un-maeiutical, disallowing outright the collective anamnesis or recollection typical of Socratic pedagogy, depending, as the latter does, on an objective time completely at odds with the fearful futurity experienced by Abraham alone, in an "essential solitude" which, as Maurice Blanchot recognizes, has nothing to do with solipsism or loneliness, but is the product of language itself as it works itself across an exteriority or "outside" that remains forever Other. It is in the face of this unspeakable (yet spoken) alterity that Derrida returns us to precisely to those who are closest.

> And since each of us, everyone else, each other is infinitely other in its absolute singularity, inaccessible, solitary, transcendent, nonmanifest, originarily nonpresent to my *ego* (as Husserl would say of the *alter ego* that can never be originarily present to my consciousness and that I can apprehend only through what he call *appresentation* and analogy), then what can be said about Abraham's relation to God can be said about my relation without relation to *every other (one) as every (bit) as other*, in particular my relation to my neighbour or my loved ones who are as inaccessible to me, as secret and transcendent as Jahweh. (26, emphases in original)

7.   My Death

When my young daughter or son ask me, with an alarming directness so typical of children, about my own death, a question born of a very real anxiety that has a visible intensity---a certain look, a peculiar acuity---I am afraid. I am afraid yet I speak, I speak in order to keep fear at bay, their fear for me and their fear for themselves without me. What I say is, I hope, reassuring, it removes the sting of death and replaces pain, suffering and unrecoverable loss with words, indeed, a particular discourse of death that I have, no doubt, learnt, whether consciously or not, from the "they" who flee in the face of death's certainty. Why do I do this, and of what am I afraid? One thing is certain (or is it?), I am not afraid of death, how could I be, I will never experience my own death; and yet I am afraid, that much is undeniable---but why? Derrida comes close to answering this when he speaks of the fear of fear; he writes:

We are afraid of the fear, we anguish over the anguish, and we
tremble. We tremble in that strange repetition that ties an
irrefutable   past...to   a   future   that   cannot   be
anticipated...unpredictable; approached as unapproachable. Even if
one thinks one knows what is going to happen, the new instant of
that happening remains untouched, still unaccessible, in fact
unlivable. (27)

Even Hegel's combatants would concur with this. The "virility"
of this philosophy is as much a fear of fear as it is a fear of death, but it is
a fear of one's *own* fear that compels the "staking of life" here, a fear that,
in spite of the gulf that separates them, is shared by both Hegel and
Derrida, indeed, philosophical discourse generally. I would like to make a
different claim: in the face of my own certain but indefinite death I *am*
anxious but I am *also* afraid, not of death, nor of my own eventual fear
even if it were to arise, but of the *other's* fear, the fear of those who are
closest to me yet "as inaccessible as Jahweh". It is this mutual
inaccessibility that demands the irony of which, and *from* which I (and
they) must speak.

The impossibility and yet necessity of communication---the
ironic predicament *par excellence*---brings both a hopelessness and an
urgency to the task of providing the other with a life that must end with a
substantiality that both assuages and intensifies fear, as memory and loss,
presence and absence respectively. The above words, situated somewhere
between sound and silence, are, of course, part of this very project, part of
this responsibility, recognized so acutely by Heidegger, to introduce dying
into the temporality of one's life in a gradually accelerating
phenomenology of retention and protention for the sake of the other.
Without such a project the necessary bond between dying and death is
tragically broken, leaving the dead (and oneself among them) to evaporate
into the collective oblivion so perfectly articulated in funereal rhetoric.

Death without dying is indeed the most tragic form of death---
and I think again of the child---but even the shock of the most sudden
death can carry within it, compacted within the trauma, a temporality of
dying that can be carried over into the "heart" of an other as an irreducible
alterity that continues to speak of a life beyond its limit. This has nothing
whatsoever to do with the vain craving for immortality, but speaks instead,
of the other's life, and, in turn, the other's other. It does not concern the
content of a particular life being bequeathed to an other but, rather, a
phenomenological and existential *structure*---an exemplary model---that
might allow the fear of death to retain its sting but in such a way that it

provokes a fuller engagement with the responsibilities that attend the process of dying, and the life of death.

Notes

Plato, *Phaedo*, trans. Benjamin Jowett, Oxford: Oxford University Press, 1891), line 64a
Hegel, G.W.F, *The Phenomenology of Mind*, trans. James Baillie, (London: Allen and Unwin, 1971), p. 497
Ibid., p. 780
Hegel, G.W.F, *Science of Logic*, trans. A.V. Miller, (London: Allen and Unwin, 1968), p. 149
Rosenzweig, Franz, *The Star of Redemption,* trans., William Hallo, Holt, (New York: Rheinhart and Winston, 1971), p. 3
Ibid., p. 5
Kierkegaard, Soren, *Fear and Trembling*, trans. Howard & Edward Hong, (Princeton, N.J.: Princeton University Press 1983), p. 60
See, Hegel, G.W.F., *The Philosophy of Right*, trans. T. M. Knox, (Oxford: Oxford University Press, 1981), pp. 101-2
Kierkegaard, Soren, Op. cit., p. 52
Ibid., p. 53
Ibid., p. 119
Kierkegaard, Soren, Op cit., p. 118
Heidegger, Martin, *Being and Time*, trans. John Macquarrie & Edward Robinson, (Oxford: Blackwell, 1962), p. 302
Rosenzweig, Franz, Op.cit., p. 273
Schlegel, Friedrich, *Lucinde and the Fragments*, Trans. Peter Firchow, Minneapolis: Minnesota University Press, 1971), *Critical Fragment no. 108*
Husserl, Edmund, *Cartesian Meditations*, trans. Dorothy Cairns, (Kluwer, 1995), p. 112
Husserl, Edmund, *Ideas*, trans. W. R. Boyce Gibson, (London: Allen and Unwin, 1976), p. 241
Husserl, Edmund, *The Phenomenology of Internal Time Consciousness*, trans. James Churchill, Martinus Nijhoff, (The Hague, 1964), pp. 44 & 58
Nietzsche, Friedrich, *The Uses and Disadvantages of History for Life*, in *Untimely Meditations*, trans. R.G. Hollingdale, (Cambridge: Cambridge University Press, 1983), pp. 57-124

Husserl, Edmund, Op. cit., p. 84
Heidegger, Martin, Op cit, pp. 277ff
See, Kierkegaard, Soren, *Either/Or, Vol 1*, trans. David & Lillian
Swenson, (Princeton, N.J.: Princeton University Press, 1971), pp 215ff
See, Derrida, Jacques, *The Work of Mourning*, (Chicago: University of
Chicago Press, 2001)
Derrida, Jacques, *The Gift of Death*,   trans. David Wills, (Chicago:
University of Chicago Press, 1996), p. 76
See, Nietzsche, Friedrich, *Thus Spoke Zarathustra*, trans. Walter
Kaufmann, in *The Portable Nietzsche*, (New York: Viking Press, 1954),
p. 257
Derrida, Jacques, Op cit., p. 78
Ibid., p. 54.

Bibliography

Derrida, Jacques, *The Gift of Death*, trans. David Wills, Chicago:
University of Chicago Press, 1996
Derrida, Jacques, *The Work of Mourning*, Chicago: University of Chicago
Press, 2001
Hegel, G.W.F., *The Phenomenology of Mind*, trans. James Baillie,
London: Allen and Unwin, 1971
Hegel, G.W.F., *The Philosophy of Right*, trans. T.M. Knox, Oxford:
Oxford University Press, 1981
Hegel, G.W.F., *Science of Logic*, trans. A.V. Miller, London: Allen and
Unwin, 1968
Heidegger, Martin, *Being and Time*, trans. John Macquarrie and Edward
Robinson, Oxford: Blackwell, 1962
Husserl, Edmund, *Cartesian Meditation*, trans. Dorothy Cairns, Kluwer,
1995
Husserl, Edmund, *Ideas*, trans. W.R. Boyce Gibson, London: Allen and
Unwin, London, 1976
Husserl, Edmund, The Phenomenology of Internal Time Consciousness,
trans. James Churchill, The Hague: Martinus Nijhoff, 1964
Kierkegaard, Soren, *Either/Or, Vol. 1*, trans. David & Lillian Swenson,
Princeton, N.J.: Princeton University Press,1971
Kierkegaard, Soren, *Fear and Trembling*, trans. Howard and Edna Hong,
Princeton, N.J.:, Princeton University Press, 1983
Nietzsche, Friedrich, The Uses and Disadvantages of History for Life, in,

Untimely Meditations, trans. R.G. Hollingdale, Cambridge: Cambridge University Press, 1983
Plato, *Phaedo*, trans. Benjamin Jowett, Oxford: Oxford University Press, 1891.
Rosenzweig, Franz, *The Star of Redemption*, trans. William Hallo, Holt, New York: Rheinhart and Winston, 1971
Schlegel, Friedrich, *Lucinde and the Fragments*, trans. Peter Firchow, Minneapolis: Minnesota University Press, 1971

Gary Peters teaches aesthetics and visual culture at the University of the West of England, Bristol, UK. He has published work on continental philosophy, aesthetics and music and is presently completing a book entitled *Irony and Singularity: Aesthetic Education from Kant to Levinas* to be published by Ashgate in 2004. He is also a composer and musician.

DATE DUE

AP 05 '08			

DEMCO 38-296

Please remember that this is a library book,
and that it belongs only temporarily to each
person who uses it. Be considerate. Do
not write in this, or any, library book.